THE SECRETS OF STUDYING ENGLISH

COLES EDITORIAL BOARD

Bound to stay open

Publisher's Note

Otabind (Ota-bind). This book has been bound using the patented Otabind process. You can open this book at any page, gently run your finger down the spine, and the pages will lie flat.

ABOUT COLES NOTES

COLES NOTES have been an indispensible aid to students on five continents since 1948.

COLES NOTES are available for a wide range of individual literary works. Clear, concise explanations and insights are provided along with interesting interpretations and evaluations.

Proper use of COLES NOTES will allow the student to pay greater attention to lectures and spend less time taking notes. This will result in a broader understanding of the work being studied and will free the student for increased participation in discussions.

COLES NOTES are an invaluable aid for review and exam preparation as well as an invitation to explore different interpretive paths.

COLES NOTES are written by experts in their fields. It should be noted that any literary judgement expressed herein is just that – the judgement of one school of thought. Interpretations that diverge from, or totally disagree with any criticism may be equally valid.

COLES NOTES are designed to supplement the text and are not intended as a substitute for reading the text itself. Use of the NOTES will serve not only to clarify the work being studied, but should enhance the readers enjoyment of the topic.

ISBN 0-7740-3779-2

© COPYRIGHT 1998 AND PUBLISHED BY
COLES PUBLISHING COMPANY
TORONTO - CANADA
PRINTED IN CANADA

Manufactured by Webcom Limited
Cover finish: Webcom's Exclusive **DURACOAT**

CONTENTS

. . . continued

CONTENTS (continued)

HOW TO STUDY ENGLISH

READING

As the study of English always requires reading, it is very necessary to understand the types of reading, the purposes in reading, the different rates of reading, and certain physical and mental attitudes involved in good reading.

1. THE TYPES OF READING:

a. "Intensive" — slow, very thorough, very careful reading as in proof-reading a composition or in the reading of directions as to how to do something, of difficult poems or prose passages, and of material presenting an abstruse idea.

b. "Study-type" — careful, thorough, thoughtful reading, such as of literary history, essays and poems of average difficulty, and fiction read critically.

c. "Extensive" — recreational-type reading, as of plays, novels, short stories, and magazine articles, especially those assigned for "outside" reading or those which are read for pleasure.

d. "Skimming" — rapid turning of pages and scanning of lines to find a particular piece of information (a definition in a dictionary, the names of characters involved in a particular action in a novel, the date of an author's birth or the place of his burial, etc.) or to gain a general idea of something, as is done in forming a quick impression of a book and should be done in a first reading of a "study-type" assignment.

2. PURPOSES IN READING:

There are eight main purposes in reading for English:

a. To get the main ideas in a section, chapter, essay, story, or poem. (*"Extensive"*)

b. To get detailed information: the facts supporting the main ideas. (*"Study-type"*)

c. To find the answer to a specific question or to locate a particular fact. (*"Skimming"; then "Study-type"*)

d. To gather material for a critical analysis, as for a study of an author's style or of the construction of a short story; for an evaluation of an author's ideas; etc. (*"Study-type"*)

e. To share the author's feelings or those of his characters. (*All types except "Skimming"*)

f. To find out how to do something, such as how to write a "contrast-type" essay or to diagram a compound sentence. (*"Intensive"*)

g. To increase knowledge and broaden experience. (*All types*)

h. To get pleasure. (*All types*)

3. RATE OF READING:

Your *rate* of reading must *always* be *governed by your purpose* in reading *and* the *difficulty* of the material. Generally, "intensive reading" is done at the same rate as oral reading, "study-type", from 200 to 300 words per minute; "extensive," from 300 w.p.m. on up, depending upon the skill of the reader and the difficulty level of the material; and "skimming," at almost any rate.

It is important to know that material in the same book is usually read at different rates; for example, in a novel, certain unimportant or very uninteresting parts may be almost "skimmed," most of the action and the dialogue should be read "extensively," and a few passages of important description, subtle dialogue, and philosophic comment may have to be read as "study-type" or "intensive-type" for complete understanding and full effect.

The important thing is to *vary your rate* depending upon your purpose and the type of material.

4. PHYSICAL ATTITUDES:

a. Posture:

    (1) *Sit,* don't lie in your chair.

    (2) Lean slightly forward.

b. The head:

    (1) *Move your eyes,* not your head.

    (2) Keep the book perpendicular to the line of vision and 13 to 15 inches away from the eyes.

c. The eyes:

    (1) Read by phrases, not by words. This will reduce the number of "fixations" (eye-pauses in reading a line of print). Futhermore you will get ideas, not words (will see the forest instead of just the trees).

(2) Don't let your eyes pause for long either within or at the end of a line; move them along and sweep them back to the beginning of the next line.

(3) Avoid eye "regressions"; i.e., returning to words or phrases that you have already read.

(4) Look up from time to time and focus your eyes on a distant object. This will help to prevent eye-fatigue.

d. The lips: Avoid moving them as you read except in "intensive-type" reading. Also avoid pronouncing the words to yourself even in your throat, for that will hinder comprehension and slow you down to the rate of oral reading.

e. The finger: Avoid moving the finger (or a pencil) along the line as you read.

f. If the book is worth reading at all, read it with a pencil in your hand, and *use the pencil* to underline "key" words, phrases, and sentences; to make marginal notes and personal comments; to summarize, to take notes; etc.

5. MENTAL ATTITUDES:

a. *Read actively,* not passively.

(1) Think about what you are reading.

(2) Associate it with your own experience or your past reading.

(3) Get mental pictures and other sensory images.

(4) Remember that the author is trying to tell you something through the printed word: so "listen," don't just "hear."

b. Above all, approach your reading, not as a chore, but as a pleasurable experience. You can find pleasure in anything if you will give it your close attention, and you can always learn something about people and about life from almost anything that you read for English.

CONCENTRATING

1. Get interested in English. The more that you know about it, the greater your interest will be, and the easier, accordingly, it will be for you to concentrate.

2. Don't let your mind wander (or remain blank either). Make a conscious effort to bring it back to the subject if it drifts

off. Continued practice of this will increase your powers of concentration enormously.

3. Set a definite time period in which to complete an assignment, and then complete it within the limits set. If you fail to do so, go on anyway to the next thing on your schedule. This self-penalty will help force you to concentrate on the job at hand.

4. If you find yourself unable to keep your mind on your work, get a drink of water, or sharpen your pencil, or just relax for a moment or so.

5. If a distracting thought (girls, friends, Christmas holidays, a football game, a conflict with someone, etc.) persists, write it on a piece of paper and put it into your pocket for later perusal. (As strange as it may seem, this really works!)

GETTING THE RIGHT ASSIGNMENT

1. Have an assignment notebook for all of your courses, or devote a section of your English notebook to assignments in English.

2. Write in it each assignment as it is given.

3. Have a page in it to enter special assignments, such as book reports, panel discussion, term papers, etc., which are due at a future date (and be sure to consult this page from time to time to make sure that you are planning your work properly so as to complete these special assignments on schedule).

SCHEDULING YOUR WORK

1. Have a definite time set aside each day for study.

2. Try to establish a habit pattern by studying your subjects each day in a certain order.

3. Arrange your study schedule so that, if possible, you may have time for review before class.

4. Remember that your schedule must be flexible enough to meet the special demands of review tests, compositions, and other long assignments.

5. Don't forget that setting definite time limits within which to complete an assignment will help you to concentrate.

6. On the weekends, relax and enjoy yourself, but set aside definite periods for outside reading, library research, etc.

PREPARING TO STUDY

1. Have a well-lighted room with a strong light directed at your book from the left (if you are right-handed).

2. Have no distracting influences (radio, television, telephone, a girl's picture, etc.).

3. Have a desk or a table, and use a *straight* chair.

4. Go to your study room *ready to work,* not to dawdle or play.

5. Have a loose-leaf notebook with separators, and devote a part of it to each of the following: a. Assignments; b. Literature Notes and Tests; c. Grammar Notes and Tests; d. Compositions; e. Vocabulary; and f. Spelling.

6. Clear your desk of everything except your textbook, your notebook, and writing materials.

7. Have a *good* dictionary handy.

8. Study your assignment book to see what has to be done, and plan your evening accordingly.

STUDYING LITERATURE

1. GENERAL

a. Read over the notes that you took in class that day.

b. While you are studying,

    (1) Write in the text the meanings of words that you have to look up.

    (2) Summarize and transcribe to the body of the text notes from the end of the selection or from reference works so that you will not have to look them up again when you review.

    (3) Make marginal notes referring to your past reading, such as, "Cf. Mark Twain," "Cf. 'Self-Reliance',", "Idealism like Longfellow's," "Influence of Wordsworth," "Similar to situation in *Macbeth,*" etc.

    (4) Write "?" or "??" by anything that you study and re-study, but still cannot understand. Ask your teacher about these points or passages.

    (5) Make full use of any "Study Questions" or "Suggestions for Study."

(6) Note in particular any summaries given by the editor.

c. Follow the time-tested procedure: **skim - study - outline - review.**

2. LITERARY HISTORY

a. Make a *preliminary survey* of the assignment, to include

(1) A rapid "skimming" of the whole lesson to get the "big picture."

(2) A reading of the "Suggestions for Study," the "Study Questions," and any other study helps found at the end of each section or chapter.

b. Do a *"study-type" reading* of the lesson — a topic or a paragraph or other small unit at a time.

c. Close your book or look up, and *mentally summarize at the end of each paragraph or section.*

d. Re-read each passage which you cannot mentally summarize. (You have obviously been letting your mind wander or remain blank.)

e. Mark or underline "(key" words only) what seems important. This should include such things as

(1) Topic sentences.

(2) Coordinate statements that are listed numerically, such as "This period is marked by (1) a revival of learning . . . , (2) an outburst of lyrical poetry . . . , and (3) a tendency . . . , etc."

(3) A series of points, such as the novels of an author, outstanding qualities of his style, etc.

(4) Summaries.

(5) Anything else that would be useful in an outline of the lesson such as literary types developed during the period, important public services performed by an author, his influence on the period and on later writers, etc.

f. Make marginal notes for your own use to include

(1) "NB" (*nota bene*: Latin for "note well") beside something that seems extremely important.

    (2) *1, 2,* and *3* or *a, b, c, d, etc.,* beside a series of important points, such as "qualities of Poe's poetry" or "causes of the Industrial Revolution."

    (3) Your own phrases in summary of paragraphs or portions of paragraphs, as "Effects of Darwin's Theory," "Characteristics — personal essay," "Psychological novelist," etc.

    (4) Topics to be used in outlining the assignment, as "S t y l e," "Influence," "Background," "Important political events," etc.

  g. In your notebook, make an outline of the assignment. Use the complete "Outline for Study of an Author" for each major author, and points 2, 4, and 6 for each minor author studied.

  h. In *reviewing,* scan the paragraph and section headings, and mentally summarize the main points in each. Re-read what you cannot summarize.

  i. Just before class, *review* the outline that you have made.

3. THE SHORT STORY

  a. Read the introductory material, if there is any.

  b. Read the story rapidly to get the point of view, the setting, the main character(s), and the major facts of the story.

  c. Read the "Study Questions" at the end of the story.

  d. Do a "study-type" reading of the story. Note the following as you read:

    (1) The basic conflict.

    (2) The beginning situation.

    (3) The complicating incident, the complications, the climax, the resolution, and the conclusion.

    (4) The outstanding qualities of the main character(s).

    (5) The major points of the author's style.

  e. Outline the story, using points 3-8 of the "Outline for Study of a Short Story."

  f. If you have done a good job of studying, you will now know the following also:

    (1) The purpose of the author (to entertain or amuse, to present a universal truth, to thrill, to study a psychological or social or moral problem, to "grind an axe," to study a character, to satirize, etc.)

    (2) The artistry of the author (whether there is economy of words, exposition, characters, incidents, dialogue, and description; whether he has quickly aroused interest, established the mood, and secured suspense; whether he has created a single impression).

    (3) The predominance of plot, character, setting, theme, or mood.

g. Review the "Study Questions," and answer them mentally.

h. *Review* your outline and your notes before you go to class.

4. THE NOVEL

(See also the preceding section on the short story.)

a. Leaf through the novel and note its organization: preface; chapters; other divisions, possibly by episodes. There may be "Study Questions" and "Notes" in an edition prepared for school use.

b. Read the novel "extensively," determining as quickly as possible the point of view, the basic conflict, and the initial setting, to include the general environment.

c. Read by chapter; avoid extensive interruptions in the middle of one. If you are forced to break off before the end of one, skim the previously read portion before you resume your reading.

d. After each chapter or other major division, mentally summarize its contents, and determine its purpose in the book. If you cannot do so, skim or re-read the chapter until you can. A l s o , if your book has "Study Questions" for each chapter, mentally answer them.

e. Always be on the lookout for the essential elements of the plot: complications, crises, climax, resolution, and denouement.

f. As you read, do the following:

    (1) *Get the facts of the story.*

    (2) Try to visualize the action.

    (3) Place each new character as he is introduced, and keep the characters straight. W h e r e relationships are

particularly involved, as in *Wuthering Heights,* it may be necessary to construct genealogical charts.

(4) Determine the characters' motives, and observe whether they act in consonance with their motives and their natures.

(5) Observe the character development in the protagonist and in any kinetic characters.

(6) Feel with the protagonist his victories and his defeats, his joys and his sorrows, his exciting and his boring moments, his loves and his hates, etc. The author wants you to.

(7) Try to visualize each new setting.

(8) If the author's style is unusual, like Faulkner's and Hemingway's, it will be apparent, and you should note wherein it is different.

(9) Try constantly to determine the general theme and the purpose: i.e., what is the author trying to tell me and why?

g. Note in the margin in abbreviated form such points as satire (*sat.*), symbolism (*SB*), irony (*I*), peculiarities of style (*St.*), etc.

h. If you are reading to write a paper or to participate in a panel discussion, study the questions in "Panel Discussion of a Novel" before you begin to read, and take notes from the novel on those points which you can use.

i. When you have finished the book, re-read the preface if it contains criticism of the novel. Evaluate this criticism in terms of your own reading. Futhermore, if you can find any criticism of the book in the library (in a book of critical essays or in a magazine), it will be fascinating to read that also. Usually you will get a much clearer picture of the novel from these readings.

j. Finally, turn to the questions in the section, "Panel Discussion of a Novel," and see how many you can answer. Your ability to answer these questions will be in direct proportion to your understanding of the novel.

5. THE DRAMA

The drama is much like the short story and the novel in that it has all of their major characteristics: plot, character, setting, theme, and mood. It differs from them mainly in that almost everything is told you through the dialogue and the stage directions rather than through narration and exposition. Therefore you must follow the dialogue closely and read the stage directions carefully in order to follow the plot, understand the characters, visualize the setting, discern the theme, and feel the mood. Almost all of the suggestions for study of the short story and the novel (see *3* and *4* above) apply to the drama also; however, certain additional suggestions are worth mentioning:

a. Skim the text and note the organization: introduction, dramatis personae, division into scenes and acts, notes, study questions, etc.

b. Read the introduction.

c. Study the "Dramatis Personae," and try to understand who the characters are and what their relationships may be.

d. If you are "studying" the play, read it the first time as a "study-type" assignment; read it the second time "intensively," saying the lines to yourself as you think that the characters themselves should say them; read it in review "extensively."

e. If the notes are at the end, keep one finger at the notes, as you will be constantly referring to them.

f. As you proceed with your reading, follow the general suggestions for the study of literature (1 above) and the specific ones for the study of the short story and the novel (*3* and *4* above).

g. Above all, because the drama is intended to be seen and heard, not just read, you must use your imagination to visualize the settings and the action and to interpret correctly the tone of the dialogue.

h. You will find that almost all the questions in "Panel Discussion of a Novel" apply to the drama also; so use them.

6. THE ESSAY AND THE ARTICLE

a. Read the introduction if there is one. Mark any specific points brought out.

b. Read the essay (or article) rapidly to get the main idea, the points of view, and if possible, the tone and the mood.

c. Read the "Study Questions" at the end of the essay.

d. Do a "study-type" reading of the essay. Note either in the book or on paper the following:

(1) Major steps in the development of the essay.

(2) How the writer initially catches the reader's attention.

(3) How he builds up his case (logically, chronologically, haphazardly).

(4) How he pinpoints his major ideas (topic sentences, or implied topics).

(5) How he develops each major idea (experiences, details, analyses, illustrations and examples, anecdotes, comparisons, etc.).

(6) How he carries over the thought from idea to idea (transitional devices, repetition, etc.).

(7) How he concludes the essay.

(*Note:* As you read, be critical: check the validity of the ideas, the logic of the thought, and the reliability, pertinence, and adequacy of the facts.)

e. Make an outline of the essay, including points 5-8 of the "Outline for Study of an Essay or an Article."

f. If you have done a good job of studying, you will now know the following also:

(1) The purpose of the essay or the article (to advance a theory or belief; to prove a point; to provide inspiration; to amuse or entertain; to share an experience; to give information; etc.).

(2) The appeal of the essay (to the emotions, or to the intellect).

(3) Something of the author's personality, especially if it is an informal essay (urbane, sophisticated, witty, cultured; kindly, emotional, sentimental, genial; tender, whimsical, imaginative; cold, intellectual, opinionated; cynical, vituperative, misanthropic).

(4) Something of the author's style.

(5) The type and class of essay.

(6) The character of the times.

g. Look at the "Study Questions," and see whether you can answer them. If you cannot, re-read the essay, keeping the questions in mind.

h. *Review* your notes and your outline before you go to class.

7. BIOGRAPHY

a. Skim the book, noting the table of contents, the preface or foreword, the organization of the book (by chapters or o t h e r divisions), pictures and illustrations, the bibliography, and the index.

b. Read the introduction, and if possible, determine the author's relationship to his subject and his competence to write on him.

c. Read the book "extensively," noting the following as you read:

    (1) The point of view: subjective, objective; prejudiced, impartial; author writing as relative, friend, acquaintance, contemporary, scholar.

    (2) The facts of the subject's life: ancestry and parentage; early childhood experiences; education; jobs and interests; chief friends and acquaintances; difficulties, achievements, disappointments, and his reactions to them.

    (3) His outstanding traits of character and the events that illustrate them.

    (4) His major contributions to the world and his rewards.

    (5) The documentation of the facts presented: quotes from letters and documents, statements and opinions of those who knew him, footnotes, etc.

    (6) The method of presentation: chronological, thematic, scholarly, inductive.

d. Read by chapter; avoid breaking off in the middle of one. If you are forced to do so, skim the previously read portion of the chapter before you continue your reading.

e. After each chapter, mentally summarize its contents. If unable to, skim, or re-read the chapter until you can.

f. When you have finished, reflect on the book and determine the following:

    (1) The purpose of the author (to inspire the reader; to refute another biography; to idolize the subject; to condemn the subject; to present the real life of an outstanding person; etc.).

    (2) The fairness of the author (whether the subject seems to be an idol, a scoundrel, or a real human being.)

(3) The accuracy and the clarity of the author's presentation of the times in which the subject lived.

(4) The major points of the author's style.

(5) The type of biography (historical, eulogistic, critical, novelized).

g. Make an outline of the work, following the form given in "Outline for Study of a Biography."

8. A POEM

a. Study the title; it may give you a clue to the meaning of the poem.

b. Read the introduction if there is one; it may give background information or hints as to the meaning of a difficult poem.

c. *Read by thought unit,* not by line.

d. *Read the poem rapidly* for the point of view and the general idea.

e. Read the "Study Questions" at the end of the poem.

f. *Read the poem "intensively"* for complete meaning.

(1) Look up unfamiliar words and words that seem to be used in an out-of-the-ordinary sense.

(2) Use the footnotes.

(3) Watch for and interpret figurative language.

(4) Try to catch the suggestions and the overtones.

(5) Write the topic or a brief summary by each stanza or other major thought unit. (From these topics, you can see in review how the author has developed his idea.)

(6) Determine the mood and the tone.

(7) Use your imagination: in narrative poetry, visualize the action; in dramatic poetry, try to feel with the character; in lyric poetry, feel the emotion of the author.

g. Write the theme, the mood, and the tone in your book near the title.

h. *Read the poem aloud* for complete effect.

i. Review the "Study Questions," and answer them mentally.

j. Write a precis of the poem in your notebook.

k. If asked to study the poem carefully or to analyze it, complete the "Outline for Study of a Poem."

l. *Review* your notes before you go to class.

STUDYING GRAMMAR

The study of fundamental grammar is important only as it can be applied in your speaking, your reading, and your writing. For example, it is foolish to know the term *preposition* and its definition unless you are going to put objects of *prepositions* in the objective case; for the sake of variety, occasionally begin sentences with *prepositional* phrases; not end sentences with prepositions; place *prepositional* phrases near the words which they modify; make compound objects of *prepositions* parallel in thought and structure; use proper idiomatic *prepositional* forms; insert *prepositions* where they are needed for clarity or emphasis; search for the "loose" object of a *preposition* in reading poetry; etc. Therefore, treat fundamental grammar as the tool that it is, and do not consider it an end in itself; at the same time, recognize that without a knowledge of basic grammar a student will usually have difficulty in learning to speak and to write correctively and effectively.

1. Read the assignment as given by the teacher to see exactly what you have to do.

2. If there is written work, look at the exercise and underline pertinent parts of the directions, as is suggested below:

 a. *"Underline* the *subject once* and the *direct object twice;* put the *indirect object* in *parentheses."*

 b. *"Underline* the *correct form."*

 c. "Draw a *line through* the *incorrect form."*

 d. *"Copy* the *topic sentence* of each paragraph, and *write* in *outline form* the *facts used to develop* the topic."

(Having seen what you have to do, you will have a purpose in studying the explanatory material which precedes the exercise.)

3. *Study* the introductory and explanatory material *before you attempt to do the written part* of the assignment. Go carefully through and try to understand all the examples given, and memorize the definitions and the rules.

4. Read over notes that you took in class.

5. Re-read the directions for the exercise, and do the exercise *carefully* and *neatly*.

6. Skip the "stumpers" and come back to them later. Perhaps a later sentence or example may help you to solve them, and you will certainly get more items done if you do not spend too much time on any one of them.

7. Check your completed work for accuracy and neatness.

8. *Review* the definitions and the rules just before you go to class.

BUILDING YOUR VOCABULARY

1. General: Devote a section in your notebook to *Vocabulary*.

2. *Formal Vocabulary Building* (using a vocabulary textbook):

   a. In your notebook, write each word in the lesson; its pronunciation, if unusual or difficult (*quay, schism, formidable, zoology*); its part(s) of speech; its derivation, if helpful in remembering (*cynic, pariah, bedlam, maudlin*); its specific meanings; and one or two synonyms.

   b. Write a good sentence or two illustrating its meaning(s).

   c. *Review your list* just before class.

   d. Use as many of these words as possible in your speech and writing. (*"Use a word three times, and it's yours."*)

3. *Informal Vocabulary Building* (absorbing into your vocabulary words that you run across in your reading and studying):

   a. *Become aware of words of which you do not know the meaning.*

   b. Underline the word. If overall comprehension is dependent on its meaning, work on it now; if not, put a question mark in the margin and return to it later.

   c. Pronounce the word: it may be in your speaking vocabulary, and you will then recognize it.

   d. Try to guess the meaning from the context.

   e. Look for familiar parts (roots, prefixes, and suffixes) that may give you the key to its meaning. For example, *misled* may seem strange until broken down into *mis-led; impotent* becomes clear as *im* (not)-*potent; quixotic* makes more sense when we relate it to Don Quixote, an *impractical, visionary* character; *magnification* loses its formidableness when we see its as *magnify* plus *cation,* a noun-making suffix.

f. If you are still not sure of the meaning of the word, look it up in the dictionary.

g. In your text, write the meaning above the word so that it will be there for ready reference when you review for tests and examinations.

h. Finally, if you are really interested in increasing your vocabulary, follow the procedure outlined in 2 above.

STUDYING SPELLING

1. Have such a good working knowledge of the basic spelling rules (see "Spelling" under "Composition Rules" in this book) that you can apply them immediately.

2. If you are not sure of the pronunciation or the meaning of a word, look it up in a good dictionary. It would be slightly ridiculous to learn how to spell a word that you could not pronounce and whose meaning you did not know.

3. Break the word into syllables by drawing a thin pencil line down between the syllables.

4. Pronounce the word to yourself by syllables: *al to geth er.*

5. Spell the word to yourself by syllables: *a-l t-o g-e-t-h e-r.*

6. Determine whether any spelling rules apply.

7. Underline any hard spots: co*lo*nel; couns*e*l; ta*riff,* em-ba*rra*ssing.

8. Use association whenever possible: my *pal,* the princi*pal;* B*eta, the* secr*eta*ry; a station*er* sells station*ery;* a sim*ple* princi*ple.*

9. Cover the word and write it. Compare with the book. If you have misspelled the word, study it again, trying to determine why you missed it; then write it again.

10. Have someone call the words in the lesson to you.

11. On a test, check each word orally and visually after you have written it.

12. In your notebook, keep a list of the words that you have misspelled, whether on a test or in a composition. Review this list from time to time.

MEMORIZING

1. *Get the meaning* of the rule, definition, or passage (*the most important step in memorizing*).

2. Read it again and again, keeping mentally active and *tying in the words with the meaning.*

3. Work at memorizing for only short periods at a time (ten to fifteen minutes at the most).

4. Memorize short passages as a whole, and long ones by large thought units (*never line by line*).

5. After you feel that you *know* what you are memorizing, write it out.

6. *Review* as much as possible, preferably aloud. Use proper stress and pause. Say it in such a way that the meaning will be conveyed to a listener.

CLASSROOM PROCEDURE

1. Study your teacher and his methods.

2. Be determined to learn — and *pay attention.*

3. Enter discussions voluntarily; don't just sit there and wait to be called on — *but* raise your hand and be recognized before you speak.

4. Avoid arguing unimportant points.

5. Take notes:

   a. Take your English notebook to class.

   b. Make notes *in outline form.*

   c. Pinpoint the particular topic under discussion and write it down with the significant details that support it.

   d. Write almost word-for-word what the teacher, through pause or repetition, is obviously trying to have you write down verbatim.

   e. Use abbreviations as much as possible. You will have to work out your own set of abbreviations, but here are a few that may give you ideas: *AS* for *Anglo-Saxon; JFC* for *James Fenimore Cooper; hv* for *have; w/* for *with; w/o* for *without;* etc.

    f. Learn to write notes while you are listening to the teacher's next remarks.

    g. Show by some mark (*"o" or NB*) the points that were particularly stressed.

6. If you are working with a textbook, as in going over some selection,

    a. Make your notes right in the book.

    b. Mark points covered by the teacher as follows:

        * Touched on — note in review.

        ** Explained — study in review.

        *** Explained carefully and discussed — practically memorize in review.

7. Do your best to get along with your teacher. It will be very difficult for you to learn from someone with whom you are in conflict. Remember that he is a human being too. Futhermore, your "personality conflict" may be partly or almost entirely your fault; so you might well do a little self-examination.

STUDYING FOR TESTS AND EXAMINATIONS

1. The best way is to *study your lessons from day to day.* "Cramming" is not good for three reasons:

    a. You will not retain much of what you pick up.

    b. You may not have time to cover the material properly.

    c. You will be fatigued when you take the examination.

2. Get your outside reading and your term paper finished early.

3. Begin reviewing early.

4. Schedule your study.

    a. For tests, you must adjust your d a i l y schedule to accommodate the extra study time needed.

    b. For examinations, draw up a study plan that fits your examination schedule, and apportion time within it to each division of English that you must review.

5. Try to get copies of old tests, examinations, and examination questions.

6. *Study your teacher* to determine what he is likely to ask.

7. *Review the literature.*

   a. Study your outlines of the literary history.

   b. Look in the table of contents in your text at the titles of the selections covered, and mentally summarize each selection. Re-read any which you cannot summarize.

   c. Review all your notes that you made in your text. Fix "spot" passages in your mind, relating them to the title, the author, and the overall theme of the selection.

   d. Study your class notes.

   e. Review the memory work.

   f. For the examination, review the tests which you have filed in your notebook.

   g. Review your corrected compositions. Look over your tally sheet of composition errors made, and try to avoid these errors on the test or the examination.

   h. Study the chapter, "How to Answer Questions about Literature," in this book.

   i. Compose questions typical of those that might be asked, and think through the answers. Actually outline answers to any that are almost sure "spots".

8. *Review the grammar.*

   a. Look at your outline for the study of grammar, and check whether you *know* and *are able to do* everything that has been covered during the period.

   b. Review all definitions and rules. Be sure that you *understand* and *can apply them.*

   c. Skim the daily written exercises, noting in particular the mistakes that you made.

   d. For the examination, review the grammar tests which you have filed in your notebook.

   e. Practice on sentences and parts of exercises which are in your text, but which were not assigned as homework.

9. *Review the vocabulary.*

   a. Using the words listed in your vocabulary text as a guide, see whether you can give the meaning of and a synonym for each word. Also mentally compose a good sentence containing each.

b. Turn to the "Vocabulary Section" of your English notebook, and study each word of which you are not sure.

c. Study the other words entered in the "Vocabulary Section" of your notebook which you have picked up from your study and general reading.

10. Get as much rest as you can during the examination period. Don't stay up half the night "cramming"; you won't be in fit shape to taken an examination the next day.

11. *Don't get excited.* (Be confident, and you won't. How? *Study from day to day,* and *begin reviewing early enough.*)

TAKING TESTS AND EXAMINATIONS

1. *Don't get over-excited.* A *little* nervousness will sharpen your senses, but too much will "pull the curtain down over your brain" and you may "draw a blank."

2. Look over the whole examination question sheet to see what has to be done.

3. Plan your attack.

a. Apportion the time that you expect to devote to each section. Remember to *leave time for review*.

b. Determine the order in which you will attack the sections. It may be the same order in which they appear on the examination sheet; it may not be if you prefer to answer certain types of questions first. Leave space for any sections omitted initially.

4. Read the instructions carefully. If they say, "Answer *ten* of the following," don't answer twelve or fifteen. Choose the ten that you really know.

5. Read each question carefully. Determine exactly what it demands of you. Even go so far as to underline the "key words" in a question that is the least bit involved.

6. Answer the easier questions first. The thinking inspired by a later question may give you the key to a hard one for which you don't immediately know the answer. Remember to leave space for those which you omit.

7. While working on one question, write down on a piece of paper any idea that suddenly flashes into your mind if it will help you with another question.

8. If you start to work on a discussion-type question and see that you won't have time to finish it, summarize the answer in your opening paragraph, and develop as many of the points (in descending order of importance) as time will permit.

9. After you have finished, check over your paper for

  a. Completeness — Did you answer all the questions required? (Each year students fail because they omit whole sections.)

  b. Accuracy of answers.

  c. Perfection of mechanics and sentence structure.

10. Remember that *a neat paper makes a good impression* on the teacher.

11. Above all, *keep calm.*

HOW TO ANSWER QUESTIONS ABOUT LITERATURE

There are, generally speaking, four types of questions about the literature that you may be asked on tests and examinations; discussion, identification, short-answer, and interpretation. As there are correct and faulty methods of answering each type, suggested procedures and examples from students' papers with criticism are given below:

THE DISCUSSION-TYPE QUESTION

A suggested procedure:

(a) Read the question carefully, and determine exactly what it asks for by underlining the "key words."

(b) Think about the subject.

(c) Write down on a scrap of paper the thoughts which the subject calls to your mind.

(d) Organize these thoughts into a brief outline in which the major points are emphasized and the minor ones subordinated as supporting or substantiating evidence.

(e) Write the answer to the question in essay form. Have a good beginning and a good ending. (A good beginning often is a restatement of the question.)

(f) Read over your answer and make necessary corrections before you hand in your paper.

THE IDENTIFICATION-TYPE QUESTION

A suggested procedure:

(a) If the item is a person, tell briefly who he was so that his identity is unmistakable to the reader.

Beelzebub — "Satan's lieutenant in *Paradise Lost.*"

Isaac Bickerstaff — "Pen name used by Swift and later by Steele."

(b) If the item is a place, locate it unmistakably.

Twickenham — "Pope's estate on the Thames."

Grub Street — "Street in London on which struggling authors lived."

(c) If the item is a work, give the name of its author and its chief significance.

"Lycidas" — "Great elegy by Milton on his college friend, Edward King."

The Grapes of Wrath — "Novel by Steinbeck which won him the Pulitzer Prize."

THE SHORT-ANSWER-TYPE QUESTION

A suggested procedure:

(a) Read the question very carefully.

(b) Give the *complete* answer in *as few words as possible.*

(c) If you teacher desires complete-sentence answers, begin the answer with a restatement of the question.

THE INTERPRETATION-TYPE QUESTION

A suggested procedure:

(a) Read the passage very carefully, and determine exactly what it means in terms of the selection from which it is taken.

(b) Following the line of thought of the author, paraphrase the passage into clear, simple English. Be sure to explain all figurative language, allusions, and unusual words or expressions.

HELPFUL OUTLINES

OUTLINE FOR STUDY OF AN AUTHOR

1. Name; dates of birth and death.

2. Literary group or period to which he belonged.

3. Life:
    a. Place of birth.
    b. Parentage (if significant).
    c. Education (if significant).
    d. Important events of life *that bear on his writings*.
    e. Public positions held.

4. Literary achievements:
    a. Types of literature produced.
    b. Major works, with a short comment on each.

5. Style.

6. Influence on literature; importance as a writer; honours received; etc.

OUTLINE FOR STUDY OF A SHORT STORY

1. Title: suitability; effect.

2. Author.
    a. Brief biographical sketch.
    b. Outstanding characteristics.

3. Characters:
    a. Dominant (protagonist).
    b. Subordinate.

4. Setting.

5. Point of view.

6. The episode (the plot condensed into one sentence).

7. The plot:
    a. Basic conflict.
    b. Beginning situation.
    c. Complicating incident.

    d. Incidents in the rising action.

    e. Climax.

    f. Resolution and conclusion.

  8. Dominant impression.

  9. Type of story (plot, characters, setting, theme, or mood predominant).

  10. Personal comment (emotional response, etc.)

OUTLINE FOR MAKING AN SYNOPSIS OF A SHORT STORY

1. Outline the story, using sections 3-8 in the Outline for Study of a Short Story (above) as the basis for your outline.

2. Start your synopsis with the beginning situation, including the setting.

3. At some point, briefly characterize each major character.

4. Relate in order the major facts and incidents that bear on the progress of the story. Be sure to include the following:

    a. Basic conflict.

    b. Complicating incident.

    c. Further complications.

    d. Climax.

    e. Resolution and conclusion.

5. Omit all dialogue, description, comments, etc.

6. Read over the synopsis, and eliminate all unnecessary words and statements.

7. Re-read the story to make certain that you have included all essential elements.

8. Proof-read the synopsis, and make necessary corrections.

OUTLINE FOR A BOOK REPORT — NOVEL

(*Note: a. Do not necessarily follow the sequence given below; select an order that best fits your approach to the novel reported on. b. Emphasize that facet of the book that is particularly outstanding.*)

1. Theme.

2. Synopsis: setting, beginning situation, complications, climax, and conclusion.

3. Characters.

4. Style.

5. Personal comment (emotional response; general criticism; evaluation of the outstanding feature or failure of the novel).

OUTLINE FOR A BOOK REPORT — NON-FICTION

1. Title and theme.

2. Author, point of view, and purpose.

3. Summary, or exposition of several major points: incidents, character traits, crises, etc.

4. Personal comment (evaluation; criticism).

OUTLINE FOR STUDY OF AN ESSAY OR AN ARTICLE

1. Title: suitability; effect.

2. Brief life of author.

3. Type: narrative, descriptive, expository, argumentative.

4. Class: personal (informal, familiar), impersonal (formal); reflective, informative, satirical, impressionistic; didactic, nature, historical, biographical, scientific, philosophical, critical, character-study, editorial, of manners.

5. Central idea (summed up in one sentence).

6. Development of the idea:
   a. Introduction.
   b. Steps in the development.
   c. Conclusion.

7. Point of view.

8. Mood and tone.

9. Style.

10. Personal comment.

OUTLINE FOR MAKING A SUMMARY (BRIEF) OF AN ARTICLE OR AN ESSAY

1. Study the essay, underlining the important topics, points, and ideas as you read.

2. Outline the essay, using the underlined material as the basis.

3. From your outline, write your summary, trying to keep the same point of view, mood, and tone as is evident in the original.

4. Read over your summary, and revise it to eliminate all non-essential ideas and statements, such as illustrations, digressions, amplifications, comments, etc.

5. Re-read the original article to determine whether your summary is a true brief.

6. Proof read your summary, and make necessary corrections.

(*Caution*: A summary is not an analysis or a criticism; it is a brief restatement of what the essay says, and therefore should not be coloured by your own feelings, comments, etc. It is purely objective.)

OUTLINE FOR STUDY OF A BIOGRAPHY

(*See "Studying the Biography" in this book before attempting to complete this outline.*)

1. Title: suitability; effect.

2. Brief life of author, stressing his competence to write the book.

3. Point of view.

4. Type of biography.

5. Method of presentation.

6. Chief events of subject's life.

7. Chief traits of character.

8. Subject's contributions to society.

9. His rewards.

10. Personal comment (subject's worth; author's style; author's handling of material; etc.)

OUTLINE FOR STUDY OF A POEM

1. Author and title.
2. Background: incident, occasion, or times that inspired the poem.
3. Point of view.
4. Mood and tone.
5. Theme.
6. Précis of poem.
7. Development (a brief outline).
8. Type: narrative, lyric, dramatic.
9. Form: folk ballad, metrical tale, sonnet, elegy, dramatic monologue, etc.
10. Versification:
    a. Type of stanza: Spenserian, ballad, etc.
    b. Non-stanza: heroic couplet, blank verse, etc.
    c. Metre: trochaic trimeter, iambic tetrameter, etc.
    d. Rhyme scheme: *abcb, ababcdcd,* etc.
    e. Peculiarities of form.
11. Diction and figures of speech.
12. Quotable lines.

OUTLINE FOR ANALYSIS OF A POEM

(Before attempting the analysis, complete the "Outline for Study of a Poem.")

1. The title and the author.
2. What does the poet say? (a précis).
3. How does he say it?
   a. His point of view, mood, and tone.
   b. The development of his theme, to include explanation of symbolism and connotations.
   c. His technique:
      (1) The form used and its suitability.
      (2) Rhythm or metre.
      (3) Rhyme.

(4) Diction.

(5) Figures of speech.

(6) Sensuousness.

(7) Statement or suggestion?

(8) Restraint?

(9) Appeal to the emotions or to the intellect?

(*Note: It is not necessary or advisable to cover all the above points of technique; only those that are particularly applicable.*)

4. How well does he say it? (The emotional response of the reader; the freshness of the approach; the unity, clarity, and force of the presentation; the understanding of life gained.)

AN ADJECTIVE VOCABULARY

As students often find themselves at a loss for the right adjective to use in literary discussions, the following lists are given to aid them in the selection of the descriptive word which will help them to say exactly what they wish to say. The lists are by no means all-inclusive.

THE AUTHOR

Cultured, intellectual, erudite, well read. Sage, sensible, rational. Philosophic, analytical, imaginative, perceptive, visionary, prophetic. Optimistic, broad-minded, idealistic, religious, orthodox, sympathetic. Sophisticated, unsophisticated. Original, clever, witty, humorous, whimsical. Conservative, progressive, radical, reactionary, unprejudiced. Realistic, romantic.

Uncultured, unintellectual. Shallow, superficial. Bigoted, opinionated, intolerant, hypercritical, fanatical. Provincial, narrow-minded. Pessimistic, cynical. Egotistical. Sentimental.

THE STYLE

A. General: Lucid, graphic, intelligible. Explicit, precise, exact, concise, succinct, condensed, pithy, piquant. Aphoristic, allusive, ironical, metaphorical. Poetic, prosaic. Plain, simple, homely, pure. Vigourous, forceful, eloquent, sonorous, fluent, glib. Natural. Restrained. Smooth, polished, classical, artistic.

Bombastic, extravagant, euphuistic, rhetorical, tumid, turgid, pompous, grandiose. Obscure, vague. Diffuse, verbose, prolix. Pedantic, ponderous. Ungraceful, harsh, abrupt, laboured, awkward, unpolished, barbarous, crude, vulgar. Formal, artificial.

B. The Diction: Precise, exact, concrete. Plain, simple, homespun. Esoteric, learned, cultured. Literal, figurative. Connotative, symbolic, picturesque, sensuous. Literary, provincial, colloquial, slangy, idiomatic, neologic.

Inexact, euphemistic, non-specific. Bombastic, trite, artificial, abstruse, obscure, pedantic, grotesque, vulgar.

C. The Sentences: Loose, periodic, balanced, antithetical, inverted. Long, short. Euphonic, rhythmical. Aphoristic, epigrammatic. Forceful, emphatic.

Ungrammatical, un-unified, incoherent. Involved, rambling, tortuous, awkward, jerky. Cacophonic. Monotonously similiar.

THE CONTENT

Scholarly, profound. Significant. Cultural, didactic, utilitarian, humanistic, pragmatic, inspirational, philosophic, spiritual. Naturalistic, realistic, romantic, impressionistic, expressionistic. Subjective, objective. Dramatic, melodramatic, fanciful. Authentic, plausible, credible. Esoteric, recondite. Orthodox, controversial, radical, reactionary, liberal, conservative. Symbolic, mystical. Ironical, satirical, humorous.

Improbable, incredible, absurd. Superficial, shallow, trivial, insignificant, commonplace. Unscholarly, pedantic. Heretical. Prejudiced, intolerant.

THE CHARACTERS

A. Physical Qualities: Manly, virile, robust, hardy, sturdy, strapping, strong, stalwart, muscular, brawny. Beautiful, pretty, lovely, fair, comely, goodlooking, handsome. Dainty, delicate, graceful, elegant, exquisite. Charming, shapely, attractive, winsome, fascinating, ravishing. Neat, spruce, dapper, immaculate. Adroit, dexterous, adept, skillful, agile, nimble. Active, lively, spirited, vivacious.

Weak, feeble, sickly, frail, decrepit. Thin, spare, emaciated, cadaverous. Effeminate, unmanly, unwomanly. Ugly, hideous, homely. Coarse, unkempt, slovenly. Awkward, clumsy, gawky, ungainly, graceless. Bizarre, grotesque, incongruous, ghastly. Repellent, repugnant, repulsive, odious, invidious, loathsome, horrible.

B. Mental Qualities: Educated, erudite, scholarly, learned. Wise, astute, sage, intelligent, talented, intellectual, precocious, capable, competent, gifted, apt. Rational, reasonable, sensible. Shrewd, prudent, observant, clever, ingenious, inventive, subtle. Cunning, crafty, wily.

Unintelligent, unintellectual, unschooled, unlettered, ignorant, illiterate. Inane, irrational, puerile, foolish, fatuous, crass, obtuse, vacuous. Bigoted, narrow-minded. Ungifted, simple, shallow, dull, stupid, thickskulled, crackbrained, idiotic, witless, deranged, demented.

C. Moral Qualities: Idealistic. Innocent, virtuous, faultless, righteous, guileless, upright, exemplary. Chaste, pure, undefiled. Temperate, abstemious, austere, puritanical. Truthful, honourable, trustworthy, straightforward. Decent, respectable.

Wicked, inquitous, corrupt, degenerate, notorious, vicious, incorrigible, infamous, immoral, unprincipled, reprobate, depraved. Indecent, ribald, vulgar. Intemperate, sensual, dissolute. Deceitful, dishonest, unscrupulous, dishonourable. Base, vile, foul.

D. Spiritual Qualities: Religious, reverent, pious, devout, faithful, regenerate, holy, saintly, angelic, godlike.

Skeptical, agnostic, atheistic. Irreligious, impious, irreverent, profane, sacrilegious, blasphemous. Unregenerate, materialistic, carnal, mundane. Godless, diabolic, fiendlike.

E. Social Qualities: Civil, tactful, courteous, polite. Cooperative, genial, affable, hospitable, gracious, amiable, cordial, congenial, amicable, sociable. Cheerful, convivial, jovial, jolly. Urbane, suave, politic, debonair, elegant.

Unsociable, anti-social, contentious, acrimonious, quarrelsome, antagonistic, misanthropic. Discourteous, uncivil, impudent, impolite, insolent. Ill-bred, ill-mannered, unpolished, unrefined, rustic, provincial, boorish. Ungracious, brusque, churlish. Fawning, sniveling, unctuous, obsequious, sycophantic. Sullen, sulky, grumpy, fractious, shrewish, crusty, crabbed, peevish, petulant, waspish, perverse, malevolent; implacable, irascible. Critical, captious, cynical, caustic, sarcastic.

F. General Personal Qualities: Distinguished, noble, eminent, illustrious, admirable, influential, impressive, imposing. Well-bred, genteel, refined, aristocratic, cultured. Generous, benevolent, charitable, magnanimous, munificent, altruistic, philanthropic. Humane, merciful, gentle, kindly, patient, long-suffering, sympathetic, compassionate. Tolerant, indulgent, forbearing, Liberal, conservative, radical, reactionary. Ambitious, conscientious, persevering, industrious, persistent, efficient, assiduous, diligent, resourceful. Uncompromising, scrupulous, punctual. Earnest, zealous, enthusiastic. Strong-willed, determined, resolute. Confident, self-reliant. Plucky, valourous, intrepid, audacious, courageous, indomitable. Demure, sober, staid, solemn, serious, sedate. Discreet, cautious, wary, circumspect. Garrulous, eloquent, persuasive. Reserved, taciturn, laconic. Whimsical, witty. Sensitive, considerate, responsive. Thrifty, frugal. Coy, pert, flippant, saucy. Natural, candid, unaffected. Naive, artless, ingenuous, gullible. Shy, reticent, diffident, timid, meek. Humble, self-effacing, modest, unassuming. Docile, amenable, tractable. Placid, serene, tranquil. Impassive, nonchalant, indifferent, phlegmatic, imperturable, stoical, philosophical. Pensive, melancholic, moody, saturnine.

Mediocre, ordinary, insignificant, petty. Parsimonious, stingy, niggardly. Pompous, contemptuous, disdainful, domineering, imperious. Oppressive, cruel, vindictive, ruthless, brutish, truculent. Intolerant, dogmatic, prejudiced. Lazy, slothful, listless, lethargic, lackadaisical, parasitic. Inefficient, incompetent, bungling, worthless. Unambitious, dilatory, remiss. Fickle, unreliable, erratic, irresolute, capricious, unstable, irresponsible. Cowardly, timorous, craven. Mischievous, frivolous, silly. Headstrong, impulsive, wilful, impetuous, rash, indiscreet, imprudent, reckless. Prolix, wearisome. Apathetic, insensitive, callous, irresponsive. Prodigal, extravagant, profligate. Affected, pretentious, insincere, artificial. Hypocritical, pharisaical, sanctimonious. Overconfident, self-centered, vain, boastful, egotistical, conceited, bumptious. Arrogant, proud, haughty. Obstinate, stubborn, unruly, rebellious, obdurate, mulish, recalcitrant, refractory. Squeamish, fastidious. Self-indulgent. Mercenary, venal. Avaricious, envious, gluttonous, voracious. Perfidious, treacherous, traitorous, Eccentric, odd, quixotic. Smug, complacent. Obnoxious, reprehensible, contemptible, malicious, scurrilous, insidious, malignant.

DICTIONARY OF LITERARY TERMS

(All items in **bold type** are defined in this dictionary.)

Accent — the emphasis given one or more syllables in a word.

Act — a major division of a play, consisting of one or more **Scenes.** Before the 19th Century, there were usually five *acts* in a play: the **Exposition,** the **Complication,** the **Climax,** the **Resolution,** and the **Catastrophe** or **Dénouement.** Modern dramas usually have two or three *acts*.

Allegory — a narrative in which characters, objects, and events have underlying political, religious, moral, or social meanings. In what is probably the greatest English *allegory,* Bunyan's *Pilgrim's Progress,* the hero, Christian, represents any Christian on his way to Heaven ("The Celestial City") with a "burden of sin on his back," who meets many adversaries ("The Slough of Despond," "The Hill of Difficulty," etc.), temptations ("Vanity Fair") and worldly creatures ("Envy," "Atheist," "Mr. Worldly Wiseman,'" etc.) who try to divert him from his purpose in life: to get to Heaven. Finally through the assistance of his friends, "Hopeful" and "Faithful," he arrives at the Heavenly Gates and is admitted.

Other famous *allegories* are Spenser's *The Faerie Queene,* which combines political, religious, and moral allegory; Tennyson's *Idylls of the King;* and the morality play, *Everyman.* There is a good example of allegory in the modern comic strip, "Little Orphan Annie," in which Annie (the simple, but intelligent and ingenious American) is saved time and again from foreign powers and ideologies (Axel, etc.) through the intervention of Daddy Warbucks (Big Business under a free enterprise system).

Alliteration — the rhyme of the initial consonant sounds in words.

> "The *f*urrow *f*ollowed *f*ree."
> "*s*ilent *s*ea"

Allusion — a reference to persons, places, books, myths, etc., which the reader is supposed to recognize. They may be classified as:

1. *Classical*
2. *Biblical*

3. *Literary*
4. *Historical*

Anachronism — the term applied to anything in a piece of writing that is historically out of place. For example, clocks' striking, men's wearing hats and nightcaps, and houses' having chimney pots in Shakespeare's *Julius Caesar* are all *anachronisms,* for the Romans had no clocks that struck, nor did they wear hats or nightcaps, etc. These all belonged to a later date.

Anecdote — a brief account of an interesting, often amusing, incident. Anecdotes may be as short as the popular joke or as long as the short short-story of the modern magazine. They are usually characterized by dialogue.

Annotation — a note (usually a footnote) that explains or comments on or gives a reference for a word or a group of words in a text.

Anonymous — when used in connection with a work, means that its author is unknown.

Antagonist — the character or force in conflict with the **Protagonist** of a story, novel, or drama, as Claudius in *Hamlet;* Shylock in *The Merchant of Venice;* Chillingworth and the Puritan society in *The Scarlet Letter;* Antony, Octavius, and Caesar in *Julius Caesar.*

Antecedent Action — action which occurred before a narrative or a drama begins and which is sufficiently important to the plot to be included in the **Exposition.**

Anthology — a collection of writings in one book, as an *anthology* of short stories, or of Elizabethan English lyrics, or of Restoration English drama, or of American Literature since 1900, etc.

Anticlimax —

A. An event which is strikingly less important than the event which immediately precedes it, as the killing of the grooms in *Macbeth,* which follows the murder of Duncan.

B. It may be used of something which does not fulfill expectations. Pope was very fond of this use of *anticlimax* for satiric effect, as in *The Rape of the Lock,*

> "Not louder shrieks to pitying Heaven are cast,
>   When husbands, *or when lap dogs breathe their last."*

C. The term is also applied to a series which is in the reverse of climactic order, as: "His wife was killed, his house burned down, his dog ran away, and he had to go without his supper"; or "For God, for Country, and for Yale."

Antithesis — the use of balanced structure for emphasizing comparison or contrast.

Apostrophe — an address to the dead as if living:

> "O *Julius Caesar,* thou are mighty yet;
> Thy spirit walks abroad . . ."

to the inanimate as if animate:

> "Roll on, thou deep and dark blue *ocean* — roll!"

to the absent as if present:

> *"Romeo! Romeo!* Wherefore are thou Romeo?"

to the unborn as if alive:

> *"Brother,* that breathe the August air
> Ten thousand years from now . . ." — Millay

Argument — a formal summary of the chief points in a play (see *Hamlet,* Act III, Sc. II, lines 145 ff.) or a book, or a section of a book (see the introduction to each **Book** of Milton's *Paradise Lost.*)

Aside — a comment made by a player in a drama which is supposed to be audible only to the audience, not to other players. It is similar to the **Soliloquy** except that it is shorter and the speaker is not alone on the stage.

Assonance — the agreement of vowel sounds when the endings differ.

> "p*u*rple c*u*rtain" "m*o*lten g*o*lden n*o*tes"
> "*I*n X*a*nad*u* did K*u*bla Kh*a*n"
> lo*u*d sh*ou*t *ea*sily — gr*ee*dily

Note how Shelley in the following passage from "The Cloud" has combined **End Rhyme** ("Moon" — "strewn"), **Internal Rhyme** ("maiden" — "laden"; "o'er" — "floor"), **Assonance** ("wh*i*te" — "f*i*re"; "wh*o*m" — "M*oo*n"; "m*o*rtals" — "c*a*ll"), and **Alliteration** ("*Gl*ides *gl*immering"; "*fl*eecelike *fl*oor") to add beauty of sound to the beauty of his description.

> "That orbéd maiden with white fire laden,
>   Whom mortals call the Moon,
> Glides glimmering o'er my fleecelike floor,
>   By the midnight breezes strewn."

Autobiography — the story of a person's life written by himself.

Bibliography — a formal list of books, magazine articles, etc., about a particular subject or by a certain author.

Biography — the story of a person's life, such as Boswell's *Life of Samuel Johnson.*

Bowdlerize — to expurgate (usually prudishly) a p i e c e of writing, as Thomas Bowdler did an edition of Shakespeare in the 19th Century.

Burlesque — a form of literature which mocks by treating a serious theme in a trivial style (Gay's *The Beggar's Opera,* which mocks Italian opera and Sir Robert Walpole), or a trivial theme in a **Mock-heroic** vein (Pope's *The Rape of the Lock,* which satirizes a family feud in epical manner).

Cacophony — a generally harsh, unpleasant, clashing combinations of sounds *(The truculent Turk stood quite quiet).*

Caricature — a picture, description, characterization, etc., in which outstanding characteristics are overdrawn, such as the grandiloquence of Dickens' Micawber, the obsequiousness of his Uriah Heep, and the villainy of his Bill Sykes.

Catastrophe (or **Dénouement**) — the final event in a story or drama which completely resolves the **Conflict,** as the death of Brutus and Cassius in *Julius Caesar,* and of Hamlet, Claudius, Gertrude, and Laertes in *Hamlet.* In comedy, the *catastrophe* is happy, as it is for Portia, Bassanio, and Antonio in *The Merchant of Venice. Catastrophe* is also the term applied to the fifth act of an Elizabethan play.

Catharsis (Katharsis) — according to Aristotle a purification of the emotions through the experience of pity and fear gained from watching a tragedy. As the members of the audience live through terror and sorrow with the **Protagonist,** they are stripped of the pettiness of life, are purged of the enfeebling emotions of fear and pity, and emerge psychologically healthier.

Character Portrayal — the act or art of delineating character in fiction. The author has several means of portraying character, and the reader may determine the nature of an individual from various indications, such as the following:

1. From what he does.

2. From what he says and the way in which he says it.
3. From a revelation of his thoughts, either through **Soliloquy** or an omniscient author's words.
4. From what others say about him.
5. From what others say to him.
6. From the way that he reacts to other people and they to him.
7. From an actual description of him by an omniscient author in which physical, mental, moral, or other personal qualities are revealed.

Chorus — in Greek drama, a company of singers who in choral odes commented on or interpreted the action, gave expression to and helped to direct the emotional responses of the audience, sometimes expounded **Antecedent Action** and delivered the **Prologue** and the **Epilogue,** and generally served to divide the play into **Acts** by their songs between episodes. (See Sophocles' *Oedipus Rex.*) In modern times, T. S. Eliot revived the Greek *chorus* in his *Murder in the Cathedral,* and the Stage Manager of Wilder's *Our Town* performed many of the functions of a *chorus*.

Chronicle — a historical account of events in the order in which they happened, such as *The Anglo-Saxon Chronicle,* or Holinshed's *Chronicles,* from which Shakespeare drew the material for *Macbeth* and other plays.

Chronicle Play — a type of drama based on historical events. In early days, the *chronicle play* generally consisted of a mere series of events held together by a central character; however, Marlowe in *Edward II* and Shakespeare in *Richard II, Henry V,* etc., constructed definite plots concluding in catastrophe.

Classical — used to denote Greek and Roman authors and their works and is applied to those who imitate the style, etc., of the ancients.

Classicism — the term applied to a style and point of view similar to that of the Greeks and Romans. It is best defined by a listing of some of its characteristics. It is marked by

1. An emphasis on society rather than on the individual, on conformity by all to accepted standards, on regimentation of the individual.
2. An emphasis on perfection of form in all types of expression, on careful workmanship and polish: thus the use by the Neo-Classicists of 18th Century England of the **Heroic**

Couplet in p o e t r y, their insistence on the **Dramatic Unities,** and their delight in formalism, severity, simplicity, and regularity in art, in architecture, and even in gardens.

3. An emphasis on the intellectual rather than on the imaginative and the emotional, on the expression of eternal truths rather than of fleeting emotions, with particular stress laid on the manner of expression. This is well illustrated by the contrast shown in the lines of Pope (a Neo-Classicist):

> "True wit is nature to advantage dressed,
>   What oft was thought, but ne'er so well expressed."

and those of Wordsworth (a Romanticist):

> "And then my heart with pleasure fills
>   And dances with the daffodils."

4. Writings which appealed to the aristocracy rather than to the common people.

5. The use of satire after the manner of Juvenal and Horace.

6. Realism in subject matter.

7. A tendency toward artificiality rather than naturalness.

8. The repression of the emotions and the imagination.

Cliché (clee shay) — a trite phrase: one that has lost its force through overuse, as "to beat a hasty retreat," and "last but not least" he "regaled us with a few well-chosen words."

Climax —

A. From the *reader* point of view, the highest point of interest or of emotional intensity. From the *structural* point of view, it is that place where the **Complication** ceases and the **Resolution** *begins,* the turning point at which the fortunes of the **Protagonist** reach their peak or their nadir and from which they begin to go in the other direction, as in *Julius Caesar* when Antony begins his speech; in *Macbeth* when Banquo is killed; and in *Hamlet* when Hamlet comes upon Claudius kneeling in prayer and draws his sword to kill him.

B. *Climax* is the term often applied to the third act of an Elizabethan play.

C. *Climax* is also the term applied to a series of statements in ascending order of importance, as Hamlet Sr.'s "of *life,* of *crown,* of *queen,* at once dispatched."

Closet Drama — dramatic poetry which is intended primarily for reading rather than for production, such as Milton's *Samson Agonistes* and Browning's *Pippa Passes.*

Coincidence — the apparently accidental happening together of events. The forcing of *coincidence* is considered faulty technique; some of the best writers, such as Dickens and Hardy, however, use it to suit their purposes.

Comedy — a form of drama in which the **Protagonist** overcomes the obstacles, usually social in nature, facing him. There are a number of types:

A. **Tragicomedy** — a comedy in which the main plot is serious and might lead to catastrophe, but ends happily for the protagonist, as in Shakespeare's *The Merchant of Venice*.

B. **Farce** — a comedy primarily intended to make people laugh, as in Shakespeare's *The Taming of the Shrew* and many modern Broadway plays.

C. **Satirical Comedy** — comedy primarily interested in holding the foibles and vices of society up to ridicule, as the comedies of Artistophanes.

D. **Sentimental Comedy** — comedy in which the protagonist, no matter how dissolute, reforms in the end.

E. **Comedy of Humours** — a play in which an excess of one of the "humours" (blood, choler, phlegm, and melancholy) governs the protagonist and possibly others, with caricature rather than character portrayal as the result. Ben Jonson developed this type of play to its highest point: e.g., *Every Man in His Humour*.

F. **Comedy of Manners** — a type of comedy in which the artificialities of a sophisticated society are exposed and satirized. The plot, though cleverly contrived, is not so important as the characters, both men and women, who are urbane, somewhat immoral, and usually typed, and the dialogue, which is light, bantering, witty, brilliant, and cynical. Two good examples are Sheridan's *The School for Scandal* and Maugham's *The Circle*.

G. **Fantasy** — a form of comedy in which reality is disregarded, as in a fairy tale, and a fanciful world and situations predominate as in Shakespeare's *A Midsummer Night's Dream* and Barrie's *Peter Pan*.

Comic Relief — a comic element inserted in straight tragedy for the purpose of lightening the effect on the audience or of sharpening the emotional effect of a tragic scene by contrast. For instance, the "Drunken Porter Scene" of *Macbeth* tends to relieve the tension created by the murder of Duncan and at the same time, by contrast, makes that murder even more horrible.

Complicating Incident (sometimes called the *inciting* or *exciting force*) — in a narrative or a drama, the first incident which creates a conflict of forces or wills and thereby starts the plot on its way. In *Macbeth* the plot begins to move after Macbeth has heard the prophecies of the Weird Sisters. In *Julius Caesar* Cassius's first conversation with Brutus is the *complicating incident*.

Complication — within a narrative or a drama, an element which enters the story, causes a conflict, and thereby creates a new situation. For example, Macbeth has decided to let nature take its course until Duncan names Malcolm as his candidate for the kingship; this action changes the situation, and Macbeth's mind as well. In *Hamlet,* the first real *complication* is the meeting of Hamlet and his father's ghost. *Complication* is also the term applied to the second act of an Elizabethan play.

Conceit — in Elizabethan days, any simile or metaphor. Today *conceit* may mean a pretty or witty turn of expression, or it may be applied to an overdeveloped or far-fetched figure of speech.

Condensation — reduction to greater compactness. Most good poetry has this quality in that it expresses ideas with much greater compactness than is possible in prose.

Conflict — the struggle of opposing forces in a drama or a narrative. The *conflict* may be w i t h i n the individual himself (*internal*), as between Macbeth's ambition and his conscience; between idealism and selfishness as in Cyrano; between the forces of good and evil as in the **Morality Play.** It may be *external,* as between an individual and his heredity or his environment (*Main Street,* "To Build a Fire," *The Scarlett Letter,* and *The Emperor Jones*) or as between the wills of two individuals (*Pride and Prejudice*). It may be both *internal* and *external,* as in *Hamlet* (Hamlet's desire to act vs. his indecision, and Hamlet vs. Claudius). Without a *conflict* and its resolution, there can be no **Plot.**

Connotation of a word — includes all the ideas that are suggested by the term; e.g., "home" *connotes* comfort, love, security, privacy, etc., whereas it m e r e l y *denotes* the place where one lives. (See **Denotation.**) In Masefield's poem "Cargoes," the "Quinquireme of Nineveh," the "Stately Spanish galleon," and the "Dirty British coaster" *denote* merely three types of ships, but they *connote* three separate civilizations and all that we associate with those civilizations.

Context — the part of a passage in which a word or expression occurs and which helps to explain the meaning of the word or expression.

Convention — an accepted way of doing something. Thus in the **Epic** it is *conventional* to have a statement of the theme, an invocation to the Muse, the intermingling of the Gods in human affairs, etc. It was *conventional* in courtly love that the lover idealize womanhood, be humble before and completely loyal to his beloved, and be inspired by her to perform courageous and noble deeds. It was *conventional* in Elizabethan tragedy that the noblest individual left alive make the concluding speech, as did Octavius in *Julius Caesar* and Malcolm in *Macbeth*.

Crisis — a moment in a narrative or a drama when opposing forces are brought into intense struggle. There are usually a number of *crises* preceding the **Climax.** For example, in *Julius Caesar,* the discussion as to whether to kill Antony as well as Caesar; the scene in which Calpurnia persuades Caesar not to go to the Capitol and Decius Brutus makes him change his mind; Artemidorus' paper, the Sooth-sayers' words to Portia, and Popilius Lena's strange behaviour at the Capitol, which show that the conspirators and their designs are known to some; the death of Caesar; and the argument as to whether Antony will be allowed to speak at Caesar's funeral are all minor *crises* leading to the **Climax,** Antony's speech, which changed completely the positions of the conspirators.

Criticism (Literary) — the act or the art of passing judgment on the merits, as well as the deficiencies, of a literary work.

Denotation of a word — its exact meaning (Cf. **Connotation.**)

Deus Ex Machina (God out of the machine") — When the later Greek playwrights ran into a plot difficulty insoluble by logical means, they would use a mechanical crane to lower a god to the stage, who would then solve the problem by unnatural means. The term is now applied to any improbable method used by a writer to bring his plot to the desired solution, such as the last-second and almost impossible saving of the protagonist by General Lasalle in Poe's "The Pit and the Pendulum."

Dialogue — the conversation between characters in a literary work, or it may be an entire literary work in the form of conversation, as Plato's *Dialogues*.

Doggerel — verse that is irregular in metre, undignified in style, trivial in content, and often humorous or burlesque in tone, as the

44

following by Southey, which tells of the Russians' harassing the French in Napoleon's retreat from Moscow:

>"And Kutousoff he cut them off,
>And Parenzoff he pared them off,
>And Worronzoff he worried them off,
>And Doctoroff he doctored them off, . . . (*ad nauseam*)"

Drama — a form of composition either in prose or in verse which portrays life and character through dialogue and action, and is intended to be presented on a stage before an audience. There are many types of drama, the more important of which are defined in this section.

Dramatic Reverse — the incident in a drama or a narrative which usually immediately follows the climax and in which the fortunes of the protagonist reverse. In *Hamlet,* for example the *dramatic reverse* occurs when Hamlet kills Polonius, for it is his first mistake of action, it puts the King on his guard, it sends Hamlet away from Denmark, and it alienates Laertes. In *The Ancient Mariner,* the mariner blesses the water-snakes, and immediately his fortunes, which have reached their nadir, begin to rise.

Dramatic Unities — involved unity of time (action contained within a 24-hour period), unity of place (action laid in one general locality), and unity of action (action governed by one central idea, mood, or plot, with no sub-plots, digressions, or deviations from the theme permitted).

Dramatis Personae — the people of the drama; the list of characters usually found immediately following the title of the play.

Epigram — a short pithy saying, such as the following by Pope:

>"A little learning is a dangerous thing."
>"Hope springs eternal in the human breast."

As defined by Coleridge,

>"What is an epigram? A dwarfish whole;
>Its body brevity, and wit its soul."

It may be a short, pointed poem, often satirical or humorous, dealing with a single thought, such as those of Dorothy Parker or the following, a favourite of Alexander Woollcott's:

>"The golf course lies so near the mill
>That almost every day
>The laboring children can look out
>And watch the men at play." — Cleghorn

Epilogue (cf. **Prologue**) — (a) a short speech or poem addressed to the audience after the conclusion of a play (see *The School for Scandal*); or (b) a concluding section of a work, such as a novel, serving to complete the plan of the work (see *Moby Dick*).

Episode — a group of related incidents forming a definite part of the plot of a drama or a narrative. (Cf. **Incident.**)

Epitaph — an inscription on a tomb (or one suitable for inscription on a tomb) as that on Shakespeare's gravestone:

"Good friend, for Jesus' sake forbeare
To dig the dust enclosed here;
Bleste be the man that spares these stones,
And curst be he that moves my bones."

Or the *epitaph* written by Dryden for his wife:

"Here lies my wife. Here let her lie.
Now she's at rest. And so am I."

Essay — a form of prose in which the author expresses his personal opinion on almost any subject. The **Formal Essay** is an essay in which the author hides his own personality, writing as **objectively** as possible (See Bacon's *Essays*); the **Informal Essay**, or **Personal Essay** as it is sometimes called, is one in which the author becomes familiar, writes in a conversational tone, and reveals his own personality (See E. B. White's "Once More to the Lake," Thurber's "University Days," and the essays of Addison and Lamb).

Euphemism — a mild, even vague expression used instead of a harsh, unpleasant one, such as *perspire* for *sweat, pass away* for *die, lay to rest* for *bury*.

Euphony is produced by a generally pleasing combination of sounds. (Cf. **Cacophony.**)

"A damsel with a dulcimer
In a vision once I saw."

Euphuism — an affected style of writing established by John Lyly in his *Euphues,* which is characterized by **Alliteration**, extravagant **Similes**, frequent **Antithesis**, and parade of obscure learning.

"Be valyaunt, but not too venturous. Let thy attyre be
comely, but not costly." — Lyly

Today the term is applied to any ornate, artificial, elegant style of writing.

Exposition — the process of giving the reader or the audience necessary information about characters and **Antecedent Action**

before the plot begins. It is also the term applied to the first act of an Elizabethan drama.

Fable — a short secular *allegory,* such as *Aesop's Fables,* in which the actions of animals are used to illustrate moral lessons.

Fiction — the name for stories dealing with imaginary people and imaginary events.

Figurative — expressing one thing in terms of another with which it is analogous. (Cf. **Literal.**)

Figure of Speech — a form of expression in which words are used out of their usual sense in order to make the meaning more specific by (a) *clarifying* ("Muscles as *strong as iron bands*,"; "The road was *a ribbon of moonlight*"); (b) *ornamenting* ("My luve is like *a red, red rose*", "Like *girls at their first communion* the pear trees stand") or (c) *adding emotional force* ("She is *a real beast*"; "The *icy hands* of Death"). **Mixed Figure of Speech** — two incongruous or inconsistent **Figures of Speech** combined to make one: e.g., "Keep your eye on the ball, and don't get off the track," and "Put your shoulder to the wheel, and you'll climb the ladder of success." In the following, Shakespeare has been inconsistent in his **Metaphor** in that "ambition" is first a *spur* and then the *rider* himself vaulting into the saddle:

> "   I have no spur
> To prick the sides of my intent, but only
> Vaulting ambition, which o'erlaps itself
> And falls on th' other side." (*Macbeth*)

Focus — The centre around which an author organizes his material and builds his story. It may be a character (Hamlet or Thomas a Becket), a setting (Egdon Heath in *The Return of the Native* or the jungle in *Green Mansions*), the plot (*The Count of Monte Cristo* or *Treasure Island*), or the theme (London's *The Sea Wolf*).

Foil — a character who, because of his qualities, tends to emphasize by contrast the qualities of another character. In *Oedipus,* Creon is a *foil* to Oedipus because he is circumspect and reasonable, whereas Oedipus is rash and passionate. In *Hamlet,* both Laertes and Fortinbras serve as *foils* to Hamlet, for their situations are similar to his, but their natures and actions are entirely different.

Foot — a portion of a line of poetry, usually consisting of one accented and either one or two unaccented syllables.

The number of feet in a line determines the type of line. Note that division into poetic feet is marked with a vertical line (|).

1. **Monometer** (one foot): "To arms!" |

2. **Dimeter** (two feet): "Life must | go on; |
   I forget | just why." |

3. **Trimeter**: "He made | and lov | eth all." |

4. **Tetrameter:** "I have | a ren | dezvous | with Death." |

5. **Pentameter:** "I'd rath | er be | a dog | and bay | the moon." |

6. **Hexameter:** "That doth | this Red | crosse Knight's ensam | ple plain | ly prove." |

7. **Heptameter:** "Oh East | is East, | and West | is West | and nev | er the twain | shall meet."

8. **Octameter.** "Take | thy beak | from out | my heart | and take | thy form | from off | my door."

Poetic feet have been given technical names according to the number and arrangement of the accented and unaccented syllables within a foot.

1. **Iambus** (adjective — **Iambic**): unaccented — accented.
   ĕm bárk   rĕ láte   dĕ fér

2. **Trochee** (adjective — **Trochaic**): accented — unaccented.
   fránk lў   qués tiŏn   díf fĕr

3. **Spondee:** accented — accented
   blóod-réd   lífe líke   gréy stónes

4. **Pyrrhic Foot**: Unaccented — unaccented.
   "Thĕ sáil | ŏf thĕ | dĕpárt | ĭng shíp." |

5. **Anapaest** (adjective — **Anapaestic**): unaccented —unac-cented — accented.
   cĭg ă rétte   ĭn tĕr rúpt   ĕn gĭ néer

6. **Dactyl** (adjective — **Dactylic**): accented — unaccented — unaccented.
   láugh ă blĕ   mí crŏ scŏpe   sén tĭ mĕnt

7. **Amphibrach** (adjective — **Amphibrachic**): unaccented — accented — unaccented.
   spĕ cí fĭc   ĕl líp sĭs   ĕn jóy mĕnt

Foreshadowing — the process in a drama or a narrative of giving the audience or the reader a hint about a coming event. In *Julius Caesar,* for instance, the scene between Portia and the Soothsayer and the scene in which we meet Artemidorus both *foreshadow* the murder of Caesar. The Weird Sisters of *Macbeth,* by their prophecies, *foreshadow* the major actions in that play.

Frame Story — one in which there is a basic story (the *frame*) from which other stories develop, such as those told by the ten young noble people escaping from the plague in Boccaccio's *Decameron Tales* and by the pilgrims going to Canterbury in Chaucer's *Canterbury Tales.* Later *frame stories* include Irving's *Tales of a Traveller,* Longfellow's *Tales of a Wayside Inn,* and Whittier's *Tent on a Beach.*

Genre (zhan'-r) — in its broadest sense, literaray works similar in form, style, content, or purpose, such as the novel or drama (form), Elizabethan sonnets (form and style), poetry expressing the "death wish" (content), the "muckraking" novels of the early 20th Century in America (form and purpose).

Gothic Novel (Romance) — a **Genre** introduced by Horace Walpole's *The Castle of Otranto,* in which there is much of the supernatural for blood-chilling, spine-tingling effect. Haunted castles, secret passageways, ghosts, statues and portraits that came alive, strange cries and shrieks, etc., were characteristic. Later *Gothic novels* include Mary Godwin Shelley's *Frankenstein* and Bram Stoker's *Dracula.* They were the forerunners of the modern horror story.

Hyperbole — an obvious exaggeration for the sake of effect without any attempt at deception.

> "Will all great Neptune's ocean wash this blood
> Clean from my hand? No, this *my hand will rather*
> *The multitudinous seas incarnadine,*
> *Making the green one red."*

> "Here once the embattled farmers stood
> And fired *the shot heard round the world."*

Idyl(l) — a pastoral poem that presents an incident of natural simplicity in a rustic setting, such as Burns' "The Cotter's Saturday Night" and Whittier's *Snowbound.*

Image — a word, expression, or idea that appeals to the senses and clarifies by creating a mental picture with sensory implications, as in Shakespeare's "Sonnet 73," in which the *images* of the dying year, the dying day, and the dying fire suggest the shortness of life remaining and imply the urgency of loving strongly before death comes.

Imagery — the use of words that appeal to one of the senses —sight (gleaming knives), smell ("the clean pine-board of created produce"), taste (candied apples), hearing (roaring fire), touch (satin skin), or the kinesthetic —muscular — sense (squirming eels). Keats was particularly fond of *imagery,* as is illustrated from "The Eve of St. Agnes":

> "blanchéd linen, smooth, and lavendered" (sight, touch, smell)
>
> "lucent sirups . . . spicéd dainties" (taste)
>
> "music yearning like a God in pain" (hearing)
>
> "silver, snarling 'gan to chide."
>
> "The maiden's chamber, silken, hushed, and chaste."

Imagists — a group of 20th Century poets, including Amy Lowell and Ezra Pound, who generally used *Free Verse* and who believed in writing on any subject, expressing their ideas and emotions in clear, precise images, and using concrete words from the language of common speech. See Amy Lowell's "A Lady" and "Patterns" as examples of their type of work.

Incident — something that happens, a single event. A number of incidents usually go together to form an **Episode.** For example, the notes' being thrown into Brutus' study is one *incident* in the whole *episode* of the winning of Brutus to the conspiracy in Shakespeare's *Julius Caesar.*

In Medias Res ("into the midst of the thing") — A writer is said to have "plunged *in medias res"* if he begins his narrative with an important incident rather than the first incident in order of time. Milton's *Paradise Lost* begins with Satan and the other fallen angels' rising from the Lake of Fire and plotting revenge against God, who has cast them out of Heaven. It is not until Book V that Milton, through Raphael, relates the story of their rebellion, which caused their loss of Paradise.

Interlude — a farcical type of short drama designed to be presented between the acts of a miracle or morality play, or even between the courses of a banquet. The best-known is John Haywood's *The Four P's.*

Inversion — a change in the normal order of words in a sentence, which is quite common in poetry. Emily Dickinson in

"I Never Saw a Moor" says,

> "Yet *certain am I* of the spot . . ."

rather than in the normal order of subject, verb, subjective complement:

> " Yet *I am certain* of the spot . . ."

Irony — A. A statement in which the opposite is said from what is actually intended (called **Verbal Irony**). In *Julius Caesar,* Antony called the conspirators "honourable men" when he really meant they were "dishonourable." Pope actually meant "uninstructive hours" when he said in *The Rape of the Lock* concerning the nobility who frequented Hampton Court:

> "In various talk th' instructive hours they passed:
> Who gave the ball, or paid the visit last."

In "The Shortest Way with the Dissenters" Defoe, in an attempt to plead for tolerance by showing the Anglicans and the Tories, who were very violent against the Dissenting churches, how ridiculously extreme they had become, advocated hanging all Dissenting ministers and exiling all members of non-Anglican churches. Unfortunately, his *irony* was so realistic that both the Dissenters and the Tories took him literally.

B. When the opposite to the expected occurs or when one does not get what he deserves, there is **Situation Irony.** In O. Henry's "The Cop and the Anthem," Soapy reforms and decides not to try again to be sent to jail for the winter. Just at that moment, a policeman arrests him for vagrancy, and a judge sentences him to jail for the winter months. In *Oedipus Rex,* Oedipus pronounces a curse on the slayer of Laius; ironically, he himself is the slayer. Macbeth trusts implicitly in the statement of the Witches that no man born of woman can harm him; then, at the last he discovers that Macduff, his mortal enemy, was not "of woman born."

C. When the audience or the reader knows more than do the characters, **Dramatic Irony** occurs. A Grecian audience knew the whole story of a play before they ever saw it; thus they knew exactly what was going to happen and were always "ahead of" the characters. The audience hears the prophecy of the Witches regarding Macbeth's safety "Till Birnam Forest come to Dunsinane"; they learn that Birnam Wood will be used by Malcolm's soldiers as camouflage on the march against Dunsinane; thus they know more than either Macbeth or Malcolm and await with suspense the former's reaction when he learns that the wood *"is* come to Dunsinane."

Kenning — a metaphorical compound word used in Anglo-Saxon poetry for, or in addition to, the usual name of a person or thing: e.g., "wave-skimmer" for a *boat;* "swan-road'" for the *sea;* etc.

Legend — a story which is considered to be based on fact, although proof of its truth is unavailable. The most famous English *legends* are those about King Arthur, on which are based many English works, such as Spenser's *The Faerie Queene,* Malory's *Morte d'Arthur,* and Tennyson's *Idylls of the King.* (Cf. **Myth.**)

Limerick — a five-line nonsense stanza of **Anapaestic** feet, the first, second, and fifth lines being **Trimeter** and the third and fourth **Dimeter.** The **Rhyme Scheme** is *a a b b a.*

> "There was once a faith-healer of Peele
> Who said, 'Although pain isn't real,
> If I sit on a pin
> And I puncture my skin,
> I dislike what I fancy I feel,' " — Anon.

Literal — conveying the primary meaning.
Dove — (*Literal*) a kind of pigeon.
  (*Figurative*) the symbol of the Holy Spirit.
Laurel — (*Literal*) a kind of shrub.
  (*Figurative*) a symbol of victory over achievement.

Local Colour Story — one in which the quaint and interesting peculiarities of a particular locale are emphasized, such as its customs, its dialect, etc. Bret Harte's stories of the West, Cable's *Old Creole Days,* and Joel Chandler Harris' Uncle Remus stories are good examples.

Malapropism — the ridiculous misuse of a word, as Mrs. Malprop did so often in Sheridan's *The Rivals*: e.g., "You forfeit my *malevolence* (benevolence) forever" and "that she may *reprehend* (apprehend) the true meaning of what she is saying." Perhaps her most delightful *malapropisms* occur in her misquotation of Hamlet's speech to his mother regarding his father:

> "Hesperian curls — the front of Job himself! —
> And eye, like March, to threaten at command! —
> A station, like Harry Mercury . . ."

Masque — a form of spectacular drama with a loosely constructed allegorical plot usually given at court or at some manor house on a special occasion, such as a visit by Queen Elizabeth. It was characterized by a certain amount of dialogue, much singing and dancing, and very ornate costuming and stage settings, somewhat like the modern musical comedy. Although the most famous *masque* is Milton's *Comus,* Ben Jonson is probably the best known writer of *masques.*

Melodrama — a highly sensational or romantic play in which reality is suspended to give the audience thrills, to create emotional excitement, such as O'Neill's "Where the Cross Is Made" and *The Emperor Jones.*

Metaphor — a comparison, either expressed or implied, without the use of *like* or *as.*

> "My father, he was a mountaineer
> His *fist* was a *knotty hammer."* — Benét
> "Life's but a *walking shadow,* a *poor player*
> *That struts and frets his hour upon the stage . . ."*

In the following *metaphors,* the comparison is implied: first, between the "middle mind" and a pleasant cat, and second, between Claudius' murder of Hamlet Sr. and something stinkingly rotten.

> "But O beware the middle mind
> That purrs and never shows a tooth." — Wylie
> "O, my offence is rank; it smells to heaven."

Sometimes the comparison will be used throughout a whole poem (an **Extended Metaphor**) as in Tennyson's "Crossing the Bar," Sandburg's "Prayers of Steel," and Longfellow's "Hymn to the Night."

Metonymy — the use of a word for another with which it is intimately associated. (**Metaphor** is based on resemblance between two dissimilar things; *metonymy,* on association, the part being used for the whole or the whole for the part.)

> "*Grey hair* (old people) should be respected."
> "To read *Chaucer* (i.e., his works) is to dwell with genius".
> "Strike for your *altars* and your *fires."*

The altar and the fire are associated with and here stand for religion and the home respectively.

Metre — the pattern of rhythm in a line of poetry (see **Scansion**).

Metrical Pattern — the accent pattern set in the first line of a poem and expected in succeeding lines.

Metrical Variations — If a poem rigidly adheres to the metrical pattern set in the first line, much of its charm is often lost in the inflexible and monotonous recurrence of the same rhythm; therefore poets vary the meter in different ways.

1. They will use a type of foot which is different from the prevailing one in the line, such as a trochee in an iambic line:

"Sŏmethĭng | thĕre ĭs | thăt dóes | nŏt lóve ǀ ă wáll." |

2. Or a **Truncated (Catalectic) Foot**, one in which a pause is substituted for an unaccented syllable, as in Tennyson's

"Brĕak, | brĕak, | brĕak, . . ." |

3. Or a **Feminine Ending**, which is a syllable added to the end of a line, as in

Tŏmór | rŏw ánd | tŏmór | rŏw ánd | tŏmórrŏw . . ." |

4. In blank verse, there are several methods of producing metrical variations other than the use of different types of feet, feminine endings, and truncated feet. A **Caesura** is a "sense" pause in the middle of a line. It is marked in scansion with parallel vertical lines (||). A **Run-on Line** is a line that does not end with a pause or with a complete thought, as opposed to an **End-Stopped Line,** which does. Note how Milton's skillful use of *caesuras* and *run-on lines* in the following prevents the lines' being sing-songy, precise, and rigid:

"Of man's first disobedience, || and the fruit *(Run-on)*
Of that forbidden tree whose mortal taste *(Run-on)*
Brought death into the World, || and all our woe, *(End-stopped)*
With loss of Eden, || till one greater Man *(Run-on)*
Restore us, || and regain the blissful seat, *(End-stopped)*
Sing, Heavenly Muse." ||

Miracle Play — a medieval drama which related stories about the lives of the saints and the miracles which they had performed.

Mock-Heroic — the term applied to poetry which treats a trivial subject in the epic manner. It is often used interchangeably with **Mock Epic.** A good example of a *mock-heroic poem* is Chaucer's "Nun's Priest's Tale," which is the old "Cock and the Fox" story told in the manner of the epic with many of the epic conventions.

Mood — the emotional state of the author as he expresses what he has to say; it is his attitude toward his subject. (Cf.

Tone.) Sometimes the author's mood and tone may be identical; often they are not. For example, the mood may be *disgusted,* and the tone *sarcastic;* the mood *sympathetic,* and the tone *inspirational;* the mood *bitter,* but the tone *ironically gay;* the mood *hopeless,* but the tone *hysterically defiant.* The attitude of writers towards Death varies greatly. Seeger's mood in "I Have a Rendezvous with Death" is *tragic*; Browning's in "Prospice" is *optimistic* and *triumphant;* Bryant's in "Thanatopsis" is *philosophical;* Keats' in "When I Have Fears" is *doleful*; and Lanier's in "The Stirrup Cup" is *heroic.*

Moral — the practical lesson taught by a piece of writing, especially by **Fables** and other didactic writings. The *moral* of "The Ancient Mariner" is expressed by the lines:

> "He prayeth best who loveth best
> All things, both great and small;
> For the dear God loveth us,
> He made and loveth all."

Morality Play — a type of allegorical drama in which the characters were personified abstractions, such as Charity, Faith, Good Deeds, Fellowship, Jealously, Vice, etc. It generally was involved with a struggle between Virtue and Vice for the possession of a man's soul, and had as its purpose the imparting of a moral lession; thus Marlowe's *Dr. Faustus* has many of the elements of a *morality play.* The most famous *morality* is *Everyman.*

Motive — a reason which causes a character to act as he does. For instance, in *Julius Caesar,* Cassius' motive is envy of anyone greater than himself; therefore he is *motivated* to overthrow Caesar. In romantic literature, characters are usually impelled by a single motive, as Dantes is by revenge in *The Count of Monte Cristo* and Faustus is by pride; in realistic literature (*Hamlet* for example), the characters have mixed motives, as they do in real life.

Mystery Play — a medieval drama which presented stories from the Bible, usually centering about the redemption of man.

Myth — a story, usually involving the supernatural, which explains some practice, belief, or natural phenomenon. The myth of Ceres and Prosperpina explained to the ancients the mystery of vegetation during six months of the year and its absence during the other six months.

Narrative — a story of any kind.

Naturalism — a form of **Realism** in which man is looked upon as just another animal governed almost entirely by nature — by physical and chemical forces. He cannot rise above his materialistic world; he has no free will, for he is controlled by overpowering forces, and therefore he is relieved of moral responsibility. For examples, see Dreiser's *An American Tragedy*, Dos Passo's *U.S.A.,* and London's *The Call of the Wild*. Sometimes the exponent of *naturalism,* in his preoccupation to "tell all" and portray "life in the raw," becomes tedious with too many intimacies and unpleasant details which might well have been omitted. (Adj. — **Naturalistic**.)

Novel — extended prose **Fiction** in which fictitious characters and actions similar to those of real life are portrayed in a **Plot**. (Cf. **Romance**.) Unfortunately, there are so many different types of *novels* — the **Gothic**, the **Naturalistic**, the **Picaresque**, the **Problem,** the **Propaganda**, the **Psychological**, the **Realistic**, the **Stream-of-consciousness,** etc. — that a detailed, accurate definition is almost impossible.

Novelette — a short novel, usually of less than forty thousand words, designed to be read at a single sitting to create a single effect, as Hemingway's *The Old Man and the Sea*.

Objective — the term applied to an attitude which is detached, impersonal, unprejudiced in its approach to a subject. **Subjective,** on the other hand, is applied to a personal attitude. A photograph of a landscape would be *objective*; a painting of it would probably be *subjective* because the impressions of the artist would be injected into it. Milton seems almost entirely *objective* in *Paradise Lost* because he seldom introduces ideas which the reader recognizes as those of the writer; in his sonnet, "On Having Arrived at the Age of Twenty-three," he is entirely *subjective*, for he writes about himself from his own personal point of view.

Occasional Poem — a poem written for a special occasion. Good examples are "The Boys" which Oliver Wendell Holmes wrote for the thirtieth reunion of his college class, and Mr. Willoughby Reade's "Centennial Ode," which he composed for the celebration of the hundredth year of Episcopal High School.

One-Act Play — just what its name implies: a play in one act. Just as the full-length play is often compared with the novel, the one-act play is comparable to the short story in that it should deal with a *single* crisis in the life of a *single* character, and should develop a *single* theme and create a *single* effect.

Onomatopoeia — the imitation of sounds by words either directly (*buzz, bang, splash*) or suggestively (the swish of "ladies' skirts across the grass," and "the silken sad uncertain rustling of each purple curtain").

Parable — a short religious allegory, such as "The Good Samaritan," "The Prodigal Son," "The Sower," etc.

Paradox — a statement that either seems to or actually does contradict itself.

> "If a man would save his life, he must lose it."
>
> "I could not love thee, Dear, so much,
> Loved I not Honor more."
>
> "Here lies our sovereign lord, the King,
> Whose word no man relies on;
> He never says a foolish thing
> Nor ever does a wise one."

Paraphrase — a restatement of a passage in one's own words.

Parody — a work mimicking the language, style, or ideas of another for comic or satiric effect. Note the following parody of Hamlet's famous "To be or not to be" soliloquy:

> "To study or not to study — that is the question;
> Whether 'tis better at my age to suffer
> The demerits of my outraged teachers,
> Or to take my suitcase in my hand
> And by running away, end them."

Pastoral (from the Latin *pastor* — shepherd) — dealing with shepherds or simple rural life. For examples of *pastoral* writings, see Spenser's *The Shepherd's Calendar,* Marlowe's "The Passionate Shepherd to His Love," Shakespeare's *As You Like It,* and Milton's "Lycidas."

Pathos — a quality in a piece of literature which excites pity, sorrow, or sympathy in the reader. In *Hamlet,* Claudius' soliloquy beginning, "O, my offence is rank, it smells to heaven," awakens the feeling of sympathy in the audience; therefore it is said to have *pathos.* When the attempt to stimulate the emotion falls flat or becomes ludicrous, the result is called **Bathos.**

Personification — the giving of personality or life to inanimate objects or to ideas.

> "The *sea* creeps to pillage,
> She leaps on her prey . . ." — Wylie
>
> "But look, the *morn,* in russet mantle clad,
> Walks o'er the dew of yon high eastward hill."

"When *Duty* whispers low, 'Thou must,'
The Youth replies, 'I can.' "

Picaresque — a term meaning "characteristic of rogues," from the Spanish *picaro* (rogue). The **Picaresque Novel** is the story of a rogue, told generally in the first person. Because of poverty and mistreatment in childhood, he is motivated by the baser instincts and by a desire to "make good in the world" by any means other than work; but he reforms and lives respectably before the end. Outstanding examples are Defoe's *Moll Flanders* and *Colonel Jack*. Fielding, Smollett, and Dickens have *picaresque novel* qualities in many of their works.

Plot — the *plan* of the author of a narrative or a drama to bring his characters through a conflict to an inevitable conclusion. In a typical dramatic plot, the **Protagonist** comes into conflict with the **Antagonist** in a **Complicating Incident.** There is then a series of incidents (the **Complication** or rising action) in which the struggle of the protagonist with the opposing force increases in intensity, perhaps with minor **Crises,** until a **Climax** is reached. Then occurs the **Dramatic Reverse,** with resultant falling action (**Resolution**), which leads to the **Dénouement** or **Catastrophe.**

There are certain essentials of any good plot:

1. There must be a **Conflict** which is sufficiently intense and interest-arousing to create **Suspense.**

2. Only **Incidents** and **Episodes** which are important to the development and the resolution of the conflict should be included.

3. The incidents which occur should be in keeping with the characters of those who participate in them and should arise because of the nature of their characters.

4. The **Dénouement** must be natural, even inevitable, and not forced by some **Deus ex machina.**

Poetic Justice — the term applied to the proper operation of justice (so common in poetry and fiction) in that the good are rewarded and the evil punished. It is most impressive when a culprit is ironically snared in his own trap, as Laertes is by the poisoned sword and Claudius by the sword and the poisoned cup in *Hamlet,* for as Hamlet says,

"   'Tis the sport to have the enginer
Hoist with his own petar."

Poetic License — the right of a poet to depart from the normal for purposes of effect. For instance, Pope says, "Drink *deep* (rather than *deeply*) or taste not the Pierian spring", and Shakespeare writes, "Wishing *me* (rather than *myself*) like to one more rich in hope." Such departure from grammatical rules would never be permitted in prose, particularly by English teachers. Even errors of fact are excused under *poetic license*, as when Keats gave credit to Cortez rather than to Balboa for discovering the Pacific Ocean in his "On First Looking Into Chapman's Homer."

Point of View — the position from which something is observed, a matter is considered, a story is told, etc.; it is extremely important in governing the selection of material.

A. In a description, the writer chooses a *point of view* (such as a hilltop or a sand dune) and tells what he sees from that position.

B. A matter may be considered either **Objectively** or **Subjectively,** *optimistically* or *pessimistically,* in a debate either *affirmatively* or *negatively,* etc.

C. An author may tell his story from any one of several different *points of view*: i.e., the person through whose eyes and mind the reader "sees" the story may be any one of several people.

1. *First person* — The narrator is the "I" of the story. He may be the major character (Huck Finn), the author himself (Maugham in *The Razor's Edge*), or a minor character (the narrator in *The Virginian*). By using this *point of view,* the author limits himself in his selection of material in that he can relate only what the narrator himself thinks, observes, and hears.

2. *Third person*:

a. *Limited* — The author tells his story with the focus on one character, usually the main one (Robert Jordan in *For Whom the Bell Tolls* and Henry in *The Red Badge of Courage*); the author can see into the mind of this character only and can narrate only those actions and scenes at which he is actually present unless someone else tells this character what happened in his absence. An extremely *limited point of view* is the "dramatic objective." The author takes the position of a mere observer and tells only what happened and what was said, and leaves the reader to infer what the characters thought (Hemingway's "The Killers").

b. *Omniscient* — The author selects the *point of view* of a person who knows everything that happens, who can see into the very consciences and motives of the characters, and who even inserts his own comments (*The Scarlet Letter* and *Vanity Fair*).

Sometimes the *point of view* in a story will change; e.g., from "third person omniscient" to "first person" (Conrad's *Lord Jim*), or from one "first person" to another (Mr. Lockwood and Mrs. Dean in *Wuthering Heights*).

Précis — a brief summary. (Cf. **Paraphrase.**)

Problem Play or Novel — one written primarily to delineate some problem of human relationships as they are affected by social laws and customs. As examples see Ibsen's *A Doll's House* and Hawthorne's *The Scarlet Letter*.

Prologue — An introduction to a play, a novel, or a poem. It may serve many purposes; e.g., to give **Antecedent Action,** as in Marlowe's *Dr. Faustus;* to lay the **Setting,** as the Stage Manager, serving as the prologue, does in Wilder's *Our Town;* to expound the **Theme,** as in *Everyman;* or to establish the **Mood,** as in Sheridan's *The School for Scandal.* (*Cf.* **Epilogue.**)

Propaganda — writings that stress "a message" usually at the expense of fact and logic. The **Propaganda Novel** can be as extreme as Stowe's *Uncle Tom's Cabin* or as mild as Dickens' *Oliver Twist* and *Nicholas Nickleby*.

Prose — that which is written in the ordinary language of conversation, newspapers, textbooks, etc., and is distinguished from poetry by its typographical form and by the irregularity of its rhythm.

Prose Statement — a **Paraphrase** of a poem or part of a poem.

Prosody — the science of versification. It includes **Metre, Rhyme,** etc.

Protagonist — the character who takes the leading part in a play (Brutus in *Julius Caesar*), a novel (Sidney Carton in *A Tale of Two Cities*), or a short story (Pepé Torres in "Flight"). (Cf. **Antagonist.**)

Proverb — a brief, epigrammatic saying that has become a by-word. The terms **Adage** and **Maxim** are used synonymously with *proverb.*

"A rolling stone gathers no moss."
"Liars should have good memories."
"He that spareth his rod hateth his son."

Psychological Novel (Story) — one in which what goes on in the characters' minds and why they act as they do are of more importance than what happens. See Hawthorne's and George Eliot's works as examples. An extreme form is the **Stream-of-Consciousness Novel (Story)**.

Pun — a play on words that sound alike, usually for the sake of humour. Although the pun is considered "the lowest form of wit," it was often used by Shakespeare and other Elizabethan playwrights, probably to please the "pit" crowd. In the opening scene of *Julius Caesar,* when Marullus asks the Cobbler his trade, he is told, "A mender of bad *soles,*" which may mean that the Cobbler is either a priest or a shoemaker. When Flavius questions him further, he replies, "Truly, sir, *all* that I live by is with the *awl.*"

Realism — a theory of writing which emphasizes that *real,* not idealized, life must be presented in a story or a drama.

Realistic — the term applied to writing which presents life as it is; which tells not only of the good, but also the evil; which describes not only the heroic achievements, but also the dismal failures of its characters; which treats of not only the existing moments in a character's life, but also the drab and commonplace ones; which deals with ordinary, average people, not just heroes. See Jane Austen's *Pride and Prejudice* as an example of a *realistic* novel, Ibsen's *A Doll's House* as an example of a *realistic* drama. (Cf. **Romantic** and **Naturalistic.**)

Refrain — a group of words, a line, or a group of lines which recurs regularly at the end of successive stanzas in a poem, as the familiar

> "On our way rejoicing,
> As we homeward move,
> Harken to our praises,
> O thou God of love."

which is repeated at the end of each stanza of the **Hymn,** "On Our Way Rejoicing."

Repetition — the repeating of a word or phrase for emphasis or rhetorical effect.

> "Alone, alone, all, all alone.
> Alone on a wide, wide sea."

> "The war is inevitable — and let it come! I repeat it, sir, let it come!"

Resolution — the part of a drama or a narrative in which the problems created by the complications are solved and the stage is set for the **Dénouement.** It is also the term often applied to the fourth act of an Elizabethan drama.

Restraint — control over and repression of feelings, a quality of good poetry. Lack of restraint leads to sentimentality or over-ornate language. An excellent example of *restraint* may be seen in Amy Lowell's "Patterns," in which not only Miss Lowell, but also the subject of the poem shows the power to control her emotions.

Rhetorical — the term applied to writing which emphasizes style, usually at the expense of thought.

Rhetorical Device — an expression used by orators and writers to secure effect, often at the expense of thought, such as **Antithesis, Climax,** the **Rhetorical Question, Hyperbole, C o n c e i t s,** and **Repetition.**

Rhetorical Question — a question to which no answer is expected or which implies its own answer.

> ". . .   O Wind,
> If Winter comes, can Spring be far behind?"
>   "Is life so dear, or peace so sweet, as to be
> purchased at the price of chains and slavery?"

Rhyme — the similarity between the sounds of words or syllables. For there to be perfect *rhyme,* (a) the vowel sounds must be similar and accented; (b) the sounds following the vowel must be similar; (c) the sounds preceding the vowel must be different.

cr — y	comm — u — nity
b — uy	imp — u — nity
l — ie	opport — u — nity

Types of Rhymes:

A. **End Rhyme** — the correspondence between the sounds of words at the end of lines.

> "The woods are lovely, dark, and *deep,*
> But I have promises to *keep.*
> And miles to go before I *sleep*." — Frost

B. **Masculine Rhyme** — one that is single.

> run — fun — one — sun — done

C. **Feminine Rhyme** — one that is multiple with the first rhyming syllable accented and the following ones not accented.

showers — flowers — bowers; impulsively — convulsively

D. Internal Rhyme — rhyme of words in the same line or between a word in one line and one within the next.

> "We were the *first* that ever *burst* . . ."
> "The trees were black where the bark was *wet.*
> I see them *yet,* in the spring of the year. . . .
> The rooks went up with raucous *trill.*
> I hear them *still,* in the fall of the year." — Millay

E. Consonance — the agreement of ending consonant sounds when the vowel sounds differ.

gro*ss* - cra*ss*	na*ture* - fea*ture*
li*ve* - do*ve*	a*ngrily* - hu*ngrily*

F. Imperfect Rhyme — the use, where rhyme is expected, of words that do not strictly rhyme. (See also **Assonance** and **Consonance**.)

1. **Visual Rhyme** — the use of words which appear to the eye to rhyme, but which are pronounced differently.
   good - food; sword - word; breast - feast

2. **Strained Rhyme** — the use of words which must be forced to rhyme by changing the accent.
   cry - silent*ly;* mak*ing* - *sing; die* - memo*ry*

G. Rhyme Scheme — the pattern of rhymes in a stanza. It is usually marked by the use of the letter of the alphabet, beginning with *a* and using the same letter to denote all lines which rhyme. The following is an example from Keats' "The Eve of St. Agnes" of the rhyme scheme in the Spenserian stanza.

"They glide, like phantoms, into the wide hall,	a
Like phantoms, to the iron porch, they glide;	b
Where lay the Porter, in uneasy sprawl	a
With a huge empty flagon by his side:	b
The wakeful bloodhound rose, and shook his hide,	b
But his sagacious eye an inmate owns:	c
By one, and one, the bolts easy slide: —	b
The chains lie silent on the footworn stones; —	c
The key turns, and the door upon its hinges groans."	c

Rhythm — the recurring rise and fall of sounds in a line of poetry.

Romance — a kind of novel that deals with people, events, and places that are unreal or out of the ordinary. It emphasizes adventure, surprising incidents, improbable situations, etc., rather than character, and serves the reader as an escape from the world of reality. A rather good example of the modern *romance* is Stevenson's *The Black Arrow* with its imprisoned ladies in distress, battles, shipwrecks, underground passageways, peepholes, outlaws, avaricious nobles, and final triumph of virtue. Malory's *Morte d'Arthur* is possibly the best of the medieval *prose romances*. Sir Walter Scott may be considered the typical *romancer*.

Romantic — the term applied to that which in literature is not essentially true to life. (Cf. **Realistic**). The basic differences between *realistic* and *romantic* are well illustrated in the companion poems of Marlowe and Raleigh, "The Passionate Shepherd to His Love" and "The Nymph's Reply to the Shepherd," in which the shepherd sees the world through rose-coloured glasses, picturing a life of pleasure lived in an eternal summertime, whereas the utterly practical nymph sees life as it is, with its responsibilities, its sorrows as well as its joys, its winter as well as its summer.

Romanticism — a literary movement which reacted against the regimentation of the 18th Century. It is best defined by a listing of its characteristics. It was marked by

1. An interest in the individual rather than in society.
2. A rebellion against all things which limit or hamper the individual.
3. An interest in the lives of common people and things.
4. Sympathy for the downtrodden.
5. Hatred of war.
6. Belief in the brotherhood of man.
7. Love of Nature.
8. The concept that God was to be found in Nature.
9. The concept that Nature was a means of escape from the evils of human society.
10. Expression of emotion.
11. Use of the imagination.
12. Interest in the supernatural.
13. A sense of awe and wonder concerning the universe.
14. Hatred of hypocrisy and outward show.
15. Freedom in versification.
16. The use of concrete, commonplace language in poetry.
17. An interest in the past, especially of Medieval Britain.

Sarcasm — a bitter remark intended to hurt the feelings of the individual at whom it is aimed. It may be **Ironical** ("You really are ready to play a football game, all right!") or direct ("Why, you couldn't run the length of the field without resting twice!")

Satire — a form of writing in which human follies and vices are held up to ridicule, generally with the intention of reform. It may be gentle (Addison and Steele), sharp and pointed (Pope, Dryden, and Byron), or extremely bitter (Swift). It may be religious (Defoe's *The Shortest Way with the Dissenters*), political (Dryden's *Absalom and Achitophel*), social (Addison's *Sir Roger de Coverley Papers*), personal (Byron's *English Bards and Scotch Reviewers*), or all inclusive (Swift's *Gulliver's Travels*).

Scansion — the distinguishing of the metrical feet in a line of poetry by oral accent or by written marks.

Lines of poetry are given technical names according to the number of feet and the prevailing type of foot. The following lines have been scanned and given their technical names:

1. *Iambic pentameter*:
   "Whĕn Í | sĕe bírch | ĕs bénd | tŏ léft | ănd ríght ..."

2. *Trochaic trimeter*:
   "Téach mĕ | hálf thĕ | gládnĕss ..." |

3. *Anapaestic tetrameter*:
   "Ănd thĕ míght | ŏf thĕ Gén | tĭle ŭnsmóte | bў thĕ swórd ..." |

4. *Amphibrachic dimeter*:
   "Ă tréachĕr ŏus smílĕr ... |
   Ă sávagĕ | bĕguílĕr ..."

5. *Dactylic hexameter*:
   "Thís ĭs thĕ | fórĕst prĭ | mévăl, thĕ | múrmŭrĭng | píñes
   ănd thĕ | hémlŏck ..."

Scene — a minor division of a play, generally dealing with a single situation or episode.

Sentiment — delicate and refined expression of emotion. **Sentimentality,** on the other hand, is affected, gushing feeling — cheap *sentiment*. The former may be found in Edna St. Vincent Millay's "Lament," which shows real restraint; the latter, in Hood's "Song of the Shirt," which is a "tear-jerker."

Setting — in a drama or a narrative, the time and place in which the action occurs: e.g., in *Julius Caesar,* the *setting* is Rome, 44 B.C. *Setting* often includes the so-called "Moral Environment," as *Puritan* New England in *The Scarlet Letter*. The term is also used for the scenery, the properties, and the costumes used in staging a play.

Short Story — a narrative which, like the novel, carries its main character through a **Conflict** to a **Climax** and **Dénouement,** but which, unlike the novel, is brief, has few characters, concerns a single crisis only, and creates a single impression.

Simile — a comparison of two persons, things, or other elements with the use of *like* or *as.*

> "You are beautiful and faded
> *Like an old opera tune*
> *Played upon a harpsichord."* — Amy Lowell

> "And ice, mast-high, came floating by,
> *As green as emerald."* — Coleridge

> "Mary Lou Wingate, *as slightly made*
> *And as hard to break as a rapier blade."* — Benét

Socratic Method — a method used by Socrates of leading another, especially an opponent in argument, to the desired conclusion through the use of an orderly sequence of questions. It was used by both Oedipus and Creon in *Oedipus Rex,* lines 562-586.

Soliloquy — a speech by a character in a play when he is alone (*solus*) on the stage. In it he reveals to the audience what he is thinking or what the audience needs to know which is not revealed by the dialogue or the action. Probably the best known in all of literature is the "To be or not to be . . ." *soliloquy* of Hamlet.

Stichomythy — a succession of sharp single-line speeches in the dialogue of a play. It was one of the **Conventions** of Greek drama (see *Oedipus Rex,* lines 1039-1059) and was often used by the Elizabethans at tense moments in their dramas, as in *Hamlet,* Act III, Scene IV, lines 9-12:

> "Queen: Hamlet, thou hast thy father much offended.
> Hamlet: Mother, you have my father much offended.
> Queen: Come, come, you answer with an idle tongue.
> Hamlet: Go, go, you question with a wicked tongue."

Stock Character — a conventionalized character whom one expects to find in a particular type of fiction. Elizabethan drama has as stock characters high-minded, noble heroes (Hamlet and Brutus), ghosts (of Hamlet Sr. and Julius Caesar), verbose old counsellors (Polonius) and villainous murderers (Claudius and Macbeth). We look for the adventurous knight, the beautiful lady in distress, and the sorceress in the metrical romance; the clean living cowboy, the rancher's comely daughter, and the unscrupulous saloon owner in the Western; etc. In the modern movie, certain actors and actresses always seem to play the sultry siren, the drunken newspaper reporter, the snobbish mother-in-law and the weak younger brother. All these are *stock characters*.

Stock Response — the usual and common emotional response to some word, phrase, or topic, such as a feeling of tenderness inspired by "mother" and "dear little baby," of deep sympathy for those who are exploited by their fellow men ("The Man With the Hoe"), etc. Following are two passages that illustrate the appeal to the *stock response*:

> "Oh, Men with Sisters dear!
> Oh, Men with Mothers and Wives!
> It is not linen you're wearing out,
> But human creatures' lives." — "The Song of the Shirt"
> "Death was cruel to one so little —
> Less than a rose, a loosened petal."

Stock Situation — a **Plot** or part of one that has become trite through overuse, such as the "Boy meets girl," the "Poor boy makes good," and the "Love triangle" plots of the modern theatre.

Stream-of-Consciousness Novel (Story) — one in which the reader sees the other characters and every incident through the mind of one of the characters; is told his momentary opinions and impressions, his recollections, his ideas, his reactions, his significant and insignificant thoughts — everything that "streams" through his "conscious." The result is a psychological study of the character in **Focus**. The method was used by Dostoievsky and developed to its full height by James Joyce (*Ulysses*) and Virginia Woolf.

Stress — the emphasis given the more important words or accented syllables in a sentence or a line of poetry. In the following, the italicized words and syllable would, in a reading, receive the stress:

> *"He* gave *his money; I* gave *my blood."*

Style — the particular manner of expression of a writer which distinguishes him from other writers. In general terms, a writer is said to have a *journalistic* style if he writes like a reporter; a *scholarly* style if he is heavy, prosaic, exact; a *vivid* style if the impressions he gives are very sharp because he always uses the exact word, the right phrase, the perfect figure; an *ornate* or *euphuistic* style if he uses fancy conceits, antithesis, elegant language; or his style may be classified as *bookish, poetic, pedantic, literary, dramatic, homely, classical, Miltonesque* or *Hemmingwayish*. Actually, it is probably wrong to try to categorize styles. The best method of analyzing an author's style is to examine his sentence structure, his choice of words, the imagery that he uses, his dialogue, his description, the rhythm of his writing, his moods and tones to determine exactly how he is different from other writers.

Sub-Plot — a minor conflict in a drama or a narrative which usually serves to help advance the main plot or to give emphasis or relief to the main plot, such as the Hamlet-Laertes conflict, which is subordinate to, but helps to advance the Hamlet-Claudius plot; or the Lorenzo-Jessica love plot in *The Merchant of Venice;* or the Templar-Rebecca *sub-plot* of *Ivanhoe. Sub-plots* are very common in narratives and dramas; as a matter of fact, *Othello* is one of the few well-known Elizabethan plays that have no sub-plots.

Suspense — a combination of two things: uncertainty on the part of the reader or audience as to the outcome of a conflict, and a genuine interest in that outcome. *Suspense* may be secured in a number of ways; through **Foreshadowing;** through effective chapter or scene endings, as when Hamlet says,

> "   The play's the thing
> Wherein I'll catch the conscience of the King."

or by effective description, such as that of the sombre, brooding heath at the beginning of *The Return of the Native* which casts an atmosphere of gloom over the whole action. It must be remembered that *suspense* is held only if the opposing forces are so evenly balanced that the outcome is in doubt right to the very end. After the climax, the reader should be aware of the inevitable conclusion; the author must therefore delay the climax until near the end of his work, as Hawthorne does in *The Scarlet Letter* (and thousands of detective story writers also do), or he should keep the reader's interest by withholding from him until the last how the catastrophe will occur, as Shakespeare does in *Macbeth.*

Syntax — the grammatical construction of a word in a sentence. Syntax is important to a reader because he must often determine the grammatical use of a word or phrase before he can understand the meaning of a sentence, particularly in poetry. For an outstanding example, see Shelley's "Ozymandias," line 8.

Symbol — a figure in which a concrete object is used to stand for an abstract idea. Conventional symbols are the *Cross* for *Christianity;* the *laurel* for *achievement;* the *elephant* for the *Republican Party;* etc. Note the symbolism in the following from Byron in which the *myrtle,* which was sacred to Venus, stands for *love,* and the *ivy,* associated with Bacchus, stands for *revelry*:

> "And the *myrtle* and *ivy* of sweet two-and-twenty;
> Is worth all your *laurels,* though ever so plenty."

Another kind of symbolism is that created by an author for a particular work or situation. For instance, the witches of *Macbeth* may be considered as symbolic of the evil forces which lead men to their doom. The tiny flower of Tennyson's "Flower in the Crannied Wall" is symbolic of the whole mystery of existence. Blake's "Tiger" is symbolic of evil. In the following passage from Amy Lowell's "Patterns,"

> "In summer and in winter I shall walk
> Up and down
> The patterned garden paths
> In my stiff brocaded gown . . ."

the "stiff brocaded gown" is symbolic of the austerity and composure with which the lady, because she is a member of the aristocratic and cultured class, must face the loss of her lover. Hawthorne's *The Scarlet Letter* is filled with symbolism. As an example, the "wild rose bush" in bloom outside the "beetle-browed and gloomy" door of the prison is symbolic of the beautiful product of nature in sharp contrast with the grim product of Puritan morality.

Theme — the underlying idea of a piece of writing. In the short story, "The Enemy", the *theme* is the inability of Fascist propaganda to make brutal a man who has had humanitarianism ingrained in him; in "Ring Around a Rosy," it is the universal disatisfaction of people with their own lot. In his novels Thomas Hardy stressed the *theme* of the helplessness of man in the hands of an unkind Fate. Hawthorne had as his *theme* the problem of sin and of its effect on people's lives. Poetry, of course, has varied *themes,* such as Love, Beauty, Nature or Death.

Tone — the term used for the manner of "speaking," the "tone of voice" used by an author; it helps to *reveal* his attitude toward his subject. (Cf. **Mood.**) If his tone is *sarcastic,* his mood is probably *hostile* or *contemptuous* or *disgusted;* if *ironic,* his mood is the opposite of what it may seem to be; if *cynical,* his mood may be *bitter* or *resentful* or *scornful.* Unless the *tone* is determined, it is difficult to arrive at the author's true *mood* and almost impossible to read his work with complete understanding.

Tragedy — drama in which the **Protagonist** is overcome by the obstacles facing him. It is a representation of a life brought to catastrophe, usually death , (a) through a **Tragic Flaw,** an overwhelming passion (ambition in Macbeth, jealousy in Othello, pride in Dr. Faustus) or a limitation in character (Marcus Brutus' super-idealism and possibly Hamlet's "thinking too precisely on th' event"); or (b) by forces beyond the control of the protagonist, such as Fate (in *Oedipus Rex* and other Greek tragedies), heredity (Brutus Jones), and environment (Hedda Gabler).

Tragic Flaw — the characteristic in the **Protagonist** of a tragedy (generally a good quality perverted) which ultimately leads to his destruction, as *ambition* did in the case of Macbeth. It is, as Shakespeare says in *Hamlet,* the "dram of evil" which

> "Doth all the noble substance often dout
> To his own scandal."

Tragic Force — that element in a tragedy (often the **Dramatic Reverse)** which provides the stimulus for the downfall of the **Protagonist,** as Macbeth's second visit to the Weird Sisters and Antony's concluding remarks to the Roman populace.

Understatement — an expression which actually says less than might be said, as in the middle of a terrific bombing, a Britisher said, "Jerry's making a bit of a noise tonight, what?" In *Beowulf* when Grendel had made the great mead hall unsafe for sleeping, the author says,

> "'Twas easy to find then earls who preferred
> A room elsewhere, for rest at night."

And the wounded Mercutio states in *Romeo and Juliet*:

> "No, 'tis not so deep as a well, nor so wide as a
> church-door; but 'tis enough, 't will serve."

TYPES OF POETRY

The major types of poetry are **Narrative, Dramatic,** and **Lyric.**

A. NARRATIVE POETRY

— poetry which tells a story. There are a number of types.

1. **Epic** — a long narrative poem which in dignified and elevated style tells of the mighty deeds of a great hero.

The **Folk Epic** — exemplified by the *Iliad* and the *Odyssey* of the Greeks (commonly attributed to Homer), the *Cid* of Spain, the *Chanson de Roland* of France, the *Nibelungenlied* of the Germans, and the Anglo-Saxon *Beowulf* — was an *epic* which arose from the legends and the traditions of a nation and the story of which was gradually added to by various poets as it was passed on by word of mouth until finally it was written down in its present form as it was related by some individual poet, such as Homer.

The **Literary Epic** is a conscious effort on the part of some poets, such as Virgil or Milton, to imitate the early epical poems. Examples of this type are Virgil's *Aeneid,* Dante's *Divine Comedy,* Spenser's *Faerie Queene,* and Milton's *Paradise Lost.*

There are certain **Conventions** of the *epic* which distinguish it:

a. The hero was usually a great national figure, either mythical (Achilles) or historical (Roland) or legendary (Arthur).

b. The *epic* dealt only with such matters as heroic deeds (*Beowulf*), great battles (the *Iliad*), and long journeys (the *Odyssey*), not with trivial matters.

c. Most of the classical *epics* were composed in twelve (Virgil's *Aeneid* and Milton's *Paradise Lost*) or twenty-four (the *Iliad* and the *Odyssey*) Books.

d. As to style, the verse was dignified and lofty in tone, and the poet was objective in his treatment of his subject matter. One other characteristic of style was the use of the **Epic** or **Homeric Simile.** This is a simile introduced by "as when," in which the secondary object is so graphically presented that it temporarily becomes of more importance than the primary object with which it is compared. For example, in the following from *Paradise Lost,* the reader is imaginatively transported from the description of the "dry land" in Hell and visualizes instead for a moment the eruption of a mighty volcano.

> "   till on dry land
> He lights — if it were land that ever burned
> With solid, as the lake with liquid fire,
> And such appeared in hue *as when the force*
> *Of subterranean wind transports a hill*
> *Torn from Pelorus, or the shattered side*
> *Of thundering Etna, whose combustible*
> *And fueled entrails, thence conceiving fire,*
> *Sublimed with mineral fury, aid the winds,*
> *And leave a singed bottom all involved*
> *With stench and smoke."*

e. The beginning of the classical epic was marked by:

(1) A statement of the theme.

> "Of man's first disobedience, and the fruit
> Of that forbidden tree . . ." (*Paradise Lost*)
> "Arms and the man I sing . . ." (*Aeneid*)

(2) An invocation to a Muse.

"Sing, *Heavenly Muse* . . ." (*Paradise Lost*)
"Sing, *Goddess*, the wrath of Achilles . . ."
(*Iliad*)

(3) The asking of what is termed the *epic question* of the Muse so invoked, which is followed by the story itself as though related by the Muse. Milton tells his Muse to

"   say first what cause
Moved our grand Parents, in that happy
     state,
Favoured of Heaven so highly, to fall off
From their Creator, and transgress his will
For one restraint, lords of the World
     besides.
Who first seduced them to that foul
     revolt?"

(4) The poet then plunges **In Medias Res.**

f. Finally there were certain miscellaneous conventions: the intermingling of the gods in human affairs; formal speeches, like those of Satan at the beginning of *Paradise Lost;* and the epic catalogue, such as the naming of the ships and their captains in the *Iliad* and the listing of each fallen angel as he rises from the fiery lake in *Paradise Lost.*

Mock Epic — a poem, such as Pope's *Rape of the Lock,* which mimics the style and conventions of the epic in treating a trivial matter. For instance, Pope states his theme formally and invokes the Muse; he describes "great battles" (Canto III, lines 37-100) in the epic manner; he uses the epic simile (Canto V, lines 9-16); the gods mingle in human affairs (Ariel, Umbriel, and the sylphs); etc.

2. **Folk** or **Popular Ballad** — a form of narrative poetry which was intended to be sung, told a brief story usually in the **Ballad Stanza,** was probably composed by several persons, who contributed different stanzas, and was passed on by word of mouth until it was finally written down by some collector, such as Bishop Percy or Sir Walter Scott. The Folk ballad had certain characteristics:

a. Often the incident told was the climax of a longer story, and much was left unsaid because the people who originally heard it knew the background. ("Bonnie George Campbell")

b. There is dialogue in most folk ballads. ("Bonnie Barbara Allan")

c. There is often a **Refrain.** ("Lord Randal")

d. There is much word and phrase repetition. (*"Haf owre, haf owre* to Aberdour . . ."* and *"Mak haste, mak haste, my mirry men all . . ."*

e. The tone is impersonal, probably because of the communal origin.

f. The themes were varied; love tragedy ("Bonnie Barbara Allan"); domestic tragedy ("Lord Randal"); historical tragedy ("Sir Patrick Spens"); the outlaw theme ("Robin Hood"); the humourous incident ("Get Up and Bar the Door").

3. **Literary Ballad** — an imitation of the folk ballad done by one author. It resembles the folk ballad in simplicity of story and language, metrical form, and theme, and often has other ballad characteristics, such as repetitions, a refrain, dialogue, etc. As good examples, see Benét's "The Ballad of William Sycamore," Keats' "La Belle Dame Sans Merci," Scott's "Proud Maisie," and Coleridge's "The Rime of the Ancient Mariner."

4. **Metrical Romance** — a long narrative poem of medieval times which told a story of chivalrous knights, ladies in distress, adventure and enchantments. The Arthurian legends and the stories of Charlemagne's knights were often the basis of the subject matter. *Sir Gawain and the Green Knight* is considered the best of this type of narrative poem.

5. **Metrical Tale** — merely a story told in verse. It may be as long as Benét's *John Brown's Body* and Scott's *Lady of the Lake,* or as short as Benét's "The Mountain Whippoorwill" and Tennyson's "The Lady of Shalott."

B. DRAMATIC POETRY

— poetry written in the form of a drama such as the Elizabethan plays, the **Masque,** and **Closet Drama.** In modern times, T. S. Eliot, has written a successful poetic drama *Murder in the Cathedral.* A special type of dramatic poetry is the **Dramatic Monologue,** a poem which consists of the speech of a single person. Through what he says, the action is presented, the replies of the other person or persons are suggested, and the character of the speaker is usually revealed. Browning excelled at this type of writing. For examples, see Browning's "My Last Duchess" and "Up at a Villa — Down in the City," and Tennyson's "Ulysses."

C. LYRIC POETRY

— poetry which expresses the personal feelings and thoughts of its author. In addition to being **Subjective,** it is usually emotional, imaginative, and melodious. There are many types.

1. **Lyric** — a short, simple, subjective poem which directly and forcefully expresses a single emotion. For examples, see Sandburg's "Prayers of Steel", Teasdale's "Barter," Wylie's "Velvet Shoes," Millay's "Lament," Wordworth's "My Heart Leaps Up," and Byron's "She Walks in Beauty."

2. **Song** — a short lyric poem designed to be sung. It may be *religious* (a **Hymn),** like Addison's "The Spacious Firmament on High" and Cowper's "Light Shining out of Darkness," or *secular,* like Shakespeare's "Who is Sylvia?", Jonson's "To Celia," and Burns' "Sweet Afton."

3. **Ode** — a lyric poem which treats a serious subject thoughtfully and emotionally and which is marked by a dignified style and a complex metrical pattern. For examples, see Wordsworth's "Ode on Intimations of Immortality," Shelley's "Ode to the West Wind," and Keats' "Ode on a Grecian Urn."

4. **Sonnet** — a fourteen-line lyric poem written in **Iambic Pentameter.** There are two major types: the **Italian (Petrarchan) Sonnet** and the **English (Shakespearean) Sonnet.** The Italian sonnet has eight lines (the **Octave)**for the development of a single thought, and six lines (the **Sestet)** for a comment on, a solution to, or an application of the thought. The rhyme is *abbaabba* in the octave and *cdecde* or any combination of *c* and *d,* or of *c, d,* and *e* in the sestet. As examples, see Elinor Wylie's "Pretty Words" and Keats' "On First Looking into Chapman's Homer." The English sonnet consists of three **Quatrains** (rhyming *abab, cdcd, efef)* an a concluding **Couplet** (rhyming *gg).* The three quatrains develop a single thought, and the couplet usually comments on it. As an example, see Shakespeare's Sonnet 73, "That time of year thou may'st in me behold." A **Sonnet Sequence** is a group of sonnets addressed to a single person or developing a single theme, such as Sidney's *Astrophel and Stella,* Spenser's *Amoretti,* Shakespeare's sequence, and Mrs. Brownings *Sonnets from the Portugese.*

5. **Elegy** — a poem which laments the dead. Some of the more famous elegies are Milton's "Lycidas" and Shelley's "Adonais" (both of which are called *personal elegies* because they are written about individuals) and Gray's "Elegy Written in a Country Churchyard," which mourns the poor and unlearned dead.

6. **Ballade** — a poem of three eight-line stanzas all rhyming *ababbcbc* and a four-line "envoi" rhyming *bcbc,* the last line of each stanza and of the "envoi" being a **Refrain.** See the *ballade* composed by Cyrano as he duelled the Vicomte (*Cyrano de Bergerac,* Act 1, Scene IV, lines 312-339).

UNITS OF VERSE

Verse — a single line of poetry.

Stanza — a unit of poetry consisting of a group of related verses, generally with a definite metrical pattern and rhyme scheme.

Canto — a division of a long poem, usually comparable to a chapter in a book.

Book — a major division of a long poem, usually of an epic. (Spenser's *The Faerie Queen* is divided into **Books,** the books into **Cantos,** the cantos into **Stanzas.)**

Blank Verse — unrhymed iambic pentameter.

Alexandrine — a line of iambic hexameter.

Free Verse (*Vers Libre*) — poetry with irregular meter and usually without rhyme. It has rhythm, but not the regular rhythm of traditional poetry. A quotation from *Leaves of Grass* by Walt Whitman, who was the first exponent of *free verse* in America, should illustrate this:

> "Beat! beat! drums! — blow! bugles! blow!
> Through the windows — through doors — burst like a
> ruthless force,
> Into the solemn church, and scatter the congregation,
> Into the school where the scholar is studying . . ."

Later, successful writers of *free verse* include Amy Lowell, Edgar Lee Masters, Carl Sandburg, Vachel Lindsay, Robinson Jeffers and T. S. Eliot.

Couplet — a pair of successive verses which rhyme.

> "Once or twice this side of death
> Things can make one hold his breath." — Coffin

Closed Couplet — a couplet which in its two lines expresses a complete thought.

> "She knew her Bible — and how to flirt
> With a swansdown fan and a brocade skirt." — Benét

Heroic Couplet — a couplet (usually a closed couplet) of iambic pentameter lines.

" 'Tis education forms the common mind:
    Just as the twig is bent, the tree's inclined."

Tercet — a stanza of three lines, usually with all rhyming such as the following from Thomas Hardy's "Lines on the Loss of the *Titanic*":

    "And as the smart ship grew
    In stature, grace, and hue,
    In shadowy silent distance grew the Iceberg too."

Quatrain — a stanza consisting of four lines, the most common type of stanza in English poetry.

Ballad Stanza — a **Quatrain** in which the first and third lines are iambic tetrameter, and the second fourth lines are iambic trimeter. The second and fourth lines must rhyme; the first and third may.

    "The King has written a braid letter,
    And signed it wi his hand,
    And sent it to Sir Patrick Spens,
    Was walking on the sand."

Quintain (*Quintet*) — a five-line stanza such as that used by Elinor Wylie in "Velvet Shoes," by Shelley in "To a Skylark," and by Poe in "To Helen."

Sestet — a six-line stanza. See Byron's "She Walks in Beauty," Tennyson's "Bugle Song," and Poe's "The Raven." It is also the name given the last six lines of an Italian sonnet.

The most famous *seven-line stanza* is **Rime Royal** (rhymed *ababbcc*), used by Chaucer in his *Troilus and Criseyde* and other poems. Other examples of a seven-line stanza are to be found in Holmes' "The Chambered Nautilus" and Shelley's "To Night."

Octave (*Octet*) — a stanza of eight lines, probably the second most common type of stanza in English poetry. See Burns' "A Man's A Man for A' That," Hood's "The Song of hte Shirt," and Shelley's "The Lamp is Shattered." *Octave* is also the name given the first eight lines of an Italian sonnet.

The best-known *nine-line stanza* is that invented by Edmund Spenser for use in *The Faerie Queene*. Called the **Spenserian Stanza** in his honour, it consists of eight lines of iambic pentameter with a final line of iambic hexameter (an **Alexandrine**). It is rhymed *ababbcbcc*. It was much admired and used by the Romanticists. See Burns' "A Cotter's Saturday Night," Byron's *Childe Harold's Pilgrimage,* and Keats' "The Eve of St. Agnes." For another type of nine-line stanza, see Tennyson's "The Lady of Shalott."

There is obviously no limit to the number of lines that a stanza may have; however, since there is no regularity of meter or rhyme in those of more than nine lines (except the **Sonnet)** reference is merely made to several examples: Keats' "Ode to a Nightingale" and "Ode on a Grecian Urn" (*ten lines*); Wordsworth's "She Was a Phantom of Delight" (*ten lines*); Whittier's "Skipper Ireson's Ride" (*eleven lines*).

Universality — the term applied to a piece of writing which appeals to people in every age. To have this quality, a work must usually express emotions that are common to all people (Tennyson's "Break, Break, Break") or portray human nature successfully (Chaucer's *Canterbury Tales*).

Verisimilitude — the quality of seeming to be true. Defoe's works, such as *Robinson Crusoe* and *The Journal of the Plague Year,* have *verisimilitude* and therefore lead the reader to accept them as true even though they are fiction. An author may build up *verisimilitude,* as Defoe did, by telling the story in the first person, by going into infinite details that only an eyewitness could relate, and by presenting the story as a historical account. It may also be established by life-likeness of characterization, logic of plot and incident, accuracy of setting, and naturalness of dialogue.

GLOSSARY OF GRAMMATICAL TERMS

Unless otherwise indicated, specific terms in a general class will be found under the general term: e.g., **Adjective Clause** may be found under **Clause, Coordinate Conjunction** under **Conjunction, Complex Sentence** under **sentence,** etc. There are a few exceptions: **Adjective Phrase** and **Adverbial Phrase** will be found under **Prepositional Phrase, Direct Object** under **Complement, Article** under **Adjective,** etc.

Terms printed in bold type in the definitions may be found elsewhere in the glossary.

Adjective — a word used to modify a **substantive.**
There were *five gigantic Polish* boys on *the* team.

Compound Adjective — a single adjective consisting of two or more words (e.g., a *never-ending* cycle, a *matter-of-fact* person).

Descriptive Adjective — an adjective that describes the substantive that it modifies (e.g., a *handsome, young, intellectual* student).

Limiting Adjective — an adjective that merely limits in some way the substantive that it modifies.

> *Those two* boys have been of *much* help to *the* school.

Proper Adjective — an adjective derived from a proper noun.

> The *Roman* populace jeered the *Carthaginian* prisoners.

Demonstrative Adjective — an adjective that points out.

> *This* sentence is no longer than *that* one.

Interrogative Adjective — an adjective used in asking a question, either direct or indirect.

> *Which* book do you want?
> He asked me *which* book I wanted.

Indefinite Adjective — an adjective that does not limit precisely the substantive that it modifies (e.g., *some* girls, *much* money, *several* books, etc.).

Pronominal Adjective — an adjective that may be used as a pronoun, such as the demonstrative, interrogative, and indefinite adjectives. (Cf. **Adjective Pronoun.**)

Attributive Adjective — an adjective that precedes the substantive which it modifies.

> The *spacious, well-planned* house was quite comfortable.

Appositive Adjective — an adjective that immediately follows the substantive which it modifes.

> The house, *spacious* and *well-planned,* was quite comfortable.

Predicate Adjective — an adjective **complement** that modifies the subject.

> The house was *spacious* and *well-planned.*

Article — *a* (or *an*) and *the.*

Definite Article — (*the*) points out a particular one of a class.

Indefinite Article — (*a* or *an*) designates any one of a class.

Adjective Phrase — see **Prepositional Phrase.**

Adverb — a word used to modify a verb, an adjective, or another adverb, (Adverbs of *manner* tell "how"; adverbs of *time* tell "when"; adverbs of *place* tell "where"; and adverbs of *degree* tell "how much" or "to what degree or extent.")

> The *exceedingly* violent storm abated *quite suddenly.*

Interrogative Adverb — an adverb used in asking a question, either direct or indirect.

> *Where* did you leave your sweater, Will?
> Will's mother asked him *where* he had left his sweater.

Relative Adverb — an adverb that relates an adjective clause to the word which the clause modifies, and is used to modify the verb in the adjective clause.

> Now is the time *when* patriots are needed.
> Shakespeare's command of the language is one reason
> *why* his plays are so magnificent.

Conjunctive Adverb — an adverb that joins the thought of two independent clauses and usually modifies the verb of the second clause (e.g., *thus, therefore, moreover, accordingly,* etc.) (The *conjunctive adverb* is called a "longer coordinating conjunction" by some books.)

> It was an extremely bitter day; *however,* Alicia and Ruth
> hardly felt the cold wind and the sleety snow.

Adverbial Noun — a noun used as an adverb.

> He came *home* from college a *week* ago.

Adverbial Phrase — see **Prepositional Phrase.**

Antecedent of a Pronoun — the substantive for which the pronoun stands.

> The supreme *egotist* pats *himself* on *his* own back.

Appositive — a substantive that usually immediately follows and means the same as another substantive.

> Albert Schweitzer, the famous *scientist, did* his work
> in Africa, a *continent* that needed his help.
> The fact *that we agree* is in itself a paradox.

Dangling Appositive — an appositive that does not refer to the substantive which it seems to explain.

> (*Dangling*) An able *diplomat,* Truman chose Whitney as
> ambassador.
> (*Improved*) Truman chose Whitney, an able diplomat, as
> ambassador.

Article — see **Adjective.**

Auxiliary Verb — a verb used with another to form a **verb phrase** (e.g., *is* going, *did* try, *shall* win, *can* taste, *must have* called).

Basal Parts — those sentence elements that are essential to the meaning of a sentence. They include the **subject,** the **verb,** and the **complements.**

Case — a property of a substantive that shows its relationship to other words in the sentence. There are three *cases*: nominative, objective, and possessive (e.g., *I me, my; he, him, his*).

Clause — a part of a sentence containing a subject and a predicate.

Independent Clause — a clause that would be complete in meaning if removed from the sentence.

> Because Brutus made mistakes, *the conspiracy failed.*

Dependent Clause — a clause that does not express a complete thought, but depends on the rest of the sentence to give it meaning. There are three kinds: adjective, adverbial, and noun (substantive).

Adjective Clause — a dependent clause t h a t modifies a substantive.

> The relatives *who came to dinner* stayed for a week.

Adverbial Clause — a dependent clause that modifies a verb, an adjective, or an adverb.

> *Though the gendarmes battled valiantly,* the mob over-whelmed them.

Noun (Substantive) Clause — a dependent clause used as a **substantive.**

> *Where you were last night* is *what we should like to know.*

Complement — a word in the predicate that completes the meaning of the verb. There are four types: **direct object, subjective complement, objective complement,** and **retained object.**

Direct Object — a complement that receives the action of the verb.

> He answered the *question* with ease.
> He told us *that we were free to leave at any time.*

Subjective Complement — a complement that means the same as or modifies the subject.

> That is the *reason* for my success. (*Pred. noun*)
> It is *I* who am to blame. (*Pred. pronoun*)
> He seems *sickly* and *undernourished*. (*Pred. adj.*)

Objective Complement — a complement that means the same as or modifies the direct object.

> They made their house a *home*.
> We thought the play *subversive*.
> You made me *what I am today*.

Retained Object — a direct object retained with a transitive passive verb when the **indirect object** has been made the subject.

> We were taught *English* by a real scholar.

Compound Element — a sentence element consisting of two or more parts which are of equal rank (*coordinate*), such as a compound subject, a compound appositive, a compound direct object, etc.

> *Rip and Randy* laughed *long and hard* at the *crude, but seaworthy* boat which their father had *planned and built*.

Conjugation — the orderly arrangement of the different forms of a verb in all its **tenses, persons, numbers, voices,** and **moods.**

Conjunction — a word used to join words or groups of words.

Compound Conjunction — a conjunction consisting of two or more words (e.g., *as though, so that, in order that, provided that,* etc.).

Coordinate Conjunction — a conjunction that joins sentence elements of equal rank.

> Suzanne *and* Sally were weary, *but* content.
> Flip *or* Lucy must have locked him out.
> Alf had to leave, *for* it was late.

Subordinate Conjunction — a conjunction that joins sentence elements of unequal rank.

> We shall probably not win *unless* Tim plays.
> *Because* Page procrastinated, his paper was a day late.

Correlative Conjunctions — conjunctions used in pairs (e.g., *either . . . or, neither . . . nor, both . . . and, not . . . but, though . . . yet,* etc.).

Not only Charles, *but also* Douglas has not arrived.

Coordinate Sentence Elements — sentence elements that have the same grammatical construction and are of equal rank.

Our *domineering, intolerant venal* landlord terrifies me.
Falstaff *roared* with laughter and *slapped* his sides.

Degree — a property of adjectives and adverbs.

Positive Degree — the simplest form of an adjective or an adverb (e.g., *dim, lovely, useless; slowly, easily, well*).

Comparative Degree — the form that indicates a higher or lower degree of the quality than exists in some other object (e.g., *dimmer, lovelier, more useless; more slowly, less easily, better*).

Superlative Degree — the form that indicates the highest or lowest degree of the quality (e.g., *dimmest, loveliest, most useless; most slowly, least easily, best*).

Direct Address — a substantive used in addressing a person or thing directly.

Hear our plea, O *Caesar!*   Here, *Fido!*

Direct Discourse — The repetition of the exact words of a speaker, with no change in form.

Jerry said, *"We have done everything that we can."*

Direct Object — see **Complement.**

Elliptical Clause — a clause in which words have been omitted.

She is not so intelligent *as Jane* (is).
Although (he is) *no genius,* he leads his class.

Dangling Elliptical Clause — an elliptical clause in which the omitted words are not clearly understood.

(*Dangling*) *When six years old,* Dickens' father died.
(*Improved*) When Dickens was six years old, his
                father died.

Elliptical Sentence — a sentence from which some essential part has been omitted, but the meaning of which is clear.

Thank you.   Good night.   Look! *a wreck!*
Why such a fuss over nothing?

Emphatic Form of a Verb — a verb phrase formed by using *do* or *did* with the first **principal part.** It is used for emphasis, in questions, or in negative statements.

> *I do want* you to help me.
> *Did he go?*   We *do* not *know.*

Expletive — a word used to introduce the **subject** of a sentence (*there* and *it*).

> *There* are only six apples left in the bowl.
> *It* is easy to learn to memorize.

Gender — distinction according to sex, a property of substantives. There are four genders: **masculine, feminine, neuter,** and **common.**

Masculine Gender — denotes the male sex (e.g., *John, his, king, buck, bull*).

Feminie Gender — denotes the female sex (e.g., *Joan, her, queen, doe, cow*).

Neuter Gender — denotes no sex (e.g., *tree, its, throne, building, paper*).

Common Gender — denotes either sex (e.g., *child, their teacher, deer, cattle*).

Gerund — a verbal noun ending in *ing*.

> *Seeing* is *believing.*
> *Driving* a Jaguar is somewhat like *flying* a jet plane.

Gerund Phrase — a phrase consisting of a gerund, its complement(s), and modifier(s).

> Before *entering politics,* one should have lessons in
>   *persuading others.*

Present Gerund — a gerund formed by adding *ing* to the present stem of a verb (e.g., *being, seeing, thinking, running*).

Perfect Gerund — a gerund formed by using *having* with the past participle of a verb (e.g., *having been, having seen,* etc.).

Dangling Gerund — a gerund which is used as the direct object or the object of a preposition and which does not logically refer to the subject or have a possesive modifier.

> (*Dangling*) On *arriving,* my room was ready.
> (*Improved*) When I arrived, my room was ready.
>
> (*Dangling*) Mary was flattered by *praising* her.
> (*Improved*) Mary was flattered by anyone's praising her.

Indirect Discourse — the repetition of the substance of a statement, usually with a change in form.

> (*Direct*) He said. "All is finished."
> (*Indirect*) He said that all was finished.

Indirect Object — a word in the predicate that indicates to whom or for whom the action is performed (without the use of *to* or *for*).

> The old woman gave the *treasury* two mites. (*to*)
> He built his *children* a playhouse. (*for*)

Infinitive — the root form of the verb, usually preceded by *to,* used as a noun, an adjective, or an adverb.

> *To see* is *to believe.*
> Water *to drink* is difficult *to find* in the Near East.

Infinitive Phrase — a phrase consisting of an infinitive, its complement(s), and its modifier(s).

> *To understand Einstein's writings* is sometimes difficult.

Infinitive Clause — a clause consisting of an infinitive, its subject, its complement(s), and its modifiers(s).

> The crew wanted *Ahab to abandon the whale-hunt.*
> God sometimes makes *us turn to Him.*

Present Infinitive — the root form of the verb (e.g., *to call, to wish, to be understood*).

Perfect Infinitive — the infinitive formed by using *to have* with the past participle of a verb (e.g., *to have called, to have wished, to have been understood*).

Dangling Infinitive — an infinitive expressing purpose that does not logically refer to the subject.

> (*Dangling*) *To speak* clearly, one's words must be enunciated carefully
> (*Improved*) To speak clearly, one must enunciate his words carefully.

Interjection — a word used to express strong or sudden feeling.

> *Alas,* Oedipus! How sad is thy life!
> *Bravo! Cheers! Heigh-ho,* Ben!

Modal Auxiliary — an **auxiliary verb** which with the **infinitive** is used to express permission, ability, probability, possibility, necessity, obligation, duty, or habitual action (e.g., *may, might, can, could, must, should, would* and *ought*).

Modifier — a word or a group of words that changes the meaning of another word by describing or limiting it (e.g., an **adjective**, an **adjective phrase**, an **adverbial clause**, a **participle**, an **appositive**.)

> *These two mighty* oaks grew *gradually* from the *tiny* acorns *which they once were.*

Dangling Modifier — a modifier that has no word to describe or define, or what seems to modify the wrong word.

> John was beheaded, *caused* by Herod's moral cowardice.
> He saw some white-hunters on horses *shooting antelopes.*

Restrictive Modifier — a modifier that limits the meaning of the word modified and that is essential to the sentence.

> The man *who has no music in him* misses much in life.
> The division *advancing on our right* met stiff resistance.

Non-Restrictive Modifier — a modifier that merely adds informaton about the word modified and that is not essential to the sentence.

> Cassius, *who had no music in him,* did not appreciate the aesthetic.
> The Sixth Armored Division, *advancing on our right,* met stiff resistance.

Mood — a property of verbs that indicates the manner in which the thought is expressed. There are three *moods*: indicative, imperative, and subjunctive.

Nominative Absolute — a **substantive,** usually with a modifying **participle,** used independently of the rest of the sentence to express time, circumstance, or cause.

> *Night having fallen,* we retired.
> He staggered into the house, *his clothing in shreds.*

Noun — a word used as the name of a person, a place, or a thing (e.g., *man, girl, city, church, book, love*).

Compound Noun — a noun consisting of two or more words (e.g., *patrol leader, lampshade, secretary-treasurer*).

Proper Noun — a noun that names a particular person, place or thing (e.g., *Stuart Saunders, T. S. Eliot, Chicago, Oregon, Eiffel Tower, Kiwanis Club*).

Common Noun — a noun that names any one of a class of persons, places, or things (e.g., *uncle, scoundrel, capital, street, idea, dictionary*).

Collective Noun — a noun which even in the singular denotes a number of persons or things (e.g., *crowd, jury, herd, covey*).

Abstract Noun — a noun which names a quality (e.g., *virtue, strength, fear, freedom, grace*).

Number — a property of substantive and verbs that indicates whether one or more than one is meant. There are two *numbers*: **singular** and **plural**.

Singular Number — denotes one (e.g., *man, wife, hero, box, datum; is, has, runs, sweeps*).

Plural Number — denotes more than one (e.g., *men, wives, heroes, boxes, data; are, have, run, sweep*).

Object of a Preposition — a **substantive** which follows a **preposition** and is related to some other word by the preposition (e.g., the man on the *beach;* a place under the *sun;* went to the *city;* struggled with his *conscience*).

Objective Complement — see **Complement.**

Paragraph — a unit of thought, usually a group of related sentences developing a single topic.

Parenthetical Element — a sentence that has no grammatical construction in the sentence, but is used to provide transition of thought or to colour the meaning of the sentence.

> I believe, *on the contrary,* that academic freedom is indispensable. There is, *I am sure*, another reason for his aggressiveness.

Participle — a verbal adjective.

> The soldier *standing* there resembles Napoleon.
> We saw him *crouching* in the bushes.

Participial Phrase — a phrase consisting of a participle, its complement(s), and its modifier(s).

> *Knowing parliamentary procedure well,* he was able to control the course of the meeting.

Dangling Participle — a participle (a) that precedes and does not logically modify the subject, (b) that does not logically modify the word which it seems to modify, (c) that has no word to modify, or (d) that modifies a whole idea.

> (a) *Turning* toward me, I heard him shout, "Wait!"
> (b) The policeman held off the mob *brandishing* his gun.
> (c) The parade was easily seen, *watching* from the window.
> (d) He was late for school, *caused* by the sleety roads.

Present Participle — the participle formed by adding *ing* to the present stem of a verb (e.g., *shooting, wishing, being called*).

Past Participle — the third principal part of a verb (e.g., *shot, wished, called.*) (It is always **passive voice.**)

Perfect Participle — the participle formed by using *having* with the past participle of a verb (e.g., *having shot, having wished, having been called*).

Parts of Speech — the eight classes into which all words in a sentence (except **expletives)** may be divided according to usage; namely, **nouns, pronouns, adjectives, verbs, adverbs, prepositions, conjunctions,** and **interjections.**

> The *well* is dry.   (*noun*)
> She is *well* today.   (*adjective*)
> The waters *well* and recede.   (*verb*)
> She certainly sings *well*.   (*adverb*)
> *Well* who would have thought that?   (*interjection*)

Person — a property of substantives and verbs that indicates whether the person speaking, the person spoken to, or the person or thing spoken about is meant.

First Person — denotes the speaker.

> *I, Dwight Eisenhower, do* solemnly swear that . . .

Second Person — denotes the person spoken to.

> *Thou, David, son* of Jesse, *art* the man.

Third Person — denotes the person or thing spoken about.

> *They* by *their stupidity have* destroyed *themselves.*

Phrase — a group of related words not containing a subject and a predicate. (See **prepositional phrase, verb phrase,** and **verbal phrase.)**

Predicate — the part of the sentence that tells something about the subject.

Quietly but firmly the mother *admonished her children.*

Simple Predicate — the verb.

> Langhorne *was* not *disturbed* by his poor class grades.

Complete Predicate — the verb with its complement(s) and modifier(s).

> They *unanimously chose Warner Chairman of the Honour Committee.*

Compound Predicate — a predicate consisting of two or more verbs.

> Caesar said that he *came, saw,* and *conquered.*

Preposition — a word used to show the relation between its **object** and some other word in the sentence.

> The dust *in* the road *from* their farm *to* the village was settled *by* the rain *during* the evening.

Compound Preposition — a preposition consisting of two or more words (e.g., *on account of, because of, with reference to, in consideration of*).

Prepositional Phrase — a phrase consisting of a preposition, its object, and the modifier(s) of the object (e.g., *on a very calm night, in addition to our present assets.) Prepositional phrases* are classified as **adjective** or **adverbial.**

Adjective Phrase — a prepositional phrase that modifies a substantive.

> A dog *with a stubby tail* was chasing a crowd *of boys.*

Adverbial Phrase — a prepositional phrase that modifies a verb, an adjective, or an adverb.

> *On Mondays* he is usually intolerant *of his students.*

Principal Parts — the first person singular *present tense,* the first person singular *past tense,* and the *past participle* of a verb, called *principal parts* because all tenses, moods, etc., are formed from them (e.g., *go, went, gone; bring, brought, brought; walk, walked, walked; laugh, laughed, laughed*).

Progressive Form of a Verb — a **verb phrase** formed by using the proper tense form of the verb *to be* with a **present participle** to express continuing action or present intention of future action.

> He *is sleeping* at present.

He *has been sleeping* since eight o'clock last night.
He *is leaving* for New York in the morning.

Pronoun — a word used in place of a noun.

Larry has ruined *himself* by *his dissipation*.

Personal Pronoun — a pronoun that indicates its **person** by its form (e.g., first person: *I, me, our;* second person: *you, thee, your;* third person: *him, she, its, their*).

Compound Personal Pronoun — a pronoun formed by adding *self* or *selves* to the possessive case of the personal pronoun in the first and second persons, and to the objective case in the third person (e.g., *myself, yourself, himself, themselves*).

Demonstrative Pronoun — a pronoun that points out (e.g., *this, that, these,* and *those.*) (Cf. **Demonstrative Adjective.**)

This is better than *those.*

Relative Pronoun — a pronoun that relates an **adjective clause** to its antecedent and is used in the adjective clause as subject, direct object, subjective complement, object of a preposition, or possessive modifier (e.g., *who, whom, whose, which, what,* and *that*).

This is the sheep *which* was lost.
There is the boy *whose* father gave the trophy.
He is not the man *that* you are.

Compound Relative Pronoun — a pronoun formed by adding *ever* or *soever* to a relative pronoun. (It is used only in a noun clause.)

They wish to see *whoever* was a witness to the accident.
You may think *whatsoever* you wish.

Interrogative Pronoun — a pronoun used in asking a question, either direct or indirect. (Cf. **Interrogative Adjective.**)

Who do men say that I am?
He asked me *what* I was doing.

Indefinite Pronoun — a pronoun that does not stand for any definite person, place, or thing (e.g., *someone, many, few, several, everybody*).

Intensive Pronoun — a **compound personal pronoun** used in apposition.

The French *themselves* have never known true democracy.
We did the work *ourselves.* (appositive to *We*)

Reflexive Pronoun — a **compound personal pronoun** used as part of the predicate to refer to the subject.

> He has injured *himself* severely.
> He is *himself* today.

Adjective Pronoun — an interrogative, demonstrative, or indefinite pronoun, so called because it may be used as an adjective also. (Cf. **Pronominal Adjective.**)

> Whose book is *this?*   *Whose* is this book?

Properties of a substantive — **person, number, gender,** and **case.**

> *He* was duly rewarded. (*He*: third *person,* singular *number,* masculine *gender,* nominative *case*)

Properties of a Verb — **person, number, tense, mood** and **voice.**

> He *was* duly *rewarded.* (*was rewarded:* third *person,* singular *number,* past *tense,* indicative *mood,* passive *voice*)

Retained Object — see **Complement.**

Sentence — a group of related words expressing a complete thought. Sentences may be classified as to form (**simple, compound,** etc.) and as to meaning (**declarative, imperative,** etc.)

Simple Sentence — a sentence containing one subject and one predicate, either or both of which may be compound.

> *Moses and Aaron led the Israelites out of Egypt.*

Compound Sentence — a sentence containing two or more **independent clauses.**

> *Esau liked to hunt, but Jacob preferred the life of a shepherd.*

Complex Sentence — a sentence containing one **independent clause** and one or more **dependent clauses.**

> *When the doorbell rings, please answer it if you are dressed.*

Compound-complex Sentence — a sentence containing two or more **independent clauses** and one or more **dependent clauses.**

> *When there was peace and prosperity, the Tories usually held the power in the House of Commons; but when troublous times came, the Whigs almost always supplanted them.*

Declarative Sentence — a sentence that states a fact.

> *Pontius Pilate proved to be a moral coward.*

Imperative Sentence — a sentence that gives a command or makes a request.

> *Be quiet, and pay attention.*   (command)
> *Please close the door.* (request)

Interrogative Sentence — a sentence that asks a direct question.

> *What do people desire more than liberty?*

Exclamatory Sentence — a sentence that expresses strong feeling.

> *Shakespeare? What an odd name that is for a dog!*

Sentence Element — a word or a group of words that forms an integral part of a sentence (e.g., the subject, the verb, the object of a preposition, a prepositional phrase, a noun clause, a verbal phrase.)

Sentence Fragment — a group of words not expressing a complete thought — an incomplete sentence.

> *When he saw the results of his reckless driving.* He swore
> never to drive a car again.

Split Infinitive — an infinitive which has an adverbial modifier between the sign *to* and the infinitive itself.

> He was told *to* immediately *report* to the office.

Subject — the part of a sentence that names what is talked about.

> Before daylight *many of the ducks* left the ricefield.

Simple Subject — the **substantive** that names what is talked about in the sentence.

> A very old family *Bible* will often contain vital records.

Complete Subject — the simple subject with all its modifiers.

> *A very old family Bible* will often often contain vital records.

Compound Subject — a subject consisting of two or more simple subjects.

> *Jack and Mary* now live in a converted garage.

Subject of an Imperative Sentence — usually *you* understood.

> (*You*) Bring your books to class tomorrow.

Subject of an Infinitive — a substantive in an **infinitive clause** that would be the subject of the verb if the infinitive clause were changed to a **dependent clause.**

> We know the *author* to be him. (*subj. of inf.*)
> We know that the *author* is he. (*subj. of verb*)

Subjective Complement — see **Complement.**

Substantive — a noun or a pronoun.

Tense — a property of verbs that indicates the time of the action. The tenses are the *present,* the *past,* the *future,* the *present perfect,* the *past perfect,* and the *future perfect.*

Topic Sentence — the sentence in a **paragraph** that states the central thought of the paragraph.

Transitional Element — a word or a group of words used to show the relation in thought between successive sentences or paragraphs.

> The sun had gone down behind the mountain. The chill of night, *however,* had not yet come to soothe the parched bodies of the desert travellers. *In addition,* the semi-darkness now tended to obscure . . .

Verb — a word used to assert something.

> Although we *have* not *unpacked,* we *will join* you at once.

Transitive Verb — a verb that has a receiver of its action.

> The mere thought of dancing school *sickened* the youth.
> The shore *was battered* by the storm-driven waves.

Intransitive Verb — a verb that does not have a receiver of its action or that expresses a state of being.

> If he *comes,* he *will be* welcome.

Intransitive Complete Verb — an intransitive verb that does not have a **subjective complement.**

> I *think;* therefore I *am.*
> Daedalus *escaped,* but Icarus *fell* into the sea.

Intransitive Copulative (Linking) Verb — an intransitive verb that has a **subjective complement.**

> Because Macbeth *was* a tyrant, his subjects *grew* disloyal.

Regular Verb — a verb that forms its past tense and past participle by adding *ed, d,* or *t* to the present stem (e.g., talk, talk*ed,* talk*ed;* dive, div*ed,* div*ed*; burn, burn*t,* burn*t*).

Irregular Verb — a verb that forms its past tense and past participle in any other way than by adding *ed, d,* or *t* to the present stem (e.g., *am, was, been; drive, drove, driven; think, thought, thought.*)

Verb Phrase — a group of words used as a verb (e.g., *shall live, was skiing, has been arranged, will have been travelling.*)

Verbal — a form of a verb that does not by itself assert anything. *Verbals* are classified as **participles, gerunds** and **infinitives.**

Verbal Phrase — see **Participial Phrase, Gerund Phrase,** and **Infinitive Phrase.**

Dangling Verbal — see **Dangling Participle, Dangling Gerund,** and **Dangling Infinitive.**

Voice — a property of verbs that indicates whether the subject is the actor or the receiver of the action of the verb.

Active Voice — the form of a verb which indicates that the subject is the actor.

> Columbus *discovered* America in 1492.
> Jack's wife *drove* him to the station.

Passive Voice — the form of a verb which indicates that the subject is the receiver of the action of the verb. It is formed by using the correct tense form of the verb *to be* with the past participle of the main verb (e.g., *to be understood, was broken, shall have been expelled, having been announced*).

> America *was discovered* by Columbus in 1492.
> Jack *was driven* to the station by his wife.

GRAMMAR RULES
PARTS OF SPEECH

The part of speech of a word is determined by its use in the sentence.

> *Wrong* sometimes seems to triumph. (*noun*)
> That is the *wrong* answer. (*adjective*)
> This problem is solved *wrong*. (*adverb*)
> George never *wronged* even his enemies. (*verb*)

SUBSTANTIVES

A pronoun must agree with its antecedent in person, number, and gender. (Its case is dependent on its use in the sentence.)

> *Everyone* has *his* book with *him.*
> *All* had *their* books with *them.*
> *Neither* of the girls had changed *her* dress.
> This is one of the *horses which* were racing last Saturday.
> Hutch is the only *one* of my students *who* was prepared today.

The case of a substantive is determined by its use in the sentence.

Following are the uses of the nominative case: (a) subject of a verb; (b) subjective complement (except of an infinitive with a subject); (c) a substantive used in direct address; (d) a substantive used in the absolute construction; (e) an appositive to a substantive in the nominative case.

The possessive case is used to show ownership or relationship.

1. To form the possessive case of a compound noun, make the last element of the noun possessive (e.g., my *brother-in-law's* car, the *attorney-general's* secretary).

2. Avoid using the possessive case of an inanimate object.

> (*Poor*) The *building's* windows, the *tree's* branches.
> (*Better*) the windows *of the building,* the branches *of the tree.*

3. In certain cases, the possessive of a substantive is used as the object of the preposition *of.* This use is called the *double possessive* (e.g., that car *of mine,* an uncle *of Henry's,* etc.).

Following are the uses of the objective case: (a) direct object; (b) object of the preposition; (c) indirect object; (d) objective complement; (e) subject of an infinitive; (f) subjective complement of an infinitive with a subject; (g) an appositive to a substantive in the objective case.

A pronoun introducing a dependent clause gets its case from its use in the clause.

> George is the boy *whom* I saw leading the group.
> We know *who* you think did it.
> You may ask to the party *whoever* is socially acceptable.

A subjective complement has the same case as the subject to which it refers.

The best-behaved *people* here are *they*.
He pretended to be *I*.
We thought the *culprit* to be *him*.

Every pronoun must have a definite antecedent that is immediately clear to the reader.

1. Avoid the indefinite use of *it, you* and *they*.

(*Poor*) In this book, *it* says that foxes are dangerous.
(*Better*) This book states that foxes are dangerous.
(*Poor*) In China *you* cannot always choose your occupation.
(*Better*) In China an individual cannot always choose his occupation.
(*Poor*) At my school *they* have six periods a day.
(*Better*) At my school there are six periods a day.

2. If a pronoun seems to refer to either one of two antecedents, recast the sentence so that the reference is clear.

(*Poor*) John's father told him that *he* would have to stay in bed.
(*Better*) John's father told him, "I shall have to stay in bed" or "You will have to stay in bed."

3. A pronoun must not have a whole idea as its antecedent.

(*Poor*) The team played poorly, *which* made the coach angry.
(*Better*) The team's poor playing made the coach angry.
(*Poor*) Our car would not start, and *this* made us late.
(*Better*) Because our car would not start, we were late.

4. A relative pronoun should not refer to a substantive in the possessive case.

(*Poor*) Wendy is in *Mr. Johns'* classroom, who teaches biology.
(*Better*) Wendy is in the classroom of *Mr. Johns, who* teaches biology.

Use *each other* in referring to two, *one another* in referring to more than two.

Hester and Dimmesdale loved *each other*.
The three roommates helped *one another* keep the room clean.

ADJECTIVES AND ADVERBS

Use *a* before a word beginning with a consonant sound, *an* before a word beginning with a vowel sound (e.g., *a* horse, *a* year, *a* union; *an* onion, *an* heiress, *an* uncle).

The article and the possessive pronoun should be repeated before each part of a compound element if different persons or things are meant (e.g., one person: *the* secretary and treasurer, *my* father and best friend; two persons: *the* secretary and *the* treasurer, *my* father and *my* best friend).

Kind of and *sort of* should not be followed by *a* or *an*.

> (*Poor*) He is a strange *sort of a* person.
> (*Better*) He is a strange *sort of* person.

When used with numbers, *first* and *last* should precede the numbers.

> (*Poor*) The ˙*two first* pages of the book are missing.
> (*Better*) The *first two* pages of the book are missing.

Use *fewer* to denote number; use *less* to denote quantity or amount (e.g., *fewer* dimes, but *less* money; *fewer* headaches, but *less* sickness).

After verbs such as *smell, taste, look, sound, feel, stand, sit,* and the like, use an adjective to modify the subject if the subject is not performing an action; use an adverb to modify the verb if the subject is performing an action.

> Because the setter needed a bath, he smelled *bad*.
> Because the setter had a cold, he smelled *badly*.
> He appeared *slower* in a race than he actually was.
> For the second encore he appeared *more* slowly than he had for the previous one.

Use *other* or *else* when comparing a person, a place, or a thing with the general class to which it belongs.

> (*Poor*) Hayes is lazier than any boy in his class
> (*Better*) Hayes is lazier than any *other* boy in his class.
> (*Poor*) Howard likes girls better than anything.
> (*Better*) Howard likes girls better than anything *else*.

Do not use the double negative.

> (*Poor*) He did*n't* give us *no* excuses.
> (*Better*) He did*n't* give us any excuses.
> (*Poor*) I ca*n't* help *but* think that you are wrong.
> (*Better*) I ca*n't* help thinking that you are wrong.

Do not use the negative with *hardly, scarcely,* or *barely*.

> (*Poor*) We could *not hardly* keep our heads above water.
> (*Better*) We could *not* keep our heads above water.
> (*Better*) We could *hardly* keep our heads above water.

Use *as . . . as* in the affirmative, *so . . . as* with the negative.

> Peter is nearly *as* strong *as* John.
> Peter is *not so* strong *as* John.

Do not use *equally* with *as* in the *as . . . as* construction.

> (*Poor*) My task is *equally as* difficult *as* yours.
> (*Better*) My task is *as* difficult *as* yours.

Do not use *very* or *too* to modify a past participle; use *very much, very well, greatly,* etc.

> (*Poor*) His parents were *very impressed* by his grades.
> (*Better*) His parents were *quite* (or *very much*) impressed
> by his grades.
> (*Poor*) He was *too angered* to reply.
> (*Better*) He was *too angry* to reply.

Place *only, just, not* and *even* as near as possible to the words which they modify. Avoid placing *only* between the subject and the verb.

> *Only* you may feed the lions.
> You may *only* feed the lions.
> You may feed the lions *only*.
> (*Poor*) All of the money was *not* taken.
> (*Better*) *Not* all of the money was taken.

Almost means *nearly*; *most* means *nearly all*.

> (*Poor*) *Most all* of us were wet and miserable.
> (*Better*) *Most* of us were wet and miserable.
> (*Better*) *Almost* all of us were wet and miserable.

Do not use *nowhere near* for *not nearly*.

> (*Poor*) Fred has *nowhere near* as much ability as you.
> (*Better*) Fred has *not nearly* as much ability as you.

Do not use *kind of* and *sort of* as adverbs (e.g., *somewhat* tired, not *sort of* tired; *rather* sick, not *kind of* sick).

Do not use *some* as an adverb.

> (*Poor*) The sick old woman is *some* better today.
> (*Better*) The sick old woman is *somewhat* better today.

VERBS

A verb must agree with its subject in person and number (e.g., I *am,* you *who are,* he *who is, they are*).

1. *Either, neither, each* and compounds of *one, thing,* and *body* require singular verbs (e.g., *neither* of us *is; each* of them *has; everybody is*).

2. *Both, several, few* and *many* require plural verbs (e.g., *both are; few* of them *know*.)

3. *Most, some, all, none, any,* and *such* may be either singular or plural depending on their meaning. Their number is often indicated by the number of the object of the preposition following them.

> *Some* of the *cake is* stale.
> *Some* of the *cakes are* stale.
> *None* of the *money was* ever found.
> *None* of the *sailors* were ever found.

4. Nouns which are plural in form, but singular in meaning require a singular verb (e.g., the *news is, measles is, mumps is*).

5. Compound subjects connected by *and* which denote one person or thing require a singular verb (e.g., *ice cream and cake is* my favourite; *macaroni and cheese is;* his *contemporary and best friend was*).

6. Nouns ending in *ics* require a singular verb if they denote an art, a skill, or a subject; they require a plural verb if they denote activities (e.g., *mathematics is, civics is; athletics are, acoustics are*).

> *Politics is* taught in most universities. (*subject*)
> *Politics are* rather sordid in some communities. (*activities*)

7. Subjects modified by *each, every,* and *many a* require a singular verb.

> *Each* man, woman, and child *is* willing to help.
> *Many a* newspaper and magazine *has failed* financially.

8. When the parts of a compound subject are connected by *or, nor,* or *but,* the verb agrees with the nearer subject. (If the parts of the compound subject differ in person, it is better to recast the sentence.)

> Neither his brothers *nor he seems* to understand.
> *Do* either the *boys or* their father work for you now?
> Not only ten quail, *but* also a *rabbit was* caught in the trap.

9. *The number* requires a singular verb; *a number* requires a plural verb.

> *The number* of casulaties *is* not known.
> *A number* of students *are* outside.

10. When a verb has a collective noun in the singular as its subject, the verb is singular if the group as a whole is acting, but plural if the members of the group are acting as individuals.

> The *class has* decided to donate a clock tower to the school.
> The *class have* disagreed about what to give the school.
> The *jury has* given *its* verdict and *have* gone to *their* respective homes.

11. Subjects denoting quantity or amount require a singular verb.

> *Eleven dollars is* all the money that I have.
> *Five gallons* of gas *is* what I asked for.

The present tense is formed from the present stem (the first principal part) (e.g., he *is,* we *study,* they *sing*).

The past tense is formed from the past stem (the second principal part) (e.g., he *was,* we *studied,* they *sang*).

The future tense is formed by using *shall* or *will* with the present stem (e.g., he *will be,* we *shall study,* they *will sing*).

The present perfect tense is formed by using the present of *have* with the past participle of the main verb (e.g., he *has been,* we *have studied,* they *have sung*).

The past perfect tense is formed by using the past of *have* with the past participle of the main verb (e.g., he *had been,* we *had studied,* they *had sung*).

The future perfect tense is formed by using the future of *have* with the past participle of the main verb (e.g., he *will have been,* we *shall have studied,* they *will have sung*).

The relationship between the time of the action in the independent clause and that in the dependent clause must be made clear by the use of the proper tenses.

> Because he *studies,* he *does* well on quizzes.
> Because he *had studied,* he *did* well on this quiz.

In indirect discourse and in clauses expressing purpose, a past tense in the independent clause usually requires a past tense in the dependent clause.

He *says* that he *lives* in Ontario.
He *said* that he *lived* in Ontario.
He *is hurrying* so that he *may* not *be* late.
He *hurried* so that he *might* not *be* late.

In indirect discourse, use a present tense in the dependent clause to express a universal truth.

Our teacher *told* us that the sun *rises* in the east.
Shakespeare *said* that love is blind and lovers *cannot see*.

The passive voice is used only when it is desirable to emphasize the receiver of the action or when the doer is unknown or obvious. Otherwise the verb may be termed the "weak passive."

Three of those cars are *owned* by Mr. Latham.
Many valuable rugs *were burned* in the fire.
Lucius *was elected* captain of the soccer team.

The indicative mood is used to state a fact or to ask a direct question.

Hayes *was* lonely without his old friends.
Was that not Chris Brown whom we *saw* with you?

The imperative mood is used to express a command or a request.

Take your seats at once, and *be* quiet.
Please *help* me with my term paper, Mr. Fox.

The subjunctive mood is used to express a wish, a prayer, or a condition or supposition that is contrary to fact. It is also used after verbs of commanding or requesting, after *as if* and *as though,* and after such expressions as *it is necessary, it is wise.*

I wish that it *were not* raining. (*wish*)
Thy kingdom *come.* (*prayer*)
If I *were you,* I would leave. (*condition contrary to fact*)
He directed that we *be* on time. (*after command*)
She treats him as if he *were* her slave. (*after as if*)
It is important that we *be* there early.

In a present condition which is contrary to fact, use the past subjunctive; in a past condition which is contrary to fact, use the past perfect subjunctive.

(*Present*) If he *were playing,* we might win.
(*Past*)   If he *had been playing,* we might have won.

After *as if* and *as though* and in wishes, use the past subjunctive if the time is the same as or after that expressed in the main verb;

use the past perfect subjunctive if the time is before that expressed in the main verb.

> He looks as if he *were* sick. (*same time*)
> He looks as if he *had been* sick. (*before*)
> I wish that I *were* there now. (*same time*)
> I wish that I *had been* there yesterday. (*before*)

In clauses expressing purpose, use *may* and *might* rather than *can* and *could*.

> They worked rapidly so that they *might* finish early.

May, can, and *must* are present tense; *might, could, should,* and *would* are considered past tense.

> I hope that we *may* join you later.
> I hoped that we *might* join you later.

May and *might* are used to express permission of possibility.

> Yes, you *may* stay out until midnight. (*permission*)
> It *may* snow tonight. (*possibility*)

Can and *could* are used to express ability.

> He *can* kick a football sixty yards.
> *Could* you tell that I was nervous?

Must is used to express necessity.

> One *must* eat in order to live.

Should and *would* generally follow the rules for *shall* and *will*, each, however, has certain special uses. *Should* is used in all three persons to express duty or obligation (e.g., *Children should obey their parents*). It is used in all three persons in a simple condition (e.g., *If you should see her,* ask her to wait for me.) *Would* is used in all three persons to express habitual action (e.g., *He would take a walk almost every day.*) *If* is used in all three persons in the conclusion of a simple condition (e.g., If I were you, *I would not delay*).

Ought is used to express duty or obligation.

> Every qualified voter *ought* to cast his ballot.

Do not use *try and;* use *try to.*

> (*Poor*) We will *try and* win.
> (*Better*) We will *try to* win.

CONJUNCTIONS

Use *than* after the comparative degree only.

    (*Poor*)   This car is not much different *than* that one.
    (*Better*) This car is not much different *from* that one.

Never use *because* to introduce a noun clause.

    (*Poor*)   *Because you are lazy* is why you have never done well.
    (*Better*) *Because* you are lazy, you have never done well.

Use *when* or *where* to introduce a noun clause only when time or place is indicated.

    (*Poor*)   An adjective is *when* a word is used to modify a substantive.
    (*Better*) An adjective is a word used to modify a substantive.
    (*Poor*)   I read in the paper *where* schools will be closed next week.
    (*Better*) I read in the paper *that* schools would be closed next week.

Without, like, except, and *on account of* are prepositions and may not be used as conjunctions.

    (*Poor*)   I cannot do it *without* you help me.
    (*Better*) I cannot do it *unless* you help me.
    (*Poor*)   Do *like* I say, not *like* I do.
    (*Better*) Do *as* I say, not *as* I do.

In a comparison, do not omit a necessary conjunction.

    (*Poor*)   She is as pretty, if not prettier than Vicki.
    (*Better*) She is as pretty *as* Vicki, if not prettier.

Both parts of a correlative conjunction must precede the same type of grammatical construction.

    (*Poor*)   He is *not only* cruel to dogs, *but also* to cats.
    (*Better*) He is cruel *not only* to dogs, *but also* to cats.

In a comparison, the construction and case of the item following *than* or *as* must be the same as that of the item with which it is compared.

    (*Poor*)   The *song* of a lark is sweeter than a *thrush*.
    (*Better*) The *song* of a lark is sweeter than *that* of a thrush.
    (*Poor*)   *Hearing* is not quite the same as *to listen*.
    (*Better*) *To hear* is not quite the same as *to listen*.
    (*Better*) *Hearing* is not quite the same as *listening*.

Coordinate conjunctions may be properly used to join only sentence elements that are parallel in both thought and grammatical construction.

(*Poor*)   He faced the enemy *boldly* and *with defiance.*
(*Better*)   He faced the enemy *boldly and defiantly.*
(*Poor*)   *We finally reached home,* and *it was a welcome sight!*
(*Better*)   We finally reached home. It was a welcome sight.

COMPOSITION NOTES

GENERAL DIRECTIONS

If you expect to write a good composition, you must follow a very definite procedure, such as the following:

1. Select a subject, and limit the scope of it.

2. Secure material about the subject by observing, conversing, reading, and using your imagination.

3. Organize the material thus gained.

4. Write a rough draft of the composition.

5. Read over the rough draft, and make necessary changes and corrections.

6. Select a suitable and interesting title.

7. Write the composition in final form.

8. Wait twenty-four hours; then re-read your composition *objectively,* and correct the errors found.

In selecting a subject, you should choose one that, first, will interest you and, second, will not be too broad for the time and space allotted. For instance, "Tobacco" is a very broad subject, and "Smoking" is narrower; but "The Evils of Smoking" is the type of limited subject on which a weekly composition might be written.

Having chosen your subject, you must think about it, talk about it, and read about it, storing up material on paper as you do so. Then you must organize your material by outlining it.

Finally, you should begin to write, following your outline generally, but *giving most of your attention to the expression of your thought.* In the introduction, catch the reader's attention by being interesting as well as direct and informative. Conclude your composition in such a way that the reader will feel its completeness and its force.

If possible, complete your composition on the day before it is due. Put it aside overnight. When you read it over the next day, you can be more objective in your criticism and will find many errors that you would have overlooked if you had proof-read it immediately after having finished it. Regardless of when you do it, always re-read your composition before you hand it in.

SOME HELPFUL HINTS

1. *Keep your reader in mind.* Write so that he will understand what you are trying to tell him; don't make him struggle to get your ideas.

2. *Remember that you are communicating something to the world at large.* You are not writing just to please yourself or your teacher.

3. *Don't hand in a hurriedly done, terrible paper.* It is better to be late than to submit poor workmanship.

4. *Select a point of view, establish it early, and keep it throughout the paper* (personal, impersonal; formal, conversational; objective, subjective, sympathetic, unsympathetic; serious, humourous.)

5. *Avoid such expressions as* "I think," "in my opinion," "I shall now tell you," "I will relate in this composition," etc.

6. *Never include such statements as* "There are many other reasons why . . . but there is not time to relate them all." *The reader will immediately feel the incompleteness of the composition.*

7. *Be natural and sincere.* Don't try to be "literary." Don't try to cover a paucity of ideas with a superfluity of words.

THE OUTLINE

Every young mind is filled with interesting thoughts and ideas, but they do not occur to every young mind in clear, logical, effective sequence. Most students can avoid a disorderly, ineffective composition only by planning the work on paper *before* they begin to write.

Outlining is easy if you follow these simple directions:

1. Think about the subject.
2. Write down in any order the thoughts that the subject brings to your mind (or that you get from reading and talking about it).

3. Classify the related thoughts into groups by placing a distinctive mark (*A, B, C,* etc.) beside each of those that belong together.

4. Select a topic for each group.

5. Discard topics and groups that are not relevant or that are too minor to be included.

6. Arrange the groups in their natural and logical order.

7. Combine topics that group naturally, and form new main topics; subordinate minor topics.

8. Arrange the items in each group in logical order.

Almost any writing can be divided naturally under three distinct headings: introduction, body, and conclusion. The frame of a typical outline with topics, sub-topics, and sub-sub-topics, follows:

SUBJECT

    I. Introduction
       A.
       B.

   II. Body
       A.
          1.
          2.
             a.
             b.
       B.
       C.

  III. Conclusion
       A.
       B.

There are certain rules for form that should be observed in outlining:

1. Divisions, such as topics, sub-topics, etc. are indicated by the alternation, in a definite pattern, of letters with numerals, commencing with Roman numerals, as: I, A, 1, a, (1), (a).

2. The words *Introduction, Body* and *Conclusion* should never be included in an outline.

3. Each topic and sub-topic should begin with a capital.

4. If there is only one sub-topic, precede it with a colon and place it on the same line as the topic (for every *1,* there must be a *2;* for every *a,* there must be a *b.*)

    (*Poor*)   A. Cause of malaria
                      1. Anopheles mosquito
               B. Effects of malaria
    (*Good*)   A. Cause of malaria: anopheles mosquito
               B. Effects of malaria

5. Topics and sub-topics that are parallel in thought should be parallel in structure (noun and noun; verb, verb, and verb; participle and participle).

    (*Poor*)   A. Physical injury caused by smoking
                    1. Lung cancer
                    2. Makes you nervous
                    3. Losing appetite
                    4. You get an ulcerated stomach
               B. Smoking causes damage to property
                    1. Clothing and furniture burned
                    2. Real property
                        a. Houses and buildings
                        b. Forest fires and wheatfields

    (*Good*)   A. Physical injury caused by smoking
                    1. Lung Cancer
                    2. Nervousness
                    3. Loss of appetite
                    4. Ulcerated stomach
               B. Property damage caused by smoking
                    1. To personal property
                        a. Clothing
                        b. Furniture
                    2. To real property
                        a. Houses and buildings
                        b. Forests and wheatfields

BEGINNING AND ENDING A COMPOSITION

1. Although there are myriad ways of beginning a composition, you should always pick the one that will best fit your approach to the subject and which will *catch the reader's attention* from the very first. As students often have trouble with their opening sentences, twenty different methods of beginning are given below. Some are for narrative, some for the other types of writing. They are by no means comprehensive; they merely show a variety of ways in which you can get started.

Begin with

A. The setting ("It was one of those dark, muggy, misty New Orleans nights when gentle people avoid the back alleys.")

B. The situation ("Willie and Sarah stood looking dumbfounded at each other: their television picture tube had just gone black.")

C. The antecedent action ("Willie and Sarah had for years longed for a house in the suburbs; yet each time that they had accumulated a few savings . . .")

D. The first incident ("Joe stopped the truck and, against company orders, picked up the hitch-hiker.")

* E. The effects ("Two cars were completely wrecked, seven people were hospitalized, and three bodies were in the morgue just because Joe had gazed a trifle too long at a luscious blonde.")

F. Establishment of the point of view ("As I was walking down Legare Street last night, I saw . . ." or "The attitude of the government toward . . . has been unusually courageous and exemplary.")

* G. A summary of points ("There are four major reasons why . . .")

* H. A summary of steps ("There are four distinct steps to follow in . . .")

I. The first step ("In crossing a street, one should first . . .")

* J. The importance of the subject ("Knowing how to . . . may save your life some day.")

* K. A quotation (" 'The wicked wasp of Twickenham' — that is how people referred to Alexander Pope . . .")

* L. An evaluation of the subject ("Alexander Pope was probably the most arrogant and powerful literary dictator, and yet the most . . .")

M. An explanation of the writer's qualifications ("For seven long years I pitched for the Washington 'Senators,' and I know how loyal . . .")

* N. An informal statement ("in these troublous times, we must not be carried away by emotion.")

* O. A formal statement ("In troublous times, people are sometimes carried away by their emotions.")

P. A definition (*"Webster's Collegiate Dictionary* defines cheating as . . .")

* Q. An interest-rousing statement ("Surely man is a broom-stick!")

R. An interest-rousing question ("Have you ever considered that man is much like a broomstick?")

* S. An interest-rousing challenge ("No one can deny that actually man is quite comparable to a broomstick.")

T. A statement of preference ("Some people like their cooks to be clean and neat; others want them coloured or white; but I . . .")

2. An effective ending for a composition is just as important as an effective beginning. The vital thing is to *leave the reader with a feeling of completeness.* The asterisked methods in *1* above may be used equally well in closing the composition. If your composition is short and if the final paragraph of the body is strong, no formal conclusion is necessary.

ORDER OF DEVELOPMENT

There are six major orders in which compositions can be developed. In outlining your composition, select the method that will best help you to achieve unity, coherence, and emphasis.

1. *Chronological order* (from one detail to another in order of time) — used in narration and in exposition of how to make or to do something.

2. *Space order* (from near to far, from top to bottom, from inside to outside, etc.) — used largely in description.

3. *Logical order* (from general to specific, from specific to general, from cause to effect, from one detail to another in order of logic) — used in exposition and argumentation.

4. *Comparison and contrast order* (from one subject of comparison to the other) — used in comparing or contrasting two subjects.

5. *Climactic order* (from least important to most important, from minor good points to major bad ones, from minor bad points to major good ones.) — used in narration, character portrayal, and criticisms.

6. *Emphatic order* (from second most important reason through less important reasons to most important reason) — used in argumentation and in exposition of reasons for a belief or a stand.

OUTLINES OF THE TYPES OF WRITING

Basically, there are four types of writing: narration, description, exposition, and argumentation. Each has its purpose. Naturally there is overlapping — some description in narration, some exposition in argument — but a piece of writing will, basically, be just one of the four types.

1. NARRATION

Narration is the type of composition in which the writer relates an incident (personal or imaginative experience; anecdote), an episode (short story), a series of episodes (novel), a person's life (biography), or the story of the past (history), usually in chronological order. It involves *setting* (time and place), *characters* (the people,) and *action*.

Although it is incorrect to say that there is a basic frame for short narrative writing, a typical outline for narration developed in purely chronological order is given below. Note that narration answers the questions *who, what, when, where, how,* and *why.*

Title

I. *Introduction*: (Who, what, when, and where?)
   A. What was happening at the time? Where? When?
   B. Who was involved?
II. *Body*: (How and why?)
   A.   Relate the incident or incidents,
      1. usually in chronological order.
      2.
   B.
   C.
III. *Conclusion*: The effects.

2. DESCRIPTION

Description is a form of composition in which the writer paints in words a picture of a person, a place, or a thing from a certain point of view (both location and attitude). It should reveal the impressions made by the subject on the writer.

A typical frame outline for description is given below:

Title

I. *Introduction*: Your point of view and your first impression of the subject.

II. *Body*:
- A.   An exact description of what you saw
- B. related in space order. Include as many
- C. details and appeal to as many different
- D. senses as possible.

III. *Conclusion*: Final impressions made by the subject.

(*Caution*: Be sure to keep the same point of view or indicate changes as they occur.)

3. EXPOSITION

Exposition is a form of composition in which the writer explains, proposes, or analyzes almost anything. Because there are so many types of expository writing, it is impossible to give one outline that would be all inclusive. Below are outlines that might be used with several major types.

a. How to Make or to Do Something.

Title

I. *Introduction*:
- A. The thing to be made or done.
- B. The materials needed.
- C. The tools and skills needed.

II. *Body*:
- A. First step in the operation.
- B. Second step.
- C. Third step, etc.
- D. Cautions to be observed.

III. *Conclusion*:
- A. The finished product.
- B. Its use, value, etc.

b. **Explanation of an Idea, a Theory, or a Belief.**

Title

I. *Introduction*:
  A. Brief statement of the idea.
  B. Explanation of the idea.

II. *Body*:
  A.   Illustrations and example to
  B. show the truth of the idea.

III. *Conclusion*: A summary.

c. **Character Portrayal.**

Title

I. *Introduction*:
  A.   The identity of the character and
  B. the things generally that make him unusual or worth discussing.

II. *Body*:
  A. First quality.
     1.   Incidents from the subject's life to show
     2. that he possesses this quality.
  B. Second quality
     1. Incidents, etc.
     2.
  C. Third Quality.

III. *Conclusion*: A summary.

d. **Comparison or Contrast of Two Subjects.**

I. *Introduction*:
  A.   Introduction and general comparison
  B. or contrast of the subjects.

II. *Body*:
  A. Quality #1.
     1. In "X".
     2. In "Y".

II. *Body*:
  A. Qualities in "X"
     1. Quality #1.
     2. Quality #2.

OR

B. Quality #2.
   1. In "X".
   2. In "Y".

B. Qualities in "Y"
   1. Quality #1.
   2. Quality #2.

III.   *Conclusion*:An evaluation of the two subjects.

e. **Editorial.**

Title

I.   *Introduction*: The incident or the situation that inspires the editorial.

II.   *Body*:

A. The reason for the incident or the situation.

B. Dangers or problems inherent in the situation.

C. A remedy for the situation.

III.   *Conclusion*: The results to be obtained from the remedy.

4. ARGUMENTATION

Argumentation is a form of composition in which the writer attempts to defend or to attack the truth of a proposition. Its purpose is to convince an *intelligent* person of the validity of the writer's beliefs.

In preparing an argument, first *get all available information* on your subjects (libraries, erudite persons, government agencies, chambers of commerce, etc.)

Then *organize your material,* dropping all that is weak or not really relevant. Classify your material under simple coordinate headings so that your major points will be crystal clear. For instance, your plan might have (1) *political,* (2) *economic,* and (3) *social* advantages; or there might be (1) *physical,* (2) *mental,* and (3) *moral* benefits derived from it. In attacking the proposition, you might prove that its adoption would be (1) *politically unwise,* (2) *economically unsound,* (3) *militarily impossible,* and (4) *socially unjust.* Above all, use only a few sharply defined topics so that you will not confuse your reader.

Next, *outline your topics* in emphatic order. Under each main topic, include sub-arguments.

In writing your argument, have strong introductory and concluding statements. Both should summarize your main arguments. Topic and summary sentences should be included in each major paragraph to focus the reader's attention on your point.

Finally, a good argument must have three characteristics if it is not to fall flat on its face.

1. It must be logical.
2. It must be well grounded on facts.
3. It must be complete.

Following are certain weaknesses that should be avoided in argumentation:

1. **Arguing from insufficient evidence.** "Study hall is harmful because last year the vision of five boys was weakened between September and June."

2. **Arguing from doubtful authority.** "To prove my point that study hall is unfair, I have a petition signed by forty of the oldest boys in school, requesting the abolition of study hall on the grounds that it is unfair."

3. **Arguing from a mere assumption.** "Study hall is bad for the growing boy because it inhibits his natural desires."

4. **Begging the question** (assuming to be true what is supposed to be proved). "Study hall must be bad for boys; otherwise the question of its abolition would never have been brought up."

5. **Arguing by mere assertion.** "Study hall is unwise. The boys know it. Deep down in their hearts the teachers know it; but the teachers will not admit it because they are afraid to depart from the traditional. All progressive educators insist that supervised study hall is bad."

6. **Arguing by analogy.** "Study hall is bad because it makes boys do what they don't want to do. It is like a compulsory movie; nobody gets very much out of one which he is forced to attend."

Given below is a frame outline for argumentation.

Title

I. *Introduction*: A statement of the proposition and a summary of the points for or against it.

II. *Body*:
   A. Definition of terms.
   B. Next-to-strongest argument.
   C. Argument.
   D. Argument.
   E. Strongest argument.

III. *Conclusion*: Restatement of your position with a summary of your points.

THE RESEARCH PAPER

A research paper is a long composition in which you present information, the opinions of others, and your own opinions and conclusions which you have gained by reading rather extensively on a subject. As you will be required to write numerous research or "term" papers, you should learn now a good procedure to follow. Given below is a method that has proved itself. Follow it, and you will save much time and will submit papers that are at least well organized.

1. Choose a field, select a subject within that field and analyze the subject to find points that will require discussion in your paper.

2. Go to the library and locate all books, magazines, reference works, etc., which should contain material about your subject. Make a list of these in bibliographical form, and keep it for reference.

3. Examine each possible source, looking first at the table of contents and the index, and discard those which will not help you.

Note: Certain books will contain bibliographies which will lead you to other sources.

4. Read carefully those sources which contain useful information, and take notes as you read.

5. Take notes on 3x5 cards, one card for each note. At the top of the card, write the author's name, an abbreviation of the title, the page reference, and the topic of the note.

6. Each note should be a summary; but if it is a direct quotation that you think will be useful, *it must be in quotation marks*.

7. Sort your notes, and arrange them in piles by topic. List these topics on a piece of paper.

8. Make an outline for your paper, using as a basis these topics and any others that may have occurred to you as you read.

9. Write a rough draft of your paper, using your outline as a guide. Do not just copy your notes, but use them to verify your statements and to validate your opinions and your conclusions.

10. Wait at least a day, read over your rough draft as *objectively* as possible, make necessary changes and connections, and

write your paper in final form (on one side of the sheet only).

11. Make a title page, including on it the title of your paper, your own name, the course, the date, and your teacher's name.

12. Your second page should be an outline of the paper or a table of contents.

13. Make your final bibliography, listing only the sources which you used in your paper, and include it at the end of your paper.

14. Try to get a cheap semi-stiff binder for your paper.

15. Read your paper over and make last-minute corrections before you hand it in.

FOOTNOTING

In order to avoid deceiving the reader (and yourself) into thinking that words, expressions, and ideas gained from someone else are your own, you must, each time that you use one, insert a footnote to show the source of your information, using quotation marks when you quote directly. The greatest difficulty lies in deciding what to footnote and what not to footnote. The following may help you.

1. You need not footnote

a. Information absorbed into your knowledge so that you do not have to refer to a text or a note in order to express it.

b. Farcts which are common knowledge: e.g., the fact that Shakespeare was born in Stratford-on-Avon in 1564.

2. You should footnote

a. A direct quotation (and enclose it in quotation marks.)

b. The thoughts, opinions, and conclusions of others, even when you express them in your own words through summary or paraphrase.

The mechanics of footnoting are not difficult if you follow this procedure:

1. Number the footnotes consecutively on a page.

2. Place the footnote number just above the end of the last word of the material for which you are giving credit.

3. Place the footnote number and the work to which you are indebted at the bottom of the paper.

4. Draw a line between the bottom of the text and the first footnote.

5. The first time that you acknowledge a work in your paper, write it out in bibliographical form (excluding the publisher), and give the page number.

> *Example*: 1. Percy Lubbock, *The Craft of Fiction,* London, 1926, p. 87.

6. If the same work is cited in the *next* footnote, use the following form:

> 2. *Ibid.,* p. 93.

7. If acknowledgment of another work or other works intervenes, use the following form:

> 4. Lubbock, *op. cit.,* p. 117.

8. If you are using two works by the same author and you re-cite one of them, use an abbreviated title in the footnote:

> 2. Lubbock, *Fiction,* p. 137.

BIBLIOGRAPHY

The listing of works in a bibliography can become quite involved. If you will follow the procedure given below and imitate the examples, you can construct a perfectly adequate bibliography.

1. List all works in alphabetical order by author. If there is no author given, use the first word of the title in alphabetizing the work.

2. For most books, you give the name of the author (surname first), the title of the book, the place of publication, the publisher, and the date.

> Lubbock, Percy, *The Craft of Fiction,* London, Jonathan Cape Ltd., 1926.

3. For some books, other information is required, such as the name of the editor of a collection, the translator of a book, etc. Observe the following:

> *An edited collection*: Untermeyer, L. ed., *Modern British and American Poetry,* New York, Harcourt, Brace & Co., 1939.

> *A translation*: Silone, I., *Bread and Wine,* translated from the Italian by Eric Ross, New York, Harper and Bros., 1932.

A critical edition: Coleridge, S. T., *The Poetical Works of Samuel Taylor Coleridge,* ed. by James D. Campbell, London, Macmillan Co., 1925.

4. For magazine articles, give the author's name, the title of the article, the title of the magazine, the volume number, the date of issue, and the page numbers.

Bumstead, Newman, "Children's Art Around the World," *The National Geographic Magazine,* CXI (March, 1957), pp. 365-387.

5. For a reference work, follow the form for the magazine article, including the edition number for works of more than one edition.

"Alluvial Deposits," *Encyclopedia Britannica,* 16th ed., 1948, Vol. I, pp. 183-185.

RULES FOR FORM

1. Make an outline of your composition.
2. Make a rough draft of your composition; do all necessary correcting on this rough draft; copy the corrected composition on notebook paper; and hand in *all* your work on the assigned day.
3. All final composition work must be done in ink.
4. Put your name, the course, and the date in the upper right-hand corner of the first page.
5. Write the title on the first line.
6. Skip a line and begin the composition on the third line.
7. Indent the first word of every paragraph about one inch.
8. Leave a narrow right-hand margin.
9. Write nothing on the last ruled line of each page.
10. Do not write on the back of the page.
11. Do not include little helps like *Over* and *The End.*

SELF-EXAMINATION

From time to time, your teacher will ask you to look over your composition, keeping one or more of the following questions in mind as you do so. You will find it to your profit to examine each one of your compositions in the light of at least one of these questions, whether you are required to do so or not.

1. THE SENTENCE

a. Is every sentence grammatically complete?

b. Is each word the most vivid and expressive one that I can use?

c. Does every sentence say exactly what I want it to say?

d. Does each sentence deal with only one thought?

e. Does each sentence logically follow the preceding one or ones?

f. Have I used transition words and phrases to carry over the thought from one sentence to the next?

g. Are my facts accurate?

2. THE PARAGRAPH

a. Is each paragraph a unit of thought?

b. Do I have a topic sentence in each paragraph?

c. Does each paragraph begin and end strongly?

3. THE COMPOSITION

a. Is my opening paragraph direct and interest-catching?

b. Is each paragraph a definite and important part of the whole composition?

c. Is the order of paragraphs logical and effective?

d. Have I carried the thought easily from one paragraph to the next one by the use of good transitional devices?

e. Is any paragraph too lóng or too short?

f. Have I given the proper relative proportion to my ideas?

g. Does my closing paragraph give the reader a sense of completeness?

COMPOSITION RULES

RULES FOR PUNCTUATION

The intelligent punctuation of any sentence depends upon three fundamental requirements: an exact understanding of what we wish to say; a complete knowledge of the grammatical structure of the sentence; and comprehension of the rules for punctuation.

So that you may better understand the importance of punctuation, examine the following sentences and see what a difference the marks of punctuation make:

Why, did you ever marry John?
Why did you ever marry John?
Why, did you ever marry, John?
Why did you ever marry, John?

We'll, be ready to eat Mr. Tompkins when the bell rings.
We'll be ready to eat Mr. Tompkins when the bell rings.
We'll, be ready to eat, Mr. Tompkins, when the bell rings.
We'll be ready to eat, Mr. Tompkins, when the bell rings.

I am not to tell the truth very well today.
I am, not to tell the truth, very well today.
I am not, to tell the truth, very well today.

Now, just for fun, see what you can do with the following. Correctly punctuated and capitalized, it makes perfectly good sense.

That that is is that that is not is not that that is not is not that that is that that is is not that that is not is not that it it is.

There are several general directions for punctuation that you should keep in mind:

1. Know with understanding the rules for punctuation.
2. Punctuate each sentence as you write it, not afterwards.
3. Punctuate at the end of a line, not at the beginning of the next line.
4. In all your writing, whether for English or not, make accurate punctuation a habit.
5. Observe the punctuation used by the best authors.
6. Do not punctuate unnecessarily.
7. *Use a little common sense.*

1. THE PERIOD (.)

a. The period is used at the end of a declarative or an imperative sentence.

"A good name is rather to be chosen than great riches." (*Declarative*)

"It is more blessed to give than to receive." (*Declarative*)

"Quit yourselves like men." (*Imperative*)

"To thine own self be true." (*Imperative*)

b. The period is used after abbreviations.

A.B.; Ph.D.; P.M.; Mrs.; Sept. 10; Va.; S. C.; etc.

2. THE COMMA (,)

a. The comma is used between the independent clauses of a compound sentence if the clauses are connected by one of the simple coordinate conjunctions: *and, but, or, nor,* and *for.*

"Dust thou art, and to dust thou shalt return."

"The harvest truly is plenteous, but the labourers are few."

"All that you do, do with your might, for things done by halves are never done right."

b. The comma is used after each element of a series of coordinate words, phrases, or clauses except the last.

"His name shall be called Wonderful, Counsellor, The Mighty God, The Everlasting Father, The Prince of Peace."

"And Jesus increased in wisdom, in stature, and in favour with God and man."

(*Note*: When two coordinate adjectives not connected by *and,* precede a noun, use a comma between them.)

The tall, muscular hunter faced the charging, roaring lion.

The tall petrified hunter faced the charging African lion.

(The adjectives are not coordinate: therefore no comma.)

c. The comma is used after an introductory verbal phrase or adverbial clause.

Having done all that he could, he rested. (*Participial phrase*)

Before signing your name, read what you are signing. (*Gerund phrase*)

To finish before the bell, one must eat hastily. (*Infinitive phrase*)

"*As a man thinketh in his heart,* so is he." (*Adverbial clause*)

"*When I became a man,* I put away childish things." (*Adverbial clause*)

d. The comma is used to set off non-restrictive phrases and clauses.

(*Non-restrictive phrase*) Harry Jones, *wearing a false beard to hide his face,* boarded a plane for Toronto.

(*Restrictive phrase*) It was done by a man *wearing a false beard to hide his face.*

(*Non-restrictive clause*) Dr. Blackford, *who wore a short beard,* was once Principal of Episcopal High School.

(*Restrictive clause*) It was done by a man *who wore a short beard.*

(*Non-restrictive clause*) He did very well, *although he had never played the game before.*

(*Non-restrictive clause*) They came early, *as they had been told that there would be few seats available.*

(*Restrictive clause*) He did it *because he wanted to.*

e. The comma is used to set off parenthetical and transitional elements and other interruptions in thought.

You all know, *I suppose,* that reading is a skill which needs to be practiced.

Their action is, *furthermore,* understandable in view of the facts.

f. The comma is used to emphasize a contrast between coordinate sentence elements.

I called *Hill, not Hall.*

"I bring you *not peace, but a sword.*"

He came *not* to call *the righteous, but sinners to repentance.*

g. The comma is used to set off words used in direct address.

Willie, please do not throw water on your father.

I admit, *Mr. Thomsen,* that Yale is somewhat overrated.

"Go to the ant, *thou sluggard.*"

h. The comma is used to set off an appositive expression.

The opposing team, *bruised and beaten,* limped off the field.

Mr. Whittle, *our German teacher,* has for years posed as a weather prophet.

(*Note*: Close appositives are not set off. My brother *Jim;* the poet *Keats; etc.*)

i. The comma is used after each element of a compound date or a compound geographical expression.

It was on *September 3, 1963,* that the enemy launched their sneak attack on us.

He lives at *92 South Battery, Halifax, Nova Scotia,* in a large brick house.

j. Expressions out of their natural o r d e r in the sentence are often set off with commas.

"Whatsoever thy hand findeth to do, do with thy might."

"Even a fool, *when he holdeth his peace,* is counted wise."

k. The comma is used to set off an absolute expression.

The bridge having been built, Caesar's legions marched across.

Everything went smoothly, *preparations having been made well ahead of time.*

l. The comma is used to set off a mild interjection.

Well, you may go if you think that you must.

Oh, I suppose that there is an answer to every question.

m. The comma is used after *yes, no, certainly,* etc., in answer to a question.

Yes, you will get into the game before it is over.

Certainly, that is the way to do it.

n. The comma is used to set off a question following a statement.

That is what you meant, *isn't it?*

You do not really intend to run away, *do you?*

o. The comma is used after the salutation of a personal letter and after the complimentary close of all letters.

Dear Ruth,   My dear Mrs. Smith,   My Darling,

Very truly yours,   Sincerely yours,   Lovingly,

p. The comma is used to prevent misreading or a delay in reading.

(Ambiguous)   He moved toward his opponent shaking like a leaf.

(Clear) He moved toward his opponent, shaking like a leaf.

(Not immediately clear) Because of this friendship was out of the question.

(Clear) Because of this, friendship was out of the question.

q. The comma is used to set off *etc.* from the rest of the sentence.

Colloquialisms, slang, *etc.,* should not be used in formal writing.

r. The comma is usually used to set off the introductory material from a direct quotation that is a sentence.

"The play's the thing," *said Hamlet,* "wherein I'll catch the conscience of the King."

"My words fly up; my thoughts remain below," *said the King later.*

s. The comma is used to set off initials or titles following a proper name.

Walker, *J. L.,* and Kinsolving, *W. L.,* are wanted in the office at once.

Mr. A. R. Hoxton, *M.A., LL.D.,* was for many years our principal.

t. The comma is used to mark the omission of a verb.

A touchdown counts six points; a first down, nothing.

3. THE SEMICOLON (;)

a. The semicolon is used between the independent clauses of a compound sentence if the clauses are not joined by one of the simple coordinate conjunctions.

"Whither thou goest, I will go; where thou lodgest, I will lodge; thy people shall be my people, and thy God, my God."

"Ask, and it shall be given you; seek, and ye shall find; knock, and it shall be opened unto you."

He failed to pass the course; therefore it was necessary for him to repeat it the following year.

b. The semicolon is used between the independent clauses of a compound sentence that are joined by one of the simple coordinate conjunctions if the clauses are long or are themselves internally punctuated with commas.

The care of his own health and morals is the greatest trust which is committed to a young man; and often his degeneracy of character, his lack of self control, and his general loss of ability are due to his neglect of them.

c. The semicolon is sometimes used between the elements of a series for the sake of emphasis or because of internal punctuation of the members.

In time of war, a well-trained soldier will know how *to suffer silently; to shoot his weapon quickly and accurately;*

to hate and to kill his enemy.

These are the essentials of a successful passing attack: *a soft, easily caught pass; a crafty, nimble, loose-fingered receiver;* and *complete protection for the passer.*

d. In a quotation divided between independent clauses, use a semicolon after the introductory material if the clauses would ordinarily be separated by a semicolon.

"Train up a child in the way he should go," says the *Bible;* "when he is old, he will not depart from it.

4. THE COLON (:)

a. The colon is used to introduce a formal list at the end of a sentence, especially after such expressions as the *following, as follows,* etc.

There were three reasons for his success: *natural ability, industry,* and *perseverance.*

You should already have read the following books: *Treasure Island, Tom Sawyer,* and *Robinson Crusoe.*

b. The colon is used to introduce a formal appositive or other explanatory material at the end of a sentence.

He lacked only one thing: *good manners.*
(*Note*: The dash may be used in this construction.)

c. The colon is used between two independent clauses when the second explains the first.

The employees were exceptionally well treated: *for example, they had fifteen days' "sick leave," were allowed a month's vacation with pay, and were completely covered by insurance.*

d. The colon is used to introduce a long or a formal quotation.

Lincoln said at Gettysburg: "Four score and seven years ago . . . shall not perish from the earth."

Pope tells us: "To err is human; to forgive, divine."

e. The colon is used between the parts of titles, references, and certain numerals.

Ancient Times: *A History of the Early World.* (*Title*)
Luke 14: 23-25. (*Reference*)
It is now 6:30 P.M. (*Numerals*)

f. The colon is used after the salutation of a business letter.

Gentlemen: My dear Mr. Smith:

5. THE EXCLAMATION POINT (!)

The exclamation point is used after expressions that show strong feeling.

> Come, speak the truth!   A fine remark!
> "How are the mighty fallen!"
> "Dead for a ducat!   Dead!"

6. THE QUESTION MARK (?)

a. The question mark is used after every direct question.
> "Am I my brother's keeper?"
> What do you think of his intelligence? his character?

b. The question mark is used in parentheses to indicate that a statement is conjectural.
> Chaucer was born in 1344 (?) in London.

(*Note*: It should not be used to label humour or irony.)

> (*Poor*) After such a pleasant (?) afternoon, anyone would be tired.

7. THE DASH (—)

a. The dash is used when a sentence is broken off abruptly.
> When you have finished — by the way, when will you finish?

b. The dash is used to mark hesitation or uncertainty on the part of speaker.
> He is — er — I believe — what you might call an — er — idiot.

c. The dash is used before an expression which summarizes the preceding part of the sentence.
> "Whatsoever things are true, whatsoever things are honest, whatsoever things are just, whatsoever things are pure, whatsoever things are lovely, whatsoever things are of good report — think on these things."

d. The dash is used to set off a compound appositive or a long appositive within a sentence.
> The four Gospel writers — *Matthew, Mark, Luke, and John* — have had a greater reading public than Socrates, Plato, and Shakespeare combined.

The first applicant — *a foreign-looking person dressed in a Russian peasant's garb* — was dealt with most unceremoniously.

e. The dash is used to set off a long parenthetical expression that is somewhat remote from the main idea.

The condensed steam — all of you, I am sure, know why — will then flow back to the boiler.

f. The dash is sometimes used for emphasis.

He was weary — so weary that he could barely stand.

8. THE APOSTROPHE (')

a. The apostrophe is used to denote the possessive case of nouns and indefinite pronouns.

(*Note*: If a word does not end in *s*, add *'s;* if it does end in *s*, add only the apostrophe unless another syllable is formed when the word is made possessive.)

Not ending in s	Ending in s	Syllable added
a *lady's* hat	*ladies'* hats	a *princess's* crown
one *day's* journey	three *days'* journey	my *boss's* desk
men's furnishings	*Dickens'* novels	*James's* book
anyone's race	the *Davises'* house	*Davis's* room

b. The apostrophe is used to show joint and separate ownership. To show joint ownership, make the last element possessive; to show separate ownership, make all elements possessive.

(*Joint*) Jack and Harry's mother is here.

(*Separate*) Jack's and Harry's mothers are here.

c. The apostrophe is used to form the plural of letters and figures.

There are two *a's* in *separate*.

Dot your *i's* and cross your *t's*.

His 3's look exactly like 5's.

d. The apostrophe is used to mark the letters or figures omitted in a contraction.

don't; wouldn't; can't; let's; I'll; o'clock; the class of *'68*.

e. Avoid the use of contractions in formal writing unless quoting.

9. THE HYPHEN (-)

a. The hyphen is used between the elements of many compound words.

mother-in-law; eagle-eyed; self-righteous; forty-two.

b. The hyphen is used in dividing a word at the end of a line.

c. When dividing a word at the end of a line, always divide between syllables.

(*Incorrect*) gond-ola; illustr-ate; remain-ed.

(*Correct*) gon-dola; illus-trate; re-mained.

10. PARENTHESES ( ) AND BRACKETS [ ]

a. Parentheses are used to enclose words or groups of words that are inserted by way of comment, explanation, or tranlation.

He knows (*as does any man with battle experience*) the dangers of total war. (*Comment*)

The next year (*33 A. D.*) Jesus went up to Jerusalem for the Feast of the Passover. (*Explanation*)

"Verbum sapientibus satis" (*a word to the wise is sufficient*) has become something of a maxim at our school. (*Translation*)

b. Brackets are used to enclose explanatory material inserted in a direct quotation by an editor.

This writer avers, "He [Milton] w r o t e most of it [*Paradise Lost*] long before he became totally blind."

11. ELLIPSIS (. . .)

An ellipsis is used to mark the omission of words or groups of words, particularly in quotations.

"Our Father, who art in Heaven . . . give us this our daily bread."

12. QUOTATION MARKS (" ")

a. Quotation marks are used to enclose direct quotations.

The fool hath said in his heart, "There is no God."

Macbeth speaks of life as being "a tale told by an idiot."

b. A quotation within a quotation is placed in single quotation marks.

Costello testified as follows: "I heard Accardo say, 'My leg is broken in three places; "Greasy Thumb" Guzik stepped on it.'"

c. If a quotation consists of several paragraphs, place the quotation marks at the begining of each paragraph, but at the end of the last paragraph only.

d. In writing dialogue, make a separate paragraph for each change of speaker.

e. Always separate the words introducing the quotation from the quotation itself by suitable punctuation marks.

"I am very tired," *he said,* "of going to study hall every day."

Very deliberately the big lineman said, "I'll block that kick for the extra point"; then he picked up his helmet and ran out on the field.

f. Place the period and the comma inside the quotation marks; place the semicolon and the colon outside the quotation marks; place the question mark, the exclamation point, and the dash outside the quotation marks except when they are a part of the quotation.

Was it Jesus who said, "Remember now thy Creator in the days of thy youth"? (*Quotation is statement; introductory material is question.*)

The boy asked his teacher, "If the blind lead the blind, what happens to both?" (*Quotation is question.*)

Did Antony really ask Octavius and Lepidus, "When shall we three meet again?" (*Both are questions.*)

Were you one of the boys who shouted, "Down with the faculty!"? (*Quotation is exclamation; introductory material is question.*)

g. Use quotation marks to enclose slang, uncommon nicknames, or technical words used in general writing.

The pressure of examinations had driven *"Dopey"* completely *"off his nut."*

After four years here, a certain amount of *"endomorphism"* will have occurred even in the most *"refractory"* boy.

h. Quotation marks are used to enclose the names of houses and estates, and the titles of short poems, short stories, essays, articles, pictures, songs, and the subdivisions of books.

128

They live at "The Oaks." (*House*)

Poe's "The Pit and the Pendulum" (*Short Story*)

Bacon's "Of Studies" (*Essay*)

In the *Atlantic Monthly,* "What's Wrong with Our Schools?" (*Article*)

Gainsborough's "Blue Boy" (*Picture*)

Carmichael's "Stardust" (*Song*)

From *Adventures in American Literature,* "The Flowering of the East" (*Subdivision of book*)

THREE IMPORTANT RULES

1. Do not write a part of a sentence as though it were a complete sentence.

2. Do not use a comma between two sentences or between two independent clauses that are not joined by one of the simple coordinate conjunctions. Use a period if the clauses are not closely related in thought; use a semicolon if they are.

(*Incorrect*) "He maketh me lie down in green pastures, he leadeth me beside the still waters."

(*Correct*) "He maketh me to lie down in green pastures; he leadeth me beside the still waters."

(*Incorrect*) "Be not wise in your own conceits, recompense to no man evil for evil, provide things honest in the sight of all men."

(*Correct*) "Be not wise in your own conceits. Recompense to no man evil for evil. Provide things honest in the sight of all men."

3. Do not punctuate unecessarily.

16. ITALICS (_____)

To italicize a word in writing, draw a line under it.

a. Italicize the names of ships, aircraft, and trains, and the titles of books, plays, newspapers, magazines, and long musical compositions.

He was a passenger on the *Titanic.* (*Name of a ship*)

Silas Marner (*Book*)

Hamlet (*Play*)

The Kingston *News and Courier* (*Newspaper*)

The Atlantic Monthly (*Magazine*)

Beethoven's *Fifth Symphony* (*Long musical composition*)

b. Italicize unnaturalized foreign words and phrases. (A good dictionary will indicate which terms should be italicized.)

Many and varied have been his *res gestae*.

He completely lacked *savoir faire*.

c. Italicize letters, words, or figures when they are referred to as such.

There are too many *s's* in your spelling of *Mississippi*.

In that sentence, *hurricane* is the subject of the verb *devastated*.

d. Italicize words or phrases which are to be emphasized particularly.

For fools *rush* in where *angels* fear to *tread*.

This is most important: avoid the *overuse* of italics for emphasis.

CAPITALIZATION

1. Capitalize all proper nouns and proper adjectives.

2. Capitalize the first word of every sentence.

3. Capitalize the first word of every direct quotation *that is a sentence*.

4. Capitalize the first word of every line of poetry.

5. Capitalize the pronoun *I* and the interjection *O*.

6. Capitalize the first, the last, and every important word in a title.

A Tale of a Tub (*Title of book*)

"What Are You Laughing At?" (*Title of magazine article*)

The Society for the Prevention of Cruelty to Animals (*Organization*)

7. Capitalize all nouns and personal pronouns referring to the Deity.

Our *Father,* which are in heaven, hallowed be *Thy* name.

8. Capitalize things that are personified.

When *Freedom* cries out under the lashes of *Tyranny,* her friends rise to her aid.

9. Capitalize the first and last words of a salutation; the first only of a complimentary close in a letter.

> (*Salutation*) My dear Sir: My darling Betty,
>
> (*Complimentary close*) Yours very truly, Sincerely yours,

10. Do not capitalize unnecessarily.

UNITY, COHERENCE, AND EMPHASIS

For any composition to be an effective expression of thought, it must be composed in accordance with the principles of unity, coherence, and emphasis. Unity controls the selection of material, coherence governs its arrangement, and emphasis directs the placing of parts for proper stress.

RULES OF UNITY

The principle of unity requires that only those ideas which are related in thought shall be included in the same sentence, paragraph, or composition.

1. A sentence should contain one thought and one thought only.

2. Closely related ideas should not be divided between two sentences; they should be included in the same sentence.

3. Each statement in a paragraph should bear on the general topic of the paragraph.

4. Ideas which are closely related to the same topic should be included in the same paragraph.

5. A paragraph should usually contain a topic sentence.

6. The whole composition should contain nothing that does not help develop the general subject of the composition.

RULES OF COHERENCE

The principle of coherence requires that words, phrases, clauses, sentences, and paragraphs shall be so arranged that the relation between the ideas is immediately evident.

1. Arrange the words in a sentence in their natural and logical order.

2. Arrange the sentence and ideas in a paragraph in their natural and logical order.

3. Arrange the paragraphs in a composition in their natural and logical order.

4. Keep modifiers as close as possible to the words which they modify.

5. Avoid placing any word between the infinitive and its sign.

> (*Poor*) It will be possible *to easily remedy* the trouble.
> (*Better*) It will be possible *to remedy* the trouble *easily*.

6. Avoid separating the subject and the verb, or the verb and its complement by the insertion of a verbal phrase, an adverbial clause, or some other subordinate sentence element.

> (*Poor*) Lincoln, while attending a play at Ford's Theatre in Washington, was shot by an assassin.
> (*Better*) While attending a play at Ford's Theatre in Washington, Lincoln was shot by an assassin.

7. Avoid separating the parts of a comparison.

> (*Poor*) Vancouver is as large as, if not larger than, Hamilton.
> (*Better*) Vancouver is as large as Hamilton, if not larger.

8. Sentence elements which are parallel in thought must be parallel in structure.

> (*Poor*) He was *skinny* and *of great stature*.
> (*Better*) He was *skinny* and quite *tall*.

9. Sentence elements which are parallel in structure must be parallel in thought.

> (*Poor*) The press release told of the *valour* and the *promotion* of the sergeant to the rank of lieutenant.
> (*Better*) The press release told of the valour of the sergeant and of his subsequent promotion to the rank of lieutenant.

10. A verb must agree with its subject in person and number.

11. Every pronoun must have a definite antecedent which is immediately clear to the reader. (*Note*: In formal writing, avoid the use of *you* indefinitely.)

12. A pronoun must agree with its antecedent in person, number, and gender.

13. Make the thought flow logically from sentence to sentence.

> (*Poor logic*) Extremely fatiguing activities are not good for growing boys. Joe is a growing boy, and therefore football is not good for him.

14. Avoid the *non-sequitur* (a conclusion based on false premises).

> Extremely fatiguing activities are not good for growing boys.
> Football is extremely fatiguing to them. (*False premise*)
> Therefore it is not good for them. (*Non-sequitur*)

15. Avoid illogical statements.

> (*Poor*) Cheating is where you copy somebody's work.
> (*Better*) Cheating is the copying of someone else's work.

16. Avoid the use of incomplete, ambiguous, and illogical comparisons.

> (*Incomplete*) He is taller and just as strong as you.
> (*Improved*) He is taller than you, and just as strong.
> (*Ambiguous*) Joe kicked me harder than John.
> (*Improved*) Joe kicked me harder than John *did*. (*Or* than he kicked John.)
> (*Illogical*) The raven's plummage is blacker than any other bird.
> (*Improved*) The raven's plummage is blacker than *that of* any other bird.

17. Do not omit words essential to the thought or the structure of a sentence. (*Note*: Many students erroneously omit relative pronouns and the subordinate conjunction *that*).

> The cashier and (*the*) janitor were the last to leave.
> He searched for his book in the library and (*on*) the football field.
> I knew (*that*) the woman (*whom*) he was talking about was once an Olympic diving champion.

18. Do not omit ideas essential to the thought of a paragraph or of a whole composition.

19. Avoid the use of dangling verbals and eliptical clauses.

> (*Dangling verbal*) Having eaten our lunch, the excursion boat took us home.
> (*Improved*) After we had eaten our lunch, the excursion boat took us home. *OR* Having eaten our lunch, we went home on the excursion boat.
> (*Dangling elliptical clause*) When repaired, the mechanic will bring the car to your house.
> (*Improved*) When the car has been repaired, the mechanic will bring it to your house.

20. Keep the same point of view in a composition.

21. Do not unreasonably shift voice, tense, or mood.

(*Shift of voice*) We *drove* all night, and by morning our destination *was reached*.

(*Improved*) We *drove* all night and by morning *had reached* our destination.

(*Shift of tense*) The crowd *waited* tensely. The runners *were poised* in their starting blocks. The gun *shoots*. Jimmy *leaps* out in front and *is* never headed. It *was* a thrilling race.

(*Shift of mood*) Hold (*imperative*) the rifle firmly with one hand around the small of the stock and the other at the balance point. Then the butt is placed (*indicative*) snugly against the shoulder.

22. Do not unreasonably shift subjects.

(*Poor*) The fog lifted, and our objective came into view.

(*Better*) The fog lifted and revealed our objective.

23. Avoid the weak passive.

(*Poor*) The patient *was examined* by the doctor, and his temperature *taken*.

(*Better*) The doctor examined the patient and took his temperature.

24. Every non-parenthetical element in a sentence must have a definite grammatical construction.

(*Poor*) Kathy said that while she was talking on the telephone *that* the cake burned to a crisp.

25. Use transitional devices between clauses, sentences, and paragraphs to help make clear the relation in thought (*moreover, accordingly, in spite of this fact, on the other hand,* etc.)

26. Avoid loose thinking and general obscurity. (The violation of this rule is considered *one of the worst errors* that a writer can make.)

27. Avoid general awkwardness in sentence structure.

RULES OF EMPHASIS

The principle of emphasis requires that important words and groups of words be placed at the conspicuous points in sentences, paragraphs, and compositions. The most conspicuous, and hence the most emphatic position, is the end; and the next most conspicuous position is the beginning. Emphasis is also achieved by the proper subordination of less important ideas and elements, by the use of climax, by variations in sentence structure, and by the use of concise, specific expression.

1. Subordinate the less important ideas in a sentence.

> (*Poor*) I was crossing the street, and an automobile ran over me.
>
> (*Better*) As I was crossing the street, an automobile ran over me.

2. Avoid "upside-down" subordination.

> (*Poor*) I was crossing the street when an automobile ran over me.

3. Ideas in a sentence that are of equal importance should be made coordinate in structure.

> (*Poor*) He shot into the covey of quail, killing three.
>
> (*Better*) He shot into the covey of quail and killed three.

4. Avoid placing unimportant words or phrases at the beginning or at the end of a sentence. (Especially try to "bury" within the sentence transitional devices and parenthetical expressions as *furthermore, on the other hand, I feel sure,* etc.)

5. Avoid placing unimportant sentences at the beginning or at the end of a paragraph.

6. Avoid placing unimportant paragraphs at the beginning or at the end of a composition.

7. Arrange coordinate words and groups of words in climactic order.

> (*Poor*) He blocks ferociously, tackles hard, and runs reasonably well.
>
> (*Better*) He runs reasonably well, tackles hard, and blocks ferociously.

8. Avoid the use of short, choppy sentences except for effect.

9. Avoid the use of a series of sentences that are monotonously similar in form. Vary your sentence structure.

10. Avoid verbosity and circumlocution (excessive wordiness).

11. Avoid tautology (useless repetition of the same idea).

> Death in any *shape, form,* or *guise,* is *universally* feared *by all people.*
>
> Milton wrote a *blank verse autobiography of his life in iambic pentameter.*
>
> He kept his dogs in an area *completely enclosed* by a fence *on all sides.*

12. Use an effective title.

13. Begin your composition by coming immediately to the point in an interest-catching manner.

14. Develop each topic sufficiently for the reader to get a clear understanding of it.

15. End your composition strongly in such a way that the reader gets an idea of completeness.

16. Be sure of the accuracy of your facts, for inaccuracy will detract from the effect of your composition.

17. Avoid exaggeration, innuendo, and bombast.

18. Be specific, not general, in your expression.

GRAMMAR

1. The indicative mood is used to state a fact or to ask a direct question.

2. The imperative mood is used to express a command or a request.

3. The subjunctive mood is used to express a wish, a prayer, a condition or supposition which is contrary to fact, or an uncertainty. It is also used after verbs of commanding or requesting and after such expressions as *as if, as though, it is wise, it is necessary,* etc.

4. To express simple futurity, use *shall* in the first person and *will* in the second and third persons.

5. To express determination, willingness, or promise, use *will* in the first person and *shall* in the second and third persons.

6. In questions use the form expected in the answer.

7. The present tense is used to indicate present time, present intent of future action, habitual action, or a universal truth.

8. The past tense is used to indicate action completed in the past.

9. The future tense is used to indicate future action.

10. The present perfect tense is used to indicate action that began in the past, but either extends into the present or is connected with it.

11. The past perfect tense is used to indicate action completed in the past before a definite past time.

12. The future perfect tense is used to indicate action that will be completed before a definite future time.

13. The relationship between the times of the actions in the independent and the dependent clauses must be made clear by the use of the proper tenses.

14. Use a present verbal to indicate action at the same time as or after that of the main verb.

15. Use a past or perfect verbal to indicate action before the time of the main verb.

16. Use an adjective to modify a substantive.

17. Use an adverb to modify a verb, an adjective, or another adverb.

18. A demonstrative adjective must agree in number with the word which it modifies.

19. Adjectives and adverbs are regularly compared by adding *er* and *est* to the positive to form the comparative and the superlative degrees respectively, or by using *more* (*less*) and *most* (*least*) before the positive to form the comparative and the superlative respectively. (Avoid the double comparative or superlative.)

20. The comparative degree is used in comparing two; the superlative, in comparing more than two.

21. A substantive gets its case from its use in the sentence.

> Just between you and *me, I* think that it was *he who* told of *your* having broken the window on *Mr. Gilliam's* car.

22. A substantive preceding a gerund should be in the possessive case.

> *Your* delaying (*gerund*) the race and *his* refusing (*gerund*) to run have caused the *spectators* watching (*participle*) the meet to lose interest.

23. Use *who* to refer to persons, *which* to places or things, and *that* to persons, places, or things. (The use of *that* in referring to persons is considered inelegant by some authorities.)

> the *man who*   the *cave which*   the *answer that*

24. The compound personal pronouns may be used reflexively or intensively only.

> (*Reflexively*) The teacher hit *himself* on top of the head.
> (*Intensively*) The teacher *himself* did not know the answer.

25. Use the correct principal part.

26. Use the correct part of speech.

DICTION

1. Avoid the use of superfluous words.

   continue *on;* rise *up;* meet *up with;* etc.

2. Avoid the use of provincialisms (words peculiar to a section of the country).

   tote for *carry; poke* for *paper bag; piece* for *distance;* etc.

3. Avoid the use of colloquialisms in formal writing (words used in ordinary conversation).

   don't for *do not; exam* for *examination; fix* for *repair;* etc.

4. Avoid the use of barbarisms (words coined without authority from standard words).

   to enthuse; to suspicion; an invite; irregardless; undoubtedly.

5. Avoid the use of slang (inelegant popular language).

6. Avoid the use of trite expressions (overused expressions).

beat a hasty retreat	*dull, sickening thud*
tired but happy	*a bounteous repast*
the irony of fate	*sadder, but wiser*
a few well-chosen words	*last, but not least*

7. Avoid the use of artificial, archaic, obsolete, and poetic language in ordinary writing.

   (Artificial) *peruse* for *read; domicile* for *home; pugilistic encounter in the squared circle* for *boxing match.*

   (Archaic) *quoth* for *said; methinks* for *it seems to me.*

   (Obsolete) *bifel* for *it happened; eek* for *also.*

   (Poetic) *o'er* for *over; acold* for *cold; whilst* for *while.*

8. Avoid the monotonous repetition of the same word or phrase.

9. Use a more vivid word or expression.

   say — reply, retort, state, declare, assert, mumble, murmur, grumble, mutter, etc.

   a *good* meal — tasty, filling, savory, delicious, etc.

   a *good* book — entertaining, well-written, thought-provoking, inspiring, etc.

10. Use idiomatic language (correct expressions that are peculiar to our language).

> *agree to* (a proposal); *agree with* (a person)
> *wait on* (a customer); *wait for* (a friend)
> *off* the grass, not off *of* the grass
> *angry with* a person, not angry *at* him

11. Always use the exact word to express your meaning.

> From his remarks I *implied* (inferred) that he was unhappy.
> She walked down the *isle* (aisle) with her father.
> What will be the *affect* (effect) of the court's decision?
> He was quite *feminine* (effeminate) in his manner.

12. Avoid the use of abbreviations in formal writing.

13. Write out small numbers and numbers used as the first word in a sentence; use figures for large numbers, dates, street numbers, numbered objects and the like.

SPELLING

1. Check your spelling of a word against its pronunciation.

2. If a word accented on the final syllable ends in a single consonant preceded by a single vowel, double the final consonant before adding a suffix beginning with a vowel.

> tap — tap *p* ed, tap *p* ing   re fer' — re fer' *r* ed
> run — run *n* ing, run *n* er   im pel' — im pel' *l* ing

(*Note* 1: If the accent shifts, do not double.)

> re fer' — ref' er ence   le' gal — le gal' ity
> de fer' — def' er ence   e' qual — e qual' ity

(*Note* 2: There are a few exceptions to the rule: *chagrined, crystallize, gaseous, gasify, handicapped, handicapping,* and words ending in *w,* which is not considered a consonant at the end of a word.)

> saw — sawing, sawed   snow — snowing, snowed

3. *IE* and *EI.*

> The long-standing rule has been
> > "Use *I* before *E*
> > Except after *C*
> > Or when sounded like *A,*
> > As in *neighbour* and *weigh.*"

Following is an amplification of this rule, with certain exceptions given:

A. When the syllable has the sound of *ee* as in *seed* or *beer*, use *I* before *E* except after *C*.

I before E	*E before I after C*	*Exceptions*
ach*ie*ve	c*ei*ling	*ei*ther
bel*ie*ve	dec*ei*t	n*ei*ther
f*ie*ld	perc*ei*ve	l*ei*sure
f*ie*rce	rec*ei*pt	s*ei*ze
p*ie*r	rec*ei*ve	w*ei*rd

(*Note*: Always after *sc* and when *c* is pronounced like *sh*, use *I* before *E*: *conscience, species, proficient, sufficient.*)

B. When the syllable has the sound of *A* as in *neighbour* and *weigh, use E* before *I*.

d*ei*gn	h*ei*nous	fr*ei*ght
r*ei*gn	r*ei*n	v*ei*n

C. Some words do not by their pronunciation fit any rule and must be learned.

for*ei*gn	h*ei*ght	h*ei*r	st*ei*n
sover*ei*gn	misch*ie*f	th*ei*r	s*ie*ve
v*ie*w	handkerch*ie*f	fr*ie*nd	sl*ei*ght

4. If a word ends in *Y* preceded by a consonant, change the *Y* to *I* when adding a suffix except *ing* and *ish*.

easy — eas*i* er, eas *i* ly	*Exceptions*
happy — happ *i* er, happ *i* ness	pity — pit *e* ous
hurry — hurr *i* ed *BUT* hurr *y* ing	plenty — plent *e* ous
baby — bab *i* ed *BUT* bab *y* ish	

(*Note* 1: Monosyllables ending in *Y* preceded by a consonant usually retain the *y* before *ly, ness,* and *ward.*)

shy——sh *y* ly, sh *y* ness   sky — sk *y* ward

(*Note* 2: The *y* is usually dropped when *ist* is added to form a noun.)

biology — biolog*i*st; pharmacy — pharmac*i*st; optometry — optometr*i*st

5. If a word ends in *Y* preceded by a vowel, retain the *Y* when adding a suffix.

employ — emplo *y* ed, emplo *y* ment   day — da *i* ly   say — sa *i* d
decay — deca *y* ed, deca *y* ing   lay — la *i* d   slay — sla *i* n
essay — essa *y* ed, essa *y* ist   pay — pa *i* d

6. Final *IE* is changed to *Y* when *ing* is added.

lie — l *y* ing   die — d *y* ing   tie — t *y* ing

7. All words ending with the sound of *seed* are spelled *cede* except *exceed, proceed, succeed,* and *supersede.*

prece*de*   inter*cede*   ac*cede*   re*cede*

8. A word ending in silent *E* usually retains the *E* before a suffix beginning with a consonant.

care — care *e* ful   excite — excit *e* ment   sedate — sedat *e* ly

(*Exceptions*: acknowledgment, argument, judgment, ninth, truly, wholly.)

9. A word ending in silent *E* usually drops the *E* before a suffix beginning with a vowel.

care — caring   excite — excit ed   use — us able

(*Exception 1:* The silent *E* is retained when it is preceded by SOFT *C* or *G* and the suffix begins with *A* or *O,* in order to keep the *c* and *g* soft.)

notice — notic *e* able   courage — courag *e* ous
change — chang *e* able   advantage — advantag *e* ous

(*Exception 2:* The silent *E* is retained if confusion with another word would result.)

singe — sing *e* ing   dye — dy *e* ing

(*Exception 3:* When silent *E* is preceded by *O,* it is retained before *ing.*)

hoe — ho *e* ing   shoe — sho *e* ing   toe — to *e* ing

10. Words ending in *AC* or *IC* add *K* before *ed, ing, and y.*

shellac — shellac *k* ed   panic — panic *k* y
mimic — mimic *k* ing   picnic — picnic *k* ing

11. Most nouns form their plurals and most verbs form the third person, singular number, present tense, indicative mood, by simply adding *S.*

pipe — pipes	like — likes
angel — angels	kick — kicks
Smith — Smiths	tolerate — tolerates

12. When the plural of a noun or the third person singular of a verb contains one more syllable than the base word, its ending is *ES*.

dish — dishes	hitch — hitches
ditch — ditches	fish — fishes
box — boxes	buzz — buzzes
Jones — Joneses	hiss — hisses

13. Nouns and verbs ending in *Y* preceded by a consonant form their plurals and third person, singular number, present indicative, respectively, by changing to *Y* to *I* and adding *ES*. Verbs ending in *Y* preceded by a consonant form their past tense and past participle by changing the *Y* to *I* and adding *ED*.

| fly —fl *i* es | try — tr *i* es, tr *i* ed |
| ally — all *i* es | deny — den *i* es, den *i* ed |

14. Words ending in *O* preceded by a vowel form their plurals by adding *S*.

portfolio — portfolios   rodeo — rodeos   embryo — embryos

15. Musical terms ending in *O* preceded by a consonant form their plurals by adding *S*.

piano — pianos alto — altos solo — solos piccolo — piccolos

(*Note:* If you are in doubt about the plurals of other words ending in *o* preceded by a consonant, consult a dictionary.)

16. *The* plural of a compound noun is usually formed by making the major word plural.

        mother-in-law — mothers-in-law
        man-at-arms —men-at-arms
        man-eater — man-eaters

17. Prefixes except *TRANS* do not cause the dropping of a letter in either the prefix or the root.

dis satisfied	*BUT*
un necessary	tran shipment
mis spent	tran sept
with hold	tran substantiate
inter ruption	

18. *FUL* not *full,* is added to a noun to form a noun or an adjective.

    cup *ful*   spoon *ful*   right *ful*   youth *ful*   will *ful*

19. Words ending in *N* retain the *n* when the suffix *NESS* is added.

    green ness   sudden ness   drunken ness   open ness

20. Words ending in a single *L* retain the *l* when the suffix *LY* is added.

	BUT
final ly	dull — dul ly
cool ly	full — ful ly

EXERCISES ON COMPOSITION RULES

These exercises are designed to give you practice in the rules of composition that are most often violated.

For the Key to the Exercises see pages 186 to 225.

PUNCTUATION

Write the rule(s) involved; then copy the sentences in the exercise and punctuate them properly. *Do not change capitalization.*

Exercise 1

1. "A horse A horse my kingdom for a horse"
2. "Yond Cassius has a lean and hungry look"
3. "How forcible are right words"
4. "A wise son maketh a glad father"
5. What finally happened to Casca To Brutus To Cassius
6. Oh Oh Please Don't Why do you treat me this way
7. "It is better to dwell in a corner of the housetop than with a brawling woman in a wide house"

Exercise 2

1. Among those present were Capt and Mrs Philip Duckett, the Rev and Mrs James B Massey, Dr Trelawney, and Messrs G B Smith, H O Hunniwell, George B Hamilton, and James DeW Lang.

2. On Dec 7, 1941, at 6:00 A M Japanese airplanes under Lt Gen Hamakodo attacked the US Air Base on Luzon, PI.

3. Prof Grey received his AB degree from VPL, his MA from McGill U, a PhD from McMaster, and an LLD from the University of Montreal.

Exercise 3

1. "The wolf shall also dwell with the lamb and the leopard shall lie down with the kid."
2. "Many are called but few are chosen."
3. A decision will have to come from you or we shall be unable to act.
4. There is little to be gained by waiting for every day the enemy becomes stronger.
5. He did not have any idea of retiring nor could we persuade him even to take a vacation.
6. Some teachers can really help a dullard but bright students often seem to learn little from them.
7. The atomic fission weapons have created nervous tension throughout the world for no nation feels secure against the destruction which they can create.
8. Either he is a genius in revolutionary methods of warfare or the fates are protecting him for he has defied every rule in the tactics book.
9. Because of your slight effort in your studies you will undoubtedly fail and your classmates will go to college without you.
10. We cannot understand what electricity is nor does our teacher seem to know.

Exercise 4

1. "And now abideth faith hope charity."
2. "The winter is past the rain is over and gone the flowers appear on the earth the time of the singing of birds is come and the voice of the turtle is heard in our land."
3. His stupid bungling methods have created a disorganized unproductive state of affairs.
4. His shabby dirty old-fashioned clothes hung loosely from his twisted emaciated body.
5. Joe Harry and George have finally managed to pass Algebra II.

6. He was a leader in the classroom in the dormitory and on the athletic field.

7. Terrified lions elephants zebras and horses stampeded through the screaming milling crowd as the roaring crackling flames from the circus tent shot skyward.

Exercise 5

1. "If the blind lead the blind both shall fall into the ditch."
2. Although life seems complex while we are in school it becomes even more so in later life.
3. If God be for us who can be against us?
4. Whenever he felt like taking exercise he lay down until the feeling had passed.
5. In order to stay alive one must eat.
6. By slaying all the starlings they upset the balance of nature.
7. With the best method of producing the hydrogen bomb in their possession the Russians felt secure at the conference table.
8. Having travelled all night he was completely exhausted.
9. For informing on the tax-dodgers he was given a generous reward.
10. If you will always place a comma after an *if-clause* you will hardly ever be wrong.

Exercise 6

1. Any boy who uses his time judiciously will undoubtedly pass his work.
2. That tall man whose picture you have probably seen many times was once the Secretary of the Navy.
3. Jack Jones who uses his time judiciously is always on the Honour Roll.
4. The officer wearing the black beret is Field Marshal Montgomery.
5. Field Marshal Montgomery wearing a black beret reviewed the NATO troops.
6. The crowd was astounded by his feats of magic although he was somewhat out of practice.
7. He has always been near the top of his class as he has never shirked his academic duties.
8. We know a man who can always be trusted: Billy Smith.

9. Billy Smith who can always be trusted will be happy to invest your money for you.

10. Admiral King dressed in a white uniform watched the sailors marching past the reviewing stand.

11. The author of that maxim was Benjamin Franklin who was America's first ambassador to France.

12. Can anyone remember the name of the man who was our first ambassador to England?

13. One of the boys on the back row who was not paying attention at the time was asked the first question in the review of the lesson.

14. One of the boys on the back row who had their feet on the desks in front of them was singled out and scolded by the teacher as an example to the others.

15. Harry took a strange flower which he had found growing in his yard to the biology teacher who was able to identify it.

Exercise 7

1. There is moreover no doubt in my mind as to the letter's authenticity.

2. They will arrive I am certain before the time set for the ceremony.

3. Don't you agree in spite of your personal feelings in the matter that we should discharge the man?

4. What and please speak frankly do you think is the real reason for his defection?

5. This is I would say rather unusual; but I believe to tell the truth that it is not illegal.

Exercise 8

1. He needs a mother not a wife.

2. He served the tennis ball rather casually but drove hard to the baseline his opponent's return.

3. He actually is quite intelligent yet almost totally illiterate.

4. I requested that you come to my office not to reward you but to punish you.

5. He had always wanted a "Thunderbird" but had never been able to afford one.

Exercise 9

1. The infantry division my friends will soon be a thing of the past.
2. Messrs. Canby and Destry are you ready to begin the contest?
3. "Why don't you speak for yourself John?"
4. There is no reason mother why you should want the car today.

Exercise 10

1. My first cousin Sam Jones has been reading the collected works of the excellent modern poet W. H. Auden.
2. My counsin Sam is completely mystified by the writings of the poet Auden.
3. The fact that your mistake caused the team to lose makes no difference to your schoolmates.
4. This fact that you are not a bona fide student precludes your being allowed to play in the game.
5. He dropped the soup tureen into the teacher's lap an action that caused laughter throughout the dining room.
6. Our most genial teacher Bob Whittle once studied under the great Shakespearean teacher George Lyman Kittredge.
7. Charlie Stone president of General Motors was once an assembly-line employee of that company the largest corporation in the world.
8. His brother George once memorized the poem "Thanatopsis" in its entirety.
9. You boys should show respect to your minister a man who has devoted his life to the service of others.
10. An honest man a rarity in nature is, according to Pope, "the noblest work of God."

Exercise 11

1. On Friday June 9 1967 the final exercises were held for the graduating class.
2. Very shortly there will be a new occupant of the Prime Minister's Residence 10 Downing Street London W.1.
3. The Adjutant General gave his address as R.F.D. #1 London Ontario as of March 3 1968.
4. In August of next year Niagara, Ontario will hold an azalea festival.

Exercise 12

1. That he will be here tomorrow I am absolutely sure.
2. A true aristocrat even though he may lose his wealth will retain his dignity.
3. An army may with only slight losses to itself win a great victory.
4. Of my country's needs at this critical moment in her history I am fully aware.

Exercise 13

1. The operating room having been readied by the nurse in charge the surgeon had no technical difficulties in performing the appendectomy.
2. The old lady being about to die her family gathered around her bed.
3. The loss of the lieutenant caused only a momentary problem the leadership of the platoon being taken over almost immediately by an experienced sergeant.
4. The walls having been breached to allow the passage of the "Horse" the Greeks had no trouble in entering Troy.

Exercise 14

1. No I have not heard the score.
2. It was four to three wasn't it?
3. Indeed you should know better than that.
4. Very well we will accept your offer.
5. Yes he was one of them.
6. You don't really mean that do you?

Exercise 15

1. Ever since he has been known as the man who won the war.
2. Because of that disloyalty is now quite common in their ranks.
3. Whatever is is right.
4. When are we going to eat mother?
5. To John Smith gave his full report.
6. That that is is.
7. He faced the robber holding the pistol firmly.
8. Inside the fire blazed cheerfully.

Exercise 16

1. Beef eggs milk etc. must be kept on ice; otherwise they may spoil.
2. Your homework your weekly compositions etc. must be turned in on time.
3. He gave us the usual lecture the usual demerits the usual looks etc. before he dismissed us.

Exercise 17

1 The old man slowly replied "I have lived a full life and am now ready to die."
2. "The first rule of conduct in the OSS" he asserted "is one which most people ignore: never tell a secret."
3. "What" he asked timidly "do you want me to do?"
4. "We shall see you in the morning" they called as they drove away.
5. Did he say "It's incomprehensible"?

Exercise 18

1. Randolph G.A. and Pinckney C.C. were invited to a supper dance at National Cathedral School.
2. The Reverend James Wadsworth A.B. M.A. B.D. D.D. preached the baccalaureate sermon.
3. "The letter was signed by James F. Wright D.S.C. O.B.E. Member of Parliament Keeper of the King's Seal" the secretary told him.

Exercise 19

1. To err is human; to forgive divine.
2. Washington was a hero; Benedict Arnold a traitor to his country.
3. One brother is a mining engineer; the other a Texas ranch-owner.

Exercise 20

1. "Favour is deceitful beauty is vain."
2. "Your old men shall dream dreams your young men shall see visions."
3. "Ask, and it shall be given you seek, and ye shall find knock, and it shall be opened unto you."

4. Men make houses women make homes.
5. He gained the admiration of the world yet lost his self-respect.
6. His morning paper had not been delivered for two days therefore he called the circulation manager to determine the reason.
7. Some of the smallest trees were cut in two by the tornado on the other hand, not one of the giant oaks was badly damaged.
8. Chinese Gordon assumed greater powers than he had been granted as a result, Gladstone withdrew his support of the venture.
9. Antony wept tears of sorrow over the fallen Caesar moreover, he pledged vengeance on the assassins of his friend.
10. The conditions were quite unfavourable for a landing nevertheless, the pilot notified all aboard that he was "going to take her in."

Exercise 21

1. You have brought us famine, disease, and death but this day will, I have no doubt, see your destruction as a political force.
2. There has never, to my knowledge, been such a series of terrible thunderstorms as we have experienced the past two weeks and I am positive that never again will you have your fishing and swimming so interfered with and your vacation practically ruined by the weather.
3. In the meantime you must take every precaution not to re-injure the damaged tissue, which will heal rather slowly and you must follow to the letter the instructions which I have given you for the proper care of the burned places.
4. A good short story involves much more than just time, place, action, and people for unless plot, characterization, and theme are closely interwoven the story becomes a mere narration of events.

Exercise 22

1. He asked that the following boys meet him in his classroom: Ainslie, L.S. Maker, R.E. Calhoun, L.M. and Dandridge, G.C.
2. A quiet, secluded spot in the country a grassy, ant-free plot of ground a tall shade tree a cool, gentle breeze and a laughing, singing brook — these are the first requisites for a successful picnic.

3. Mr. Carraway, the chairman of the Senate Finance Committee Mr. Lankford, the ranking Liberal and Mr. Kennedy, the chief counsel, were the only ones present as the hearings opened.

Exercise 23

1. "Nothing matters now," said the old man sadly "no one cares whether I live or die."
2. "Life can be beautiful," the radio announcer droned "it can also be ugly without Ajax, the foaming cleanser."
3. "When we give the Senator's remarks only cursory attention, we find them very plausible," he thundered at his colleagues "but when we examine them closely, we recognize the superfluity of meaningless words and the paucity of facts!"

Exercise 24

1. There are several boys in school with French names Boileau, Racine, and Montroix.
2. These are the boys who did it Joe, Harry, and George.
3. The boys who did it are Joe, Harry, and George.
4. He rejected my plan for the following reasons it was too costly, it required more manpower than was available, and it had other earmarks of government bureaucracy.
5. Remember to take with you these essentials a comb, a toothbrush, a clean shirt, and a pair of pyjamas.

Exercise 25

1. You have only one chance of getting into college sneaking in.
2. Brutus thought that there was only one solution to kill Caesar.
3. He used only one word to apply to most of his students *stupid*.
4. This is something that you must not forget never desert a friend in need.
5. To Lee there was one sublime word in the English language *duty*.
6. Criminals incarcerated there are extremely fortunate for example they are permitted visitors daily and are allowed to participate in athletics every afternoon.

Exercise 26

1. One of the most touching statements in the *Bible* is the one made by the father of a demented boy "Lord, I believe; help thou mine unbelief."

2. He quoted from "The Declaration of Independence" "When, in the course of human events, it becomes necessary . . . declare the causes which impel them to separation."

3. Emerson is reported to have said "The world will beat a path to the door of the man who invents a better mousetrap."

Exercise 27

1. He has recently written a splendid monograph: "Three Southern Poets A Critical Analysis."

2. "The Parable of the Good Samaritan" can be found in Luke 10 33-35.

3. At 11 28 last night fires broke out simultaneously in four sections of the city.

4. One of the best American biographies — *Israfel The Life and Times of Edgar Allan Poe* — was written by Hervey Allen, a teacher of English in a secondary school.

5. Your first bibliographical entry — "Hellenism," *The Encyclopaedia Britannica,* 14th Edition, XI 385-387 — gives the wrong page reference.

Exercise 28

1. "I I just don't know er whether" he began. "No, I just er can't say."

2. He is rowdy, slovenly, boorish but why say any more about him?

3. "Do you you th think that that he will act without th th thinking?" I asked.

4. He was going to read us just what was it that he was going to read us?

Exercise 29

1. When he studies every day, when he turns in his work on time, when he pays strict attention in class when he does all these consistently, he manages to pass.

2. Joe, Henry, and George these were the boys who did it.

3. Intelligence, initiative, industry, integrity he is seeking these qualities in those whom he employs.

4. In the morning, in the afternoon, at night at any time of the day he may be found working on his silly invention.

Exercise 30

1. These boys Joe, Harry, and George are the ones who did it.
2. The captain of the team sweaty, dirty, and exhausted sat on the edge of the bench and stared at the ground.
3. The following students Ramsay Pickens, Hoxton, and McDonald are asked to remain after class.
4. This one quality of the good officer concern for those placed under him in his command was especially stressed by the general in his talk.
5. The next approach one that may not meet with the approval of all of you is to write a letter to your representative and request that they use their influence to force a decision.

Exercise 31

1. These men and I speak for all of them refuse to obey such a ridiculous order, Captain Queeg.
2. That particular statement I know that all of you will agree with me is clearly a falsehood.
3. These huskies that is, most of them have been trained to the sled.
4. Gentlemen of the jury, the defendant and this must be obvious to all of you could not possibly have committed the crime of which he is accused.

Exercise 32

1. He was a muscular and handsome but cowardly leader.
2. She had tried tried so hard to make a home for him but she had failed.
3. I told you to come tomorrow not today.
4. Fourteen survivors only fourteen out of ninety-seven passengers and crew members were brought ashore by the Coast Guard.
5. "Gentlemen may cry, Peace, Peace but there is no peace."

Exercise 33

Copy the following phrases, punctuating properly and adding *s's* as needed.

a mans world	everyones duty	a years salary
a nickels worth	the monkeys paw	the Negroes way

Joe Smiths car	girls handkerchiefs	ladies dresses
angels voices	nobodys business	two months salary
three cents worth	monkeys tails	Jim Harris house
the Smiths car	the Harrises house	foxes habits
a fox lair	*Loves Labour's Lost*	Brooks essays
that book of yours	mens furnishings	Rogers and Harts play
the lass tears	the poetess sonnet	Brooks and Warrens book
a girls handkerchief	its limbs	

Exercise 34

1. Notice that *Mississippi* is spelled with four *ss,* four *is,* and two *ps.*
2. He really doesn't know where to put the apostrophe in *dont.*
3. Youve used five *sos* and four *a lot ofs* in that one sentence.
4. When thats done, hell loaf until 5 oclock.
5. The class of 43 will celebrate its twenty-fifth reunion in 68.

Exercise 35

1. In nineteen forty eight John L. Lewis, the cigar smoking exleader of the mineworkers, called a high government official "a whiskey drinking, poker playing evil old man."
2. When Eisenhower, America's greatest soldier statesman, thought that the buildup for the Normandy breakout was almost complete, he reformed his Anglo American troops into three armies: one led by bald headed General Montgomery, one by an exclassmate at West Point, and the third by the pistol carrying Patton.
3. If we are to deemphasize athletics without a flareup in the coaching ranks, we must convince the coaches that a "point getter" in the classroom is no more to be despised than one on the football field.
4. Because of his antiadministration attitude, the hot tempered old pro-Stalinite was leading a hand to mouth existence with his thirty eight fellow conspirators, who had formed what they called a government in exile.
5. A well known Irish American labour leader has been indicted for hit and run driving by the once weak kneed grand jury.

Exercise 36

Divide the following words into syllables, using hyphens between syllables. If you are uncertain about any one of them, consult the dictionary.

lemonade	instability	righteous
college	refer	collar
infinitesimal	reference	stroller
necessity	enigma	builder
mischievous	enigmatic	bolder
caller	lender	easier
callous	tenderest	platter
derringer	leopard	bony
erring	planter	bonny
luscious	plantation	dinghy

Exercise 37

1. It is important to remember that *de gustibus non disputandum est* there can be no argument about tastes.
2. When the piston reaches top-dead-centre "T.D.C.", over half the gases in the cylinder have already burned.
3. The most important rule forgive me for mentioning it again is that good citizenship is dependent upon a respect for the rights of others.
4. A great many workers in the plant 87 by actual count have been injured since the installation of the new machinery.
5. On April 23 ?, 1564, the greatest English poet there is no argument about the term applied to him was born in the little village of Stratford-on-Avon.

Exercise 38

1. "It is rather for us to be here dedicated that government of the people, by the people, and for the people shall not perish from the earth" has real meaning for us today.
2. "   Duncan is in his grave;
                                        nothing
   Can touch him further."
3. "This other Eden, this demi-paradise,
                        this England."

Exercise 39

1. Then Jesus turned to the man and said, Go thou and do likewise.
2. Hamlet speaks of man as this quintessence of dust.
3. Was it not C. C. Pinckney who said, Millions for defense, but not one cent for tribute?

4. Render unto Caesar the things that are Caesar's Jesus told the Pharisees; and to the Herodians he said, and unto God the things that are God's.

5. Eternal vigilance, he quoted the old saying, is the price of liberty.

6. It was Adam Smith who first called the English a nation of shopkeepers.

7. The King is dead! cried the palace guard. Long live the King!

8. The saying, You can fool some of the people all of the time, and all of the people some of the time, has been ascribed to Lincoln.

9. Disraeli spoke of Gladstone as a sophisticated rhetorician inebriated with the exuberance of his own verbosity.

10. People will not look forward to posterity who never look backward to their ancestors murmured the old Charlestonian.

Exercise 40

1. That Vinegar Bend Mizell is almost as colourful as Jerome Dizzy Dean chuckled the radio announcer.

2. When you sing The Road to Mandalay, the producer told him, try to imitate the style of Lawrence Tibbett.

3. The defendant told me when I arrested him, I just borrowed the car for a little while, the detective testified at the trial.

4. The principal told John's father, The boys say, We call John The Wedge because he is the simplest tool known to man.

5. Which nation has in the past ten years revived the old adage, Might makes right? the U.S. delegate asked the Security Council of the United Nations.

Exercise 41

1. "I have never" she began; then in her usual fashion, she shifted to another subject.

2. "What should I do with these notebooks" the janitor asked.

3. "Eureka" screamed the scientist "I have found the 'Philosopher's Stone'!"

4. "This room is certainly a mess" the inspector said "Report to me as soon as you have cleaned it up."

5. "Handle it carefully" admonished the foreman "for it contains TNT."

Exercise 42

1. As the old priest murmured the final words, "forever and forever. Amen" he collapsed and died.
2. He shouted "What in the   " then the rest of his exclamation froze in his mouth.
3. Did you say, "I need four volunteers"
4. He chortled, "Willy is a real square" a rather ironical term for him to apply to anyone else.
5. Just as he was falling, did you hear him begin, "God save the"
6. He was often referred to as "Nutsy"
7. When they had finished singing "The Old Rugged Cross" they knelt for a moment of silent prayer.
8. They sang the old hymn, "Nearer, My God, to Thee" then they knelt for a moment of silent prayer.
9. Was it you who shouted, "Down with the tyrant"
10. Can you believe" they asked their scoutmaster, "that such a thing could happen at a boys camp"

Exercise 43

1. Be-bop music has succumbed to the rhythms of rock'n roll.
2. When asked the whereabouts of his accomplice, the young hood derisively replied that the jerk had kicked the bucket from a dose of plumbism.
3. The youthful toughie vowed to exenterate his teacher's eyeballs if the square didn't get off his high horse.

Exercise 44

1. Emily Dickinson's little poem, I Never Saw a Moor, is a masterpiece of condensation.
2. There is some similarity between the two short stories: Steinbeck's Flight and Conrad's The Lagoon.
3. E. B. White's essay, Once More to the Lake, is quite as nostalgic· as Charles Lamb's Dream Children, but not so full of pathos.
4. Recently a very fine article, Why We Need More Teachers, appeared in the *Saturday Evening Post*.
5. Two of Franz Hals' paintings — The Smoker and The Merry Company — show his zest for life.
6. Ben Jonson's Drink to Me Only with Thine Eyes is one of the best known songs from the days of Elizabethan England.

7. The second chapter of Cronin's *The Keys of the Kingdom* is entitled Strange Vocation.

8. The Book of Genesis in the *Bible* is often criticized as being scientifically innaccurate.

9. When one studies some of Milton's shorter works, such as L'Allegro Il Penseroso, and Lycidas, he wonders how the same man could have written *Paradise Lost*.

10. Everything about the room reeked of pseudo-culture: on one wall hung a copy of Matisse's Goldfish and Sculpture; flanking it were framed copies of Lincoln's Gettysburg Address and Kipling's Gunga Din; scattered about were miscellaneous pieces of period furniture; a phonograph in a Chippendale cabinet was playing Joyce Kilmer's Trees. What a conglomeration of bad taste!

Exercise 45

(*You may change the capitalization in these two exercises.*)

A. 1. In his mind there had never been any question about his own bravery, yet now he wavered between staying and running, as the massed tanks zigzagged across the field towards him.

2. He had suffered terribly during those two months, not once, however, had he lost faith in the doctor's ability to save him.

3. "Man is not the creature of circumstance, circumstances are the creatures of man."

4. He was distinguished for his ignorance, he never had but one original idea, and that one was wrong.

5. It is said that absence makes the heart grow fonder, that is true — if we add, "for someone else."

6. "Prose is words in their best order, poetry is the best words in the best order."

7. The law forbids a man's taking whatever he wants, do you defy that law?

8. The battle for Khartoum was lost, Gladstone had moved too late.

9. Be sure before you act, think before you speak.

10. "Is there no balm in Gilead, is there no physician there?"

B. 1. "The harvest truly is plenteous, the labourers, however, are few."

2. "The souls of kings and clerks are cast in one mold, the same reason that makes us quarrel with our neighbours causes a war between princes."

3. You can lead a horse to water, nevertheless, you cannot make him drink.

4. "Man is the only one that knows nothing, that can learn nothing without being taught, he can either speak nor walk nor eat, in short, at the prompting of nature alone, he can do nothing but weep."

5. "Can the Ethiopian change the colour of his skin, can the leopard change his spots?"

6. Never in our history has there been such peril to the nation, we must awake to the dangers before it is too late.

7. He leaned on his hoe and stared at the ground, the work that day had taken all the spirit out of him.

8. I wonder sometimes at your present lassitude, you used to be quite energetic.

9. "A poor man without a budget is like a duck without oil on his feathers, neither can hold his head above water for long."

10. "Good night, sweet Prince, flights of angels sing thee to thy rest."

Exercise 46

Rewrite each of the following, retaining only necessary punctuation marks. Do not change words or capitalization.

1. At midnight, the "policeman" walked to the "call-box", and repoted to the desk sergeant.

2. We were served: orange juice, oatmeal, bacon, and eggs, toast and coffee, for breakfast this morning.

3. The dark-skinned, Italian boy tore the clothing away from the hole, which the bullet had made in my side.

4. Few people, who have never experienced poverty, can understand the plight of these destitute, Viet-Nam refugees.

5. The *"Lusitania"* finally up-ended and sank to the bottom, of the ocean.

6. He asked me, "why I had never given any thought to the teaching of history as a profession?"

7. They kept shouting the same, dreary question: "Why did you do it?" !

8. She exclaimed, "that she did not intend to marry me!"

9. The "do-it-yourself" builder will have to procure: a hammer, a screwdriver, and some nails, and screws, before he can assemble the cabinet.

10. There is no doubt, that a superfluous comma, can hinder comprehension for a good reader.

Exercise 47

1. The true story of the sinking of the submarine Squalus was first published in the Saturday Evening Post.

2. The drama critic of the Gazette was quite scornful of the Old Vic Company's production of Shakespeare's Macbeth.

3. Thorton Wilder's three act play, Our Town, has many of the qualities of the Greek drama, according to our literature text, Adventures in American Literature.

4. The London Symphony Orchestra gave a concert which included Tschaikovsky's Fourth Symphony and the "Overture" to Romeo and Juliet.

5. A Tale of Two Cities, Ivanhoe, and Silas Marner seem to be the favourite novels of high school textbook publishers.

Exercise 48

1. My teacher considers a good dictionary a sine qua non for all his students.

2. "Noblesse oblige," murmured Duncan as Malcolm related the circumstances of the Thane of Cawdor's death.

3. His possession of the watch was considered ipso facto proof of his complicity in the crime.

4. Few people have the savoir faire of Parisians, and even fewer have their joie de vivre.

5. A vicious attack of mal de mer almost ruined his trip from New York to Bermuda.

Exercise 49

1. The noun Smith is the indirect object of the verb built.

2. The sound of too can be spelled correctly in three different ways: to, too, and two.

3. Your 8's look like 3's to me.

4. Never use don't with he as its subject.

5. Joe is the subject, hit is the verb, and home run is the direct object.

160

CAPITALIZATION

Exercise 50

Rewrite the following sentences, making necessary changes in capitalization.

1. A wild west show has come to washington, bringing with it over twenty cowboys, three brahma bulls, a number of pinto ponies, and two indian Princesses, who came along to see "the great white father."
2. Because he intends to go to college in the south, his Family sent him to a northern Preparatory School so that he might meet people from as many sections of the Country as possible.
3. When a new president enters the white house, his wife always has the rooms refurnished to suit her taste.
4. Although french, latin, mathematics, and science had all given him trouble in High School, he made straight "a's" in mathematics, physics, and comparative languages when he went to College.
5. His father and his mother had died when he was a baby, but he always called his foster parents mother and dad.
6. As He looked eastward out of the window of the big douglas transport plane, he could see the vast plains and deserts of the great southwest.
7. Last Spring the City planted Oak and Maple trees along the major avenues and in meriwether park.

Exercise 51

Rewrite the following sentences, captalizing where necessary:

1. Jack always said that he wanted "to die with his boots on."
2. "The wind has slackened," he reported over the radio; "the sea, however, is still as rough as I've ever seen it."
3. "those are the scoundrels!" he shouted. "they are the ones who stole my cattle!"
4. Hamlet speaks of man as "the paragon of animals."
5. She turned away from him and said slowly, "you go your way, and I'll go mine."

Exercise 52

Rewrite the following sentences, making necessary changes in capitalization.

1. He went to the central library, where he read *Look Back to Glory* and *Gone With the Wind*.
2. *The wind in the willows* and *Alice through the looking glass* were two of his favourite books for light reading.
3. The Prime Minister Of canada delivered a speech with the title, "what are you afraid of?"
4. Walter White was once executive secretary of the national association for the advancement of the coloured people.

Exercise 53

Rewrite the following sentences, making necessary changes in capitalization.

1. In the *Old Testament* god was called jehovah by his people.
2. O father in heaven, who art omnipotent, save thy people in their distress.
3. "Hail him, the heir of David's line,
    Whom David lord did call;
    The god incarnate, man divine,
    And crown him lord of all!"

Exercise 54

Rewrite the following sentences, making necessary changes in capitalization.

1. High School Seniors all over the country look forward with great eagerness to Commencement Exercises.
2. The President of the Company is always elected at a meeting of the Board of Directors; he then selects his Assistants, who in turn are placed in charge of the several Departments.
3. My Mother told me that her brother, my Uncle Jim, was sending me through College.
4. When you reach the Northwest corner of the County, the road will make a sharp turn South.
5. English and Mathematics are more important than Languages, History, and Sciences at most Schools.
6. At 6th avenue, the Street angles toward the East for about two City Blocks; It then again parallels the Main Highway going to the North.
7. The House Of Commons will move into its rebuilt Office Building on new year's day.

8. *The Star Of The West* was a ship fired on by the Southern Soldiers stationed on Fort Sumter in South Carolina.

9. "One confederate can whip ten yankees" was the boast of the soldiers of the South during The War Between The States.

10. The Bank on the Southeast corner of Broad and Trade Streets has a Cashier who is known all over the Business District for his Honesty and Wisdom.

GRAMMAR AND CLEAR WRITING

Exercise 55

Rewrite the following sentences to achieve unity:

1. The librarian gave him the book that he had asked for, and he met two of his friends in the hallway and went to the gymnasium with them.

2. Suddenly there were many enemy soldiers all around us, and we became confused as to what to do, but Lt. Smith rallied us around his tank, and we managed to drive them back to the street corner, but one of them slipped around behind us and hit Lt. Smith on the arm, and we had a terrible time until the reinforcements from Able Company arrived.

3. There had been lots of activity at the beach all summer, and on Labour Day we packed our bags and went back home.

4. There was a tree just in front of our house, and under the tree was a sandbox, and four children named Kathy, Alicia, Willy, and Ruthie used to play there every day, but once for a whole week I did not see them there and then I learned that they had gone away for the summer.

5. The trouble with our government is that the Liberals and the Conservatives are constantly squabbling over minor points, and we should really have a government that would pass constructive legislation.

Exercise 56

Combine elements that should be included in the same sentence.

1. There are several reasons for her academic success: she has always studied a little more than was required, and in elementary school she was given a good foundation in the fundamental subjects. Futhermore, she has considerable intelligence.

2. He had followed carefully the careers of the two boys: one had gone to Africa and had become a successful mining engineer. The other was living in Paris and had never settled down to any occupation.
3. We have very little time before class begins. Therefore we should stop chatting and do a little reviewing for the test.
4. As he sat under the old oak, he heard the call of a partridge in the woods across the river, a fish splashed noisily near the far bank, and a marsh hen screeched as she was disturbed on her nest. Moreover, he could hear the loud laughter of the dockmen as they unloaded the shrimp boats at the wharf down below him, and he felt completely enthralled by the medley of sounds.
5. He would have liked to join the fun, But he was considered *persona non grata* by everyone in the group.

Exercise 57

Rearrange the parts of the following sentences to improve the structure:

1. Be ready to attack, no matter how tired you may be, on the signal.
2. He glanced at his watch to check the time every few minutes.
3. Jack was aware of the danger involved, as well as his friend.
4. If a boy does not realize his mistakes, life will be difficult for him if his parents do not point them out to him.
5. He let himself be guided by, though he did not wholeheartedly believe in, Christian principles.

Exercise 58

Make necessary changes in the placing of modifiers to improve the sentence structure.

1. He had an overcoat over his arm that had a red lining.
2. The coach was disturbed that all the boys did not get to practice on time every day.
3. They found the dog under a taxicab without a license or a collar.
4. Worry has almost caused all of his hair to turn white.
5. They only had seven minutes before the train departed to get a sandwich.

164

6. All but him were terrified, and he even turned slightly pale.
7. The wrestlers hardly felt tired after the first day of the tournament.
8. That is an excellent plan for meeting the deadline next Tuesday which you have proposed.

Exercise 59

Correct the split infinitives:

1. By the use of the infinitron, it is now possible to quite easily and effectively split an infinitive.
2. In order to really be effective, the tennis service should cause the ball to bounce high or to sharply veer after the bounce.
3. He was able to quickly rouse his sleeping comrades by throwing icy water from the horse trough on them.

Exercise 60

Rearrange the sentence parts to improve the structure.

1. He had ruined, although he did not recognize the fact, his chances of advancing in the company.
2. Milton, while living at Horton a life of comparative ease, wrote some of his finest lyrics.
3. We can, when we know just what you want, get the job done.
4. The Assembly recognized, while they were debating the issue, the wisdom of the governor in calling the special session.
5. Most college professors, though they are underpaid and actually need higher salaries, do not complain simply because of their love for learning.

Exercise 61

Rearrange the sentence parts to improve the structure.

1. There is one of the most beautiful, if not the most beautiful, mountains in the world.
2. Jos is as intelligent as, if not more intelligent than, any other boy in his class.
3. London is just as large as, even though not so glamourous as Paris.
4. Randolph's contributions to charity have been greater than, though no so well publicized as Carter's

Exercise 62

Correct the errors in parallelism.

1. They have spent all of their money, not only on necessities, but utterly useless things as well.
2. It is neither too late, Dr. Faustus, to mend your evil ways nor to ask God's forgiveness.
3. Slowly, gradually, and without any emotion, the mill of the gods ground Oedipus to fine dust.
4. The besieged troops had been offered either an honourable surrender or to suffer death upon being captured.
5. She saw him run out of the store with a mask on his face and carrying a gun in his hand.
6. He developed a liking for broccoli through necessity rather than finding any pleasure in eating it.
7. Ackroyd is of middle age, stands straight as an arrow, and his presence is very commanding.
8. You must either park your car in one of the designated places, or the police will give you a ticket.

Exercise 63

Make necessary corrections of non-parallel thought.

1. Milton was born in 1606 and became one of England's greatest writers.
2. He likes football, baseball, and algebra.
3. That newspaper features local political and social events and has a circulation of over five thousand.
4. Mr. Rutledge was a former teacher of English and dramatics and enjoyed watching professional football.

Exercise 64

Make subject and verb agree in person and number:

1. The actual size of bathing suits vary with different manufacturers.
2. The major thing that keeps me awake at night are the children crying.
3. All that we can offer are these few dollars.
4. Neither the musicians nor the audience were satisfied with the rendition of the piece.

5. The committee have adjourned for the evening.
6. Every man and woman are expected to rise to the occasion when the demands of total war is placed upon them.
7. Four years are too long for us to be away from home.
8. She is one of those particular housekeepers who makes everyone uncomfortable by their fastidiousness.
9. There is sterness and indignation and ironic criticism all through this book.
10. One or the other of those fellows have taken it.

Exercise 65

Make the reference of pronouns clear.

1. They told us at school that Washington did not really cut down a cherry tree, which we had been led to believe in grammar school.
2. He removed the suit from the box in which it had been shipped, and deposited it in the trashcan.
3. The personnel manager told the office boy that he had done enough in his years with the company to deserve a promotion.
4. When you have finished bottling and labelling the jelly, put them in that box on the table in the corner.
5. When the umpire reproached the catcher for complaining, he took his mask off.
6. Willy told his father that he was certain to get a letter from his mother on that very day.
7. This is Mr. Callaway's book, who has been looking for it everywhere.
8. During the French Revolution, if a person disagreed with the regulations of the government, you were sent to the guillotine.
9. His worst fault was his tendency to stammer, but this was not true when he was talking with close friends.
10. He is an excellent lifeguard, which helps him to support himself during the summer months.

Exercise 66

Correct the faulty agreement of pronouns with their antecedents.

1. England expects every man to do their duty.
2. At church last Sunday, everybody was asked to bring their pledge cards to the next morning service.

3. After having been flushed six times in one week, the covey of quail deserted their usual haunts.
4. Every policeman and every fireman in the city considers it their duty to prevent fires.
5. The committee presented their report to the dean.
6. Anybody who will take their car to the local office of the highway department can have her inspected free.
7. None of the mob would accept their share of the responsibility for the damage done.
8. Nobody really understands the power of the atomic fission bomb until you have seen them exploded.
9. Everyone liked the last concert, and they all plan to attend the next one.
10. Neither Kathy nor Ruthie likes to make up their beds every morning.

Exercise 67

Make the following logical, if possible:

1. You promised to be on time, and so we did not wait for you.
2. As smoking has proved harmful to the human body, you will probably get lung cancer before you are fifty.
3. Nervous people make poor typists, and therefore she must be very nervous because she is certainly one of the worst typists that I have ever hired.
4. When Milton became blind, he was able to write *Paradise Lost*.
5. The student council has not done a good job this year; therefore it would be wise to have some other form of student government in the future.

Exercise 68

Improve the following by making the statements logical:

1. Just because you felt devilish is no reason for your dropping a block of ice down the stairwell.
2. Intoxication is when the brain is to a certain extent poisoned.
3. The reason why he was so fatigued was because he had just run three miles.
4. We boiled the nitro-glycerin until it became jelly.
5. I read in the newspaper where we can expect to have sub-normal rainfall for the next two months.

168

Exercise 69

Improve the following comparison:

1. Jack is the tallest of any boy that I know.
2. His manner of walking was as quiet as an Indian.
3. Tokyo is larger than any city in the world.
4. He liked apple pie better than anything.
5. Willy is smaller, but just as strong as Donny.
6. This is one of the longest, if not the longest bridge in Canada.
7. Ruth's hair is much blonder than Julie.
8. Charleston is nearer Bermuda than New York.
9. He loved his dog much more than his father.
10. It is much easier for Dan to make money than a friend.
11. The view from the top of Lookout Moutain is the most beautiful of any in the world.

Exercise 70

Supply the missing words:

1. He said he was going to marry any girl he could.
2. This is the man we know was the last person to see her alive.
3. They had prayers in the morning, in the evening, and on Sundays they went to church twice.
4. There go my dearest cousin and closest friend.
5. Please pass the cream and cereal.
6. Would you be sweet enough to lend me your hairbrush and comb?
7. Jerry told use he and Johnny were too tired to take us to the movie, and they were going home to bed.
8. Is that the boy you saw digging in the vacant lot?

Exercise 71

Correct the "dangling" sentence elements.

1. Having listened to the minister preach for an hour and a half, the church emptied rather rapidly after the benediction.
2. At Malmédy the SS Troopers massacred hundreds of defenseless American prisoners, laughing at their screams.
3. The bob-sled turned crosswise and flew over the bank, thus killing the driver and injuring the other members of the crew.

4. The road has been blocked for almost a week, caused by the recent two-day blizzard.

5. After having been promoted to sales manager, it became part of my job to fly all over the country on inspection trips.

6. Before removing the spark plug, the recess surrounding it should be blown out, using an air hose.

7. An elaborate classroom is not needed for teaching people to read and write.

8. Latecomers used to be locked out of college lecture halls to punish them for being dilatory.

9. While travelling through Europe on an extended tour, nylon underwear and dacron shirts are almost a necessity.

10. If unable to hear the program, some theatres are equipped with special hearing aids for deaf people.

Exercise 72

Improve the following:

1. Do the easier problems first, and then if you have time, you should work the harder ones.

2. The cab-driver assumed the duties of a policeman, and very quickly the traffic jam was unsnarled.

3. I soon finished my Latin translation, and in about another hour, my algebra problems had all been worked.

4. The more exercise we take, the stronger one becomes.

5. As we were walking along, minding our own business, suddenly a fellow in front of us goes berserk, draws a knife, and begins to slash at people near him.

6. An investigation was made by him, and the case was soon solved.

7. We had been waiting for over an hour to see the doctor. A man dressed like an important banker comes in, strides over to the receptionist, and in a loud voice demands to see the doctor at once, as his time is very important to him. She gives him priority over us. We were really furious.

8. As I stood in front of the schoolhouse, I could see my old teacher with bell in hand on the front porch. Behind the building, John, the janitor, sprawled on the back steps, as usual, sunning himself. I walked slowly down the path toward the "noisy mansion" that had meant so much to me, and greeted her with a low bow.

Exercise 73

Improve the following:

1. About that matter, there just does not seem to be any explanation for it.
2. There were a good many hunters "got their limit" on the first day of the deer season.
3. With reference to your letter, that shipment was sent by freight last week and should be delivered to you in a few days.
4. The doctor explained that whenever there were very heavy rains in an area in which people used well-water, that there was a distinct danger of an epidemic of typhoid fever.
5. That painting on the wall, if cleaned up, they can probably get a good price for it at the next art auction.

Exercise 74

Supply transitional elements to make the meaning clearer.

1. He had had trouble with mathematics in high school; he concentrated on languages, history, and philosophy in college.
2. The raging waters had torn at the bridge for more than two days; it was still standing, firm and undamaged.
3. That suit fits you perfectly and looks good on you; you might prefer one that is somewhat less expensive.
4. You must check in at the airport ticket office at least a half hour before the plane departs; your seat may be sold to another customer.
5. We did not understand exactly what he was doing; he made no attempt to explain, but kept on working.
6. They were delayed two hours by a wreck on the highway; they had made a late start; they arrived at the game during the fourth quarter.
7. He had had a serious wreck soon after he learned to drive a car, and ever since, he had been afraid to drive himself. In this crucial situation, he forgot his fears, jumped behind the steering wheel, started the engine, and raced to the hospital. He was never again bothered by driving.

Exercise 75

Subordinate the less important element in each sentence.

1. He repeated his question twice, and he realized that the student was asleep.
2. It was 5 P. M., and they closed the office and went home.
3. They were members of the local country club, and it was just across the road from their house.
4. The fog was quite heavy, and we were unable to see the lights of the approaching truck until it was almost on us.
5. There was a football game, and there she met a young teacher, and his name was Taylor, and it all happened at a preparatory school for boys.

Exercise 76

Correct the "upside-down" subordination.

1. The house was almost quiet when suddenly a scream of anguish rang out from the guest bedroom.
2. He was sitting by his television set when a bolt of lightning struck the antenna and burned out the picture-tube circuit.
3. He was about to lean back in his chair and listen to another dull lecture when it occurred to him that a review test had been assigned for that day.
4. He moved casually toward the enemy, spraying them with his sub-machine gun and forcing them to vacate their positions.
5. The old man was sitting in his boat when a huge shark seized the bait on his line and began to run with it.

Exercise 77

Make coordinate the equally important sentence elements.

1. A whirling tornado came roaring in from the south, striking the sleepy town, demolishing many of its buildings, and killing eight of its inhabitants.
2. As he walked out the door, a huge first caught him in the chest, driving him back against the door frame.
3. He picked up the unusual pebble, putting it in his pocket for later examination.
4. The arrow sped on its way, striking the deer in the shoulder and killing him instantly.

Exercise 78

Rearrange the parts of the following sentences for greater emphasis:

1. There was not any other way to solve the problem, it seemed.
2. However, the fish never seemed to be able to get off his hook.
3. They have controlled the spread of the disease to some extent, at least.
4. The boy about whom I was talking is not the criminal type, to say the least.
5. They will never again be able to put their trust in their present City Council, moreover.

Exercise 79

Rearrange the elements in each sentence in climactic order:

1. He had failed his English examination, had received no letter from his family, and had been scolded by a teacher for throwing paper at a fellow — it had been a miserable day for him.
2. We have practically gotten down on our knees to him, we have asked him, we have implored him to allow us a delay — but he has remained adamant.
3. That boy has become a superlative pass-receiver, an excellent blocker, and a good defensive man since he came to school here a year ago.
4. The town has been struck by a series of tragedies: a hurricane almost destroyed it recently, its only two doctors died last month, and the community centre burned to the ground in April.
5. That is an excellent book: the characterization is almost perfect, the setting is authentic, and the plot is quite exciting and well-developed.

Exercise 80

Improve the following:

1. The ship lay at anchor in the harbor. She was quite sleek in her lines. She had just been repainted. On her decks the sailors were polishing her brass. They were also scrubbing her decks. Some of them had their shirts off. Their bronzed backs glistened in the sun. It was a beautiful sight.
2. It was a long trip down the mountain. The fog was blinding. The road was icy. It was also very slippery. It was not protected by guard rails. It was very steep in places. There

were sharp curves every few hundred feet. There were no signs to warn motorists of them. There were two narrow bridges across deep chasms. We finally reached the bottom. I breathed a sigh of relief.

Exercise 81

Rearrange the structure of the sentences in the following paragraph to do away with the monotony:

When we first saw the bear, he had just emerged from his cave. As we approached him, he hesitated in his slow walk. When we got closer, he turned back toward the cave. Because he had chosen to "hole-up," we raced for the cave to cut him off. Although we ran as fast as we could, he got there first. Since we were afraid to follow him into the cave, we turned sadly away and continued our tramp along the mountain path.

Exercise 82

Improve the following by correcting the verbosity and the circumlocution. At the end of your improved sentence, write the number of words that you have used.

1. The City Council has been in the process of conducting an investigation in order that they may find out in what ways the problem of the disposal, in the most efficient manner, of garbage that is not burnable can be solved. (*42 words.*)

2. Pursuant to your request regarding information as to loans made by the government to individuals desiring them for implementation of soil conservation programs, I take this opportunity to advise you that a large segment of the population has also been attempting to secure the data to which you have made reference, but that we have placed your name on a high priority list and we shall be able to initiate action to secure these data for you in the very near future, at which time we shall be more than happy to accommodate you by forwarding the information requested. (*99 words.*)

3. Despite the fact that he had laboured for a long period of time with all the means available to him to prevent his firm from going into bankruptcy, he at this time reached a decision that with respect to the funding activities of the firm, there was such a large deficit that the inactivation of the company as an operating business was of the utmost necessity with the least practicable delay. (*70 words.*)

4. England anticipates that with regard to the current emergency each individual will duly implement his obligations in accordance with the several functions allocated to him. (*25 words.*)

Exercise 83

Correct the tautology.

1. Most people generally are disturbed and upset by the strange and the unfamiliar, but our pastor and minister, who is more wiser than most, is not in the least, however.
2. It was such a tiny, small bit of living organism that it was hardly visible to the eye; but by looking closely, one could see that it was rectangular in shape and red in color.
3. It was an unexpected surprise when the old lady deliberately and purposely pulled off the road so that we might pass her.

Exercise 84

Make each statement specific.

1. It was a nice day, and we had a good time.
2. Joe is a fair student and a fine boy.
3. The business failed because of inefficiency.
4. It was a very strange-looking animal.
5. He made a splendid proposition to correct the thing.

Exercise 85

Correct the incorrect verb forms.

1. If I was you, I should wait until next year to take biology.
2. He has behaved as though he was not in his right mind.
3. He behaves as if he is not in his right mind.
4. If he was not such a bore, we should invite him.
5. Suppose that he was here: would you say that about him?
6. If he was very strict, he was also very fair.
7. Hamlet obviously wished that he was dead.
8. If he were paying attention to his job, the ship would not have sunk.
9. Oh, that he was not so indifferent toward his studies!
10. If he was not so lazy, he would pass his subjects with ease.

Exercise 86

Correct the incorrect use of shall *and* will *after each of your sentences, give the reason, such as, "simple futurity" or "determination."*

1. I will be happy to take your girl to the dance.
2. I will probably not need any further tutoring.
3. If you do not help me, I will starve.
4. I shall never steal to keep famine from my door.
5. I shall gladly escort your mother to the commencement exercises.
6. My reserve troops will be committed tomorrow regardless of what you or the general or anyone else may say.
7. "Shall we win the game tomorrow?" "We will!"
8. I will probably get a cool reception, but I shall go anyway.

Exercise 87

Correct the incorrect tense forms.

1. He was tolerant toward his employees because he felt that "to err was human; to forgive, divine."
2. The teacher told us that oxygen was heavier than hydrogen.
3. We have long recognized that the best English writer of romantic novels was Sir Walter Scott.
4. At present we did not have a satisfactory answer to our question.
5. If nothing interferes, he was leaving for Berlin tomorrow.

Exercise 88

Correct the incorrect tense forms.

1. He had completed the work yesterday.
2. He always hurried to get dressed in the morning so that he may be on time for breakfast.
3. When he left us yesterday, he had complained of a pain in his upper chest.
4. Until about a year ago, he has been a model citizen.
5. Although he had never before seen such an armoured vehicle, he talks as though he were an expert on the subject of tanks.

Exercise 89

Correct the incorrect tense forms.

1. Since that time there were a number of instances of border violations by both countries.
2. He had been living in the old brownstone house for almost four years, but he will have to move next week for failure to pay his rent.
3. They will never send him to jail, for he always found a way to escape a prison sentence.
4. Kathy and Randy were close friends ever since childhood.
5. They told us that they had written to Ottawa for instructions, but we did not hear whether they ever received an answer.

Exercise 90

Correct the incorrect tense forms.

1. If I knew what awaited me on my arrival, I would never have gone.
2. Although he made good grades in high school, he had a lot of trouble just passing his courses in college.
3. He was quite elated, for he discovered a cure for the common cold.
4. It was reported that the Los Alamos scientists have invented a "clean" hydrogen bomb.
5. A member of the diplomatic corps informed us that Stalin was dead for three months before the news was announced to the world.

Exercise 91

Correct the incorrect tense forms.

1. By next week, Parliament will pass all of the Prime Minister's recommended legislation.
2. When travel by rocket ship will become safe, we shall be able to fly to Europe in two hours or less.
3. By the time that he returns, I shall finish the work for him.
4. I predict that our bureaucratic lecturer will use the term *implement* fifteen times before he finishes his speech.
5. Johnny will finish college before you get out of high school.

Exercise 92

Correct any faulty sequence of tenses.

1. They insisted that he is living in Glasgow.

2. The professor asserted that Dickens' novels were filled with propaganda.
3. After he studied his lessons, he went to bed.
4. When he asked me to recite today, I should like to have been the fellow next to me, who prepared his lesson.
5. He stopped his car to see whether his tire blew out.
6. I would not have said it if I thought that I would have shocked you.
7. He listens closely so that he might better understand.
8. They had built the boat so that it will be unsinkable.
9. He was teaching school for fifty years when he retired last June.
10. The old man told his grandchildren that blood was thicker than water.

Exercise 93

Correct the incorrect tense form of verbals.

1. I hoped to have seen you before today.
2. Those buildings are very old, being built just after the Great Fire of London.
3. Crossing the mountain at Big Gap, you will descend five miles before there is a stretch of level road.
4. Joe Collins is said to be very ill, but to be recovering rapidly now.
5. The bread was much too stale for us to have eaten it.
6. He was reported to be a leader in the prison break last week.
7. I should like to live during the "Roaring Twenties."
8. Being warned in a dream, Joseph took the young child and fled to Egypt.
9. He would prefer his next child to have been a girl.
10. Having been afraid of ghosts, he will not sleep in the attic bedroom.

Exercise 94

Correct the incorrectly used adjectives and adverbs.

1. He learned that most all of his former classmates attended church regular.
2. Although the fish tasted very badly, it appeared to have been fresh caught.

3. It was a real serious accident, although no one was bad hurt.
4. The old mountain woman felt some better after the doctor had talked frank with her.
5. That tree looks different from any other that I have ever seen.
6. Although the old setter smelled badly, he sometimes located a covey of birds.
7. He looked smilingly at me as I passed him, feeling terribly about my low grades.
8. He stood quietly for three minutes behind the door while the enemy soldiers searched the barn real careful-like.
9. He drives too fast and careless for London traffic, whereas she drives so slow that she would sure cause trouble in that city's rushing traffic.
10. When he failed to move quick enough to return the ball, his partner looked angry at him.

Exercise 95

Use the correct demonstrative adjective.

1. A study of this phenomena leads me to believe that we are being observed by people from another planet.
2. He has always despised those kind of books.
3. From this data we can assume that a falling body gathers speed every second.
4. Those sort of problems worry him more than really serious ones.
5. Please send me complimentary tickets for this prominent alumni.

Exercise 96

Correct the faulty comparatives and superlatives.

1. Of the two—the Ford and the Chevrolet—he considered the last the best.
2. The more sharper the knife, the more easily the turkey is carved.
3. Of all the soap powders tested, "Tide" cleaned better and washed clothes whiter.
4. It was the most lovely evening dress in the store and fitted Julie better.
5. Bill seems to be the more happy of all the students in class.

Exercise 97

A. *Make necessary corrections in the case of substantives.*

1. Just between you and I, there is no reason for him feeling as he does.
2. I will tell you whom I think is responsible.
3. We will send whoever you think can be trusted.
4. You are taller than her by several inches.
5. I am certain of it having been him.
6. The person who I thought to be his brother actually was his son.
7. He spoke to only two of us—namely, she and I.
8. Whomever you want to be your emissary should be named at once.
9. Who do you think me to be?
10. Whom do you think that we should select.

B. *Make necessary corrections in the case of substantives.*

1. Whom do men say that I am?
2. Let's you and I be friends, for we have a common enemy.
3. There comes the soldier whom you told me had been captured by the Koreans.
4. Is there any danger of the enemy attacking from the rear?
5. His mother has offered to send all of us to college, even you and I.
6. The windows of the store were broken again last night, apparently by someone's seeking revenge against the owner.
7. Always tackle whomever you think has the ball.
8. We sent the package of food to you and he last week.
9. Did you hear the story about Donny and I?
10. Please send to the office a boy who you are absolutely positive can be depended upon.

Exercise 98

Correct the misuse of pronouns.

1. On the way to the lake, we passed a store whose windows were filled with fishing tackle for sale.
2. The person which threw that piece of chalk is asked to see me after class.

3. He bought a second-hand automobile whose carburetor was broken and whose tires were worn down to the fabric.
4. Mr. Latham, that used to be sports editor of the *Gazette,* is now assistant director of the Local Chamber of Commerce.

Exercise 99

Make necessary corrections in pronoun form and usage.

1. Their two boys built that boat all by theirselves.
2. He promised to let Jack and myself have the next ride.
3. My father hisself made lower grades in school than I do.
4. Who besides Larry and yourself are going?
5. The forest ranger lent his gun to Woody and myself—not to you.

Exercise 100

Correct the misuse of principal parts.

1. We dove into the pool and then swum under the water until our lungs almost bursted.
2. The old man raised up in his bed and taken hold of my hand; then, after I had swore to take charge of his estate, his head sunk back on the pillow, and he give up the ghost.
3. As the sun shined dimly through the morning mist, the condemned man drunk a cup of wine, was lead by two soldiers up the steps of the gallows, and was hung for his vicious crime.
4. If I had knowed when I laid down under the blanket that Pap had stole it from the morgue, I would have froze before using it.

Exercise 101

Correct the words which are used as the wrong parts of speech.

1. I would of loaned you the five dollars if I had not suspicioned that you would never repay me without I asked you ever day.
2. It was real sweet of you to send me an invite to your party just like I was one of your closest friends.
3. On account of you walked so far in those small size shoes, you will now have to go barefooted for an awful long time, like I did.
4. Our patrol leader was loathe to stop for awhile because we had all ready wasted more time than we should of.

Exercise 102

Eliminate the superfluous words.

1. Just inside of his gate, he has put up a sign of about two feet in height: "Keep off of the grass."
2. After he had climbed up the ladder into the tree, he connected up the two lengths of rope and lowered one end down to the waiting boys.
3. When I met up with Mr. Lowe in town today, he asked me whether I would join together with him and Mr. Fox in sponsoring an oyster roast for the benefit of the church of which we are all members of.
4. To prove his point, the eccentric old teacher rose up from his chair, picked up the bucket of water, whirled it four times about his head, and then emptied it out on to the floor.

Exercise 103

Correct the provincialisms.

1. I don't reckon that we've ever been such a far piece from home before.
2. It's a right smart ways for you to have to tote that heavy poke.
3. When I slipped up behind her and bussed her on the cheek, she sloshed me with the wet mop she was holding.
4. As Sam hasted down the path in his new boughten clothes, a white-complected fellow who looked like a haunt sudden loomed up in front of him.

Exercise 104

Translate the colloquialisms into standard English.

1. A lot of folks turn in sort of early so they may be refreshed for the next day's work.
2. Any guy with the least bit of gumption wouldn't be taken in by a bunch of kids.
3. The chemistry prof told me in lab today that on Monday I'd have to take the exam I'd missed.
4. After I came back to the dorm from the gym, I found my awfully brainy roommate all enthused about a book he'd been reading, and holding forth on its merits for the benefit of a bunch of boys.

Exercise 105

Eliminate the barbarisms.

1. We humans undoubtedly will some day be able to go anyplace rockets can fly.
2. The former criminal suicided after the police became unrelentless in suspicioning him of having burgled the jewelry store.
3. I used to could wrangle an invite to the country club party most every Saturday night; but since I had that confliction with the manager, I am no longer welcome there, irregardless of whom I am with.
4. I disremember exactly when I loaned you the money, but we were somewheres downtown at the time.
5. When he was attacked that time by the octopus and drug to the bottom of the inlet, he almost drowned.

Exercise 106

Eliminate the slang.

1. It was a crummy trick for that lousy pitcher to dust off with a fast sinker such a nice guy as Mickey Mantle.
2. That cool date of mine looked so sharp that every slob in the hop-hall wanted to rock'n roll with her.
3. The blob was really plastered to the gills when the cop picked him up.
4. That chiseler really stuck his neck out when he tried to pull a phony deal that was so corny that even a nut in the booby hatch would have caught on to it.

Exercise 107

Eliminate the trite expressions.

1. It was the irony of fate that Al, a man as strong as Hercules, should have been half scared to death by a woman who was as harmless as a kitten.
2. It goes without saying that with a sense of relief we experienced this near tragedy and came through none the worse for wear.
3. When her pearly teeth flashed between her rosy lips, this member of the weaker sex was as pretty as a picture.
4. In an unguarded moment, this soul of honour who had followed the straight and narrow for years on end, was persuaded to taste

the demon rum; and all too soon he became another horrible victim of the Grim Reaper.

5. The fond parents were green with envy when their one and only and his blushing bride became such a loving couple that they neglected the old folks.

Exercise 108

Eliminate the artificial and old-fashioned expressions.

1. Hundred of women bedight in mourning weeds viewed the remains of the deceased matinee idol just before the last sad rites.

2. Prithee inform me what the leech charged for setting your broken limb.

3. When you perused the newspaper at your domicile this morning, did you remark the article about the fistic encounter between the partisan supporters of the opposing gridiron warriors in yesterday's match?

4. In these parlous time, methinks it is of the utmost importance that we inaugurate and implement plans and policies for the extinguishing of the great conflagrations that are liable to ensue in the event of an enemy rocket attack.

Exercise 109

Eliminate the unnecessary repetitions.

1. That book—a mine of information—is the reference book that I referred to constantly in composing that last composition of mine.

2. The thoughtful student, of course, soon learns that he cannot learn all the material in a course unless he studies on his own.

3. When he sat down to write his weekly theme, he was all ready to write on a theme on which he had already written four times before; but his mother changed his mind by making it a point to point out that the theme was becoming trite.

4. Before long a teacher with a long face came along and gave us a long lecture on the tragedy of living too long.

5. Well, I think that it would be well for the well to be sunk well away from the house.

Exercise 110

Replace the flat, dull (italicized) words with more vivid, expressive ones.

184

1. He *said* that it was a *good* thing to have *nice* parents.
2. We *went* quickly to the *big* window and *looked* at the big crowd gathering in the street.
3. They had a *grand* time at the *affair*.
4. The speaker had a *bad* voice.
5. History is a *thing* that I *do not like*.
6. The *animal* made a *bad* noise as it *came* toward us.
7. She is a *cute* girl.
8. We had a *terrible* time working those *awful* problems.

Exercise 111

A. *Choose the correct idiom.*

1. We (*have, have got*) to change our new policy in (*regard, regards*) to granting the employees only a half (*hour, an hour*) for their lunch period, for some of them are now so angry (*at, with*) us that I doubt (*if, whether*) they will try (*and, to*) do their work properly until the rule is changed.
2. Some of our students (*had, would*) rather die (*of, with*) influenza than be inoculated (*to, against*) it.
3. I cannot agree (*to, with*) your new policy on smoking even though it is identical (*to, with*) the one used in many other schools and may be superior (*than, to*) our present one.
4. I am ashamed (*at, of*) Shade for speaking (*aloud, out loud*) and then blaming (*it on Hayes, Hayes for it*).
5. In his talk (*to, with*) us tonight, the lecturer certainly differed (*from, with*) you about the best methods of (*raising, rearing*) children.

B. *Eliminate the incorrect (italicized) idioms.*

1. If you *plan on climbing* that high peak, I shall *wait on* you here because this is *all the farther* I can go.
2. Stuart may be an *all-around* athlete, but I doubt *if* he can get *in* college on that distinction alone.
3. Because Sarah was an unusually sweet little girl *of only about six years old* who did many helpful things *on her own accord*, her parents would not get *mad* at her even when she failed to *comply to* their wishes.
4. We *cannot help but believe* that your phenomenal success in politics has been *because of* your decision to keep yourself *independent from* any political machine.

5. I am *very interested* in the fact that you plan to *try and* write a *novel on* the people at our school.

Exercise 112

A. *Select the word that will give the exact meaning intended.*

1. (*Beside, Besides*) having the (*character, reputation*) of being (*quiet, quite*) (*frugal, stingy*) with his money, Scrooge was considered rather (*cynical, pessimistic*) about the motives of those who made it a (*custom, habit*) to sing Yuletide songs on Christmas Eve.

2. As a (*practical, practicable*) matter, it is ridiculous to (*annoy, aggravate*) at 3 P.M. on Friday a teacher who is (*all ready, already*) somewhat upset, for you may find yourself detained for the (*balance, remainder*) of the afternoon.

3. If we (*compare, contrast*) Lee and Jackson, we are (*liable, likely*) to find that they had many (*common, mutual*) attributes.

4. Many (*cynical, pessimistic*) people (*censor, censure*) those who (*discovered, invented*) the atomic fission bomb, for the fear of (*approaching, impending*) war and the bomb's (*eminent, imminent*) use has had a serious psychological (*affect, effect*) on them.

5. The (*audience, spectators*) at the baseball game shouted vituperative comments at the (*imperious, imperial*) umpire, who was supposed to be (*disinterested, uninterested*), but who apparently had a (*personnel, personal*) grudge against the home team.

B. *Select the word that will give the exact meaning intended.*

1. (*Incredulous, Incredible*) as it may seem, his (*conscience, conscious*) did not bother him at all when he was so (*contemptible, contemptuous*) as to (*desert, dessert*) his war-bride — an (*emigrant, immigrant*) to this country who understood no English — and to have nothing (*farther, further*) to do with her.

2. You must be (*quiet, quite*) (*ingenious, ingenuous*) to think that you can (*accept, except*) expensive (*presence, presents*) from a boy and not be (*obliged, obligated*) to him in some way.

3. He (*implied, inferred*) in his lecture that the Russian people are (*all together, altogether*) (*to, too*) peace-loving to support a war of (*aggression, regression*), (*and, but*) I (*expect, suspect*) that (*less, fewer*) of them than he thinks are completely (*pacific, pacifistic*).

4. It was a (*capital, capitol*) move by Senator Jackson in (*proposing, purposing*) that the senators (*defer, differ*) action on the bill until a (*later, latter*) date when they might be able to (*compare, contrast*) it with others being prepared on the same subject.

5. It is not (*healthy, healthful*) for a person to be over-(*envious, jealous*) of another's success.

C. *Substitute for each italicized word another that will give the exact meaning intended.*

1. My *principle* reason for going to the *stationary* store is to exchange this rather *course* writing paper for some that is smoother.

2. A scheming politician may have more *wisdom* than a *notorious* statesman, but he will not possess so much *knowledge*.

3. It is *unique* for a girl who is *jealous* of her *comrades* to be well liked, but it happens sometimes, *curious* to say.

4. Though *most* a year had *lapsed* since the team had won a game, its *moral* remained high.

5. The room in which the cripple *set* most of the day was very *luxuriant, while* the *balance* of the house was quite plain.

6. I *expect* that your *principle* reason for wanting to *affect* changes *continuously* is your desire to eliminate all seemingly *obsolete* features of the school.

KEY TO EXERCISES ON COMPOSITION RULES

PUNCTUATION

The following exercises have been punctuated correctly, as shown in bold type.

Key to Exercise 1

1. "A horse **!** A horse **!** My kingdom for a horse **! "**

2. "Yond Cassius has a lean and hungry look **. "**

3. "How forcible are right words **! "**

4. "A wise son maketh a glad father **. "**

5. What finally happened to Casca **?** To Brutus **?** To Cassius **?**

6. Oh **!** Oh **!** Please **!** Don't **!** Why do you treat me this way **?**

7. "It is better to dwell in a corner of the housetop than with a brawling woman in a wide house **. "**

Key to Exercise 2

1. Among those present were Capt. and Mrs. Philip Duckett, the Rev. and Mrs. James B. Massey, Dr. Trelawney, and Messrs. G. B. Smith, H. O. Hunniwell, George B. Hamilton, and James DeW. Lang.
2. On Dec. 7, 1941, at 6:00 A.M. Japanese airplanes under Lt. Gen. Hamakodo attacked the U.S. Air Base on Luzon, P.I.
3. Prof. Grey received his A.B. degree from V.P.I., his M.A. from McGill U., a Ph.D. from McMaster, and an LL.D. from the University of Montreal.

Key to Exercise 3

1. "The wolf also shall dwell with the lamb, and the leopard shall lie down with the kid."
2. "Many are called, but few are chosen."
3. A decision will have to come from you, or we shall be unable to act.
4. There is little to be gained by waiting, for every day the enemy becomes stronger.
5. He did not have any idea of retiring, nor could we persuade him even to take a vacation.
6. Some teachers can really help a dullard, but bright students often seem to learn little from them.
7. The atomic fission weapons have created n e r v o u s tension throughout the world, for no nation feels secure against the destruction which they can create.
8. Either he is a genius in revolutionary methods of warfare, or the fates are protecting him, for he has defied every rule in the tactics book.
9. Because of your slight effort in your studies you will undoubtedly fail, and your classmates will go to college without you.
10. We cannot understand what electricity is, nor does our teacher seem to know.

Key to Exercise 4

1. "And now abideth faith, hope, charity."
2. "The winter is past, the rain is over and gone, the flowers appear on the earth, the time of the singing of birds is come, and the voice of the turtle is heard in our land."

3. His stupid, bungling methods have created a disorganized, unproductive state of affairs.

4. His shabby, dirty, old-fashioned clothes hung loosely from his twisted, emaciated body.

5. Joe, Harry, and George have finally managed to pass Algebra II.

6. He was a leader in the classroom, in the dormitory, and on the athletic field.

7. Terrified lions, elephants, zebras, and horses stampeded through the screaming, milling crowd as the roaring, crackling flames from the circus tent shot skyward.

Key to Exercise 5

1. "If the blind lead the blind, both shall fall into the ditch."

2. Although life seems complex while we are in school, it becomes even more so in later life.

3. If God be for us, who can be against us?

4. Whenever he felt like taking exercise, he lay down until the feeling had passed.

5. In order to stay alive, one must eat.

6. By slaying all the starlings, they upset the balance of nature.

7. With the best method of producing the hydrogen bomb in their possession, the Russians felt secure at the conference table.

8. Having travelled all night, he was completely exhausted.

9. For informing on the tax-dodgers, he was given a generous reward.

10. If you will always place a comma after an *if-clause*, you will hardly ever be wrong.

Key to Exercise 6

1. Any boy who uses his time judiciously will undoubtedly pass his work.

2. That tall man, whose picture you have probably seen many times, was once the Secretary of the Navy.

3. Jack Jones, who uses his time judiciously, is always on the Honour Roll.

4. The officer wearing the black beret is Field Marshal Montgomery.

5. Field Marshal Montgomery, wearing a black beret, reviewed the NATO troops.

6. The crowd was astounded by his feats of magic, although he was somewhat out of practice.

7. He has always been near the top of his class, as he has never shirked his academic duties.

8. We know a man who can always be trusted: Billy Smith.

9. Billy Smith, who can always be trusted, will be happy to invest your money for you.

10. Admiral King, dressed in a white uniform, watched the sailors marching past the reviewing stand.

11. The author of that maxim was Benjamin Franklin, who was America's first ambassador to France.

12. Can anyone remember the name of the man who was our first ambassador to England?

13. One of the boys on the back row, who was not paying attention at the time, was asked the first question in the review of the lesson.

14. One of the boys on the back row who had their feet on the desks in front of them was singled out and scolded by the teacher as an example to the others.

15. Harry took a strange flower, which he had found growing in his yard, to the biology teacher, who was able to identify it.

Key to Exercise 7

1. There is, moreover, no doubt in my mind as to the letter's authenticity.

2. They will arrive, I am certain, before the time set for the ceremony.

3. Don't you agree, in spite of your personal feelings in the matter, that we should discharge the man?

4. What, and please speak frankly, do you think is the real reason for his defection?

5. This is, I would say, rather unusual; but I believe, to tell the truth, that it is not illegal.

Key to Exercise 8

1. He needs a mother, not a wife.

2. He served the tennis ball rather casually, but drove hard to the baseline his opponent's return.

190

3. He actually is quite intelligent, yet almost totally illiterate.
4. I requested that you come to my office, not to reward you, but to punish you.
5. He had always wanted a "Thunderbird," but had never been able to afford one.

Key to Exercise 9

1. The infantry division, my friends, will soon be a thing of the past.
2. Messrs. Canby and Destry, are you ready to begin the contest?
3. "Why don't you speak for yourself, John?"
4. There is no reason, mother, why you should want the car today.

Key to Exercise 10

1. My first cousin, Sam Jones, has been reading the collected works of the excellent modern poet, W. H. Auden.
2. My cousin Sam is completely mystified by the writings of the poet Auden.
3. The fact that your mistake caused the team to lose makes no difference to your schoolmates.
4. This fact, that you are not a bona fide student, precludes your being allowed to play in the game.
5. He dropped the soup tureen into the teacher's lap, an action that caused laughter throughout the dining room.
6. Our most genial teacher, Bob Whittle, once studied under the great Shakespearean teacher, George Lyman Kittredge.
7. Charlie Stone, president of General Motors, was once an assembly line employee of that company, the largest corporation in the world.
8. His brother George once memorized the poem "Thanatopsis" in its entirety.
9. You boys should show respect to your minister, a man who has devoted his life to the service of others.
10. An honest man, a rarity in nature, is, according to Pope, "the noblest work of God."

Key to Exercise 11

1. On Friday, June 9, 1967, the final exercises were held for the graduating class.

2. Very shortly there will be a new occupant of the Prime Minister's residence, 10 Downing Street, London, W.1.

3. The Adjutant General gave his address as R.F.D. #1, Point Barrow, Wisconsin, as of March 3, 1968.

4. In August of next year Niagara, Ontario, will hold an azalea festival.

Key to Exercise 12

1. That he will be here tomorrow, I am absolutely sure.

2. A true aristocrat, even though he may lose his wealth, will retain his dignity.

3. An army may, with only slight losses to itself, win a great victory.

4. Of my country's needs at this critical moment in her history, I am fully aware.

Key to Exercise 13

1. The operating room having been readied by the nurse in charge, the surgeon had no technical difficulties in performing the appendectomy.

2. The old lady being about to die, her family gathered around her bed.

3. The loss of the lieutenant caused only a momentary problem, the leadership of the platoon being taken over almost immediately by an experienced sergeant.

4. The wall having been breached to allow the passage of the "Horse", the Greeks had no trouble in entering Troy.

Key to Exercise 14

1. No, I have not heard the score.

2. It was four to three, wasn't it?

3. Indeed, you should know better than that.

4. Very well, we will accept your offer.

5. Yes, he was one of them.

6. You don't really mean that, do you?

Key to Exercise 15

1. Ever since, he has been known as the man who won the war.

2. Because of that, disloyalty is now quite common in their ranks.

3. Whatever is, is right.
4. When are we going to eat, mother?
5. To John, Smith gave his full support.
6. That that is, is.
7. He faced the robber, holding the pistol firmly.
8. Inside, the fire blazed cheerfully.

Key to Exercise 16

1. Beef, eggs, milk, etc., must be kept on ice; otherwise they may spoil.
2. Your homework, your weekly composition, etc., must be turned in on time.
3. He gave us the usual lecture, the usual demerits, the usual looks, etc., before he dismissed us.

Key to Exercise 17

1. The old man slowly replied, "I have lived a full life and am now ready to die."
2. "The first rule of conduct in the OSS," he asserted, "is one which most people ignore: never tell a secret."
3. "What," he asked timidly, "do you want me to do?"
4. "We shall see you in the morning," they called as they drove away.
5. Did he say, "It's incomprehensible"?

Key to Exercise 18

1. Randolph, G.A., and Pinckney, C.C., were invited to a supper dance at National Cathedral School.
2. The Reverend James Wadsworth, A.B., M.A., B.D., D.D., preached the baccalaureate sermon.
3. "The letter was signed by James F. Wright, D.S.C., O.B.E., Member of Parliament, Keeper of the King's Seal," the secretary told him.

Key to Exercise 19

1. To err is human; to forgive, divine.
2. Washington was a hero; Benedict Arnold, a traitor to his country.

3. One brother is a mining engineer; the other, a Texas ranch-owner.

Key to Exercise 20

1. "Favour is deceitful; beauty is vain."
2. "Your old men shall dream dreams; your young men shall see visions."
3. "Ask, and it shall be given you; seek, and ye shall find; knock, and it shall be opened unto you."
4. Men make houses; women make homes.
5. He gained the admiration of the world; yet he lost his self-respect.
6. His morning paper had not been delivered for two days; therefore he called the circulation manager to determine the reason.
7. Some of the smallest trees were cut in two by the tornado; on the other hand, not one of the giant oaks was badly damaged.
8. Chinese Gordon assumed greater powers than he had been granted; as a result, Gladstone withdrew his support of the venture.
9. Antony wept tears of sorrow over the fallen Caesar; moreover, he pledged vengeance on the assassins of his friend.
10. The conditions were quite unfavourable for a landing; nevertheless, the pilot notified all aboard that he was "going to take her in."

Key to Exercise 21

1. You have brought us famine, disease, and death; but this day will, I have no doubt, see your destruction as a political force.
2. There has never, to my knowledge, been such a series of terrible thunderstorms as we have experienced during the past two weeks; and I am positive that never again will you have your fishing and swimming so interfered with and your vacation practically ruined by the weather.
3. In the meantime you must take every precaution not to re-injure the damaged tissue, which will heal rather slowly; and you must follow to the letter the instructions which I have given you for the proper care of the burned places.
4. A good short story involves much more than just time, place, action, and people; for unless plot, characterization, and theme are closely interwoven, the story becomes a mere narration of events.

Key to Exercise 22

1. He asked that the following boys meet him in his classroom: Ainslie, L.S.; Baker, R.E.; Calhoun, L.M.; and Dandridge, G.C.

2. A quiet, secluded spot in the country; a grassy, ant-free plot of ground; a tall shade tree; a cool, gentle breeze; and a laughing, singing brook — these are the first requisites for a successful picnic.

3. Mr. Carraway, the chairman of the Senate Finance Committee; Lankford, the ranking Liberal; and Mr. Kennedy, the chief counsel, were the only ones present as the hearings opened.

Key to Exercise 23

1. "Nothing matters now," said the old man sadly; "no one cares whether I live or die."

2. "Life can be beautiful," the radio announcer droned; "it can also be ugly without Ajax, the foaming cleanser."

3. "When we give the Senator's remarks only cursory attention, we find them very plausible," he thundered at his colleagues; "but when we examine them closely, we recognize the superfluity of meaningless words and the paucity of facts!"

Key to Exercise 24

1. There are several boys in school with French names: Boileau, Racine, and Montroix.

2. These are the boys who did it: Joe, Harry, and George.

3. The boys who did it are Joe, Harry, and George.

4. He rejected my plan for the following reasons: it was too costly, it required more manpower than was available, and it had other earmarks of government bureaucracy.

5. Remember to take with you these essentials: a comb, a toothbrush, a clean shirt, and a pair of pyjamas.

Key to Exercise 25

1. You have only one chance of getting into college: sneaking in.

2. Brutus thought that there was only one solution: to kill Caesar.

3. He used only one word to apply to most of his students: *stupid*.

4. This is something that you must not forget: never desert a friend in need.

5. To Lee there was one sublime word in the English language : *duty*.

6. Criminals incarcerated there are extremely fortunate : for example, they are permitted visitors daily and are allowed to participate in athletics every afternoon.

Key to Exercise 26

1. One of the most touching statements in the *Bible* is the one made by the father of a demented boy : "Lord, I believe; help thou mine unbelief."

2. He quoted from "The Declaration of Independence" : "When, in the course of human events, it becomes necessary . . . declare the causes which impel them to separation."

3. Emerson is reported to have said : "The world will beat a path to the door of the man who invents a better mousetrap."

Key to Exercise 27

1. He has recently written a splendid monograph: "Three Southern Poets : A Critical Analysis."

2. "The Parable of the Good Samaritan" can be found in Luke 10 : 33-35.

3. At 11 : 28 last night fires broke out simultaneously in four sections of the city.

4. One of the best American biographies — *Israfel : The Life and Times of Edgar Allan Poe* — was written by Hervey Allen, a teacher of English in a secondary school.

5. Your first bibliographical entry — "Hellenism," *The Encyclopedia Britannica,* 14th Edition, XI : 385-387 — gives the wrong page reference.

Key to Exercise 28

1. "I - I just don't know - er - whether — " he began. "No, I just - er - can't say."

2. He is rowdy, slovenly, boorish — but why say any more about him ?

3. "Do you - you th - think that - that he will act without th - th - thinking?" I asked.

4. He was going to read us — just what was it that he was going to read us?

Key to Exercise 29

1. When he studies every day, when he turns in his work on time, when he pays strict attention in class — when he does all these consistently, he manages to pass.
2. Joe, Henry, and George — these were the boys who did it.
3. Intelligence, initiative, industry, integrity — he is seeking these qualities in those whom he employs.
4. In the morning, in the afternoon, at night — at any time of the day he may be found working on his silly invention.

Key to Exercise 30

1. These boys — Joe, Harry, and George — are the ones who did it.
2. The captain of the team — sweaty, dirty, and exhausted — sat on the edge of the bench and stared at the ground.
3. The following students — Ramsay, Pickens, Hoxton, and McDonald — are asked to remain after class.
4. This one quality of the good officer — concern for those placed under him in his command — was especially stressed by the general in his talk.
5. The next approach — one that may not meet with the approval of all of you — is to write a letter to your representatives and request that they use their influence to force a decision.

Key to Exercise 31

1. These men — and I speak for all of them — refuse to obey such a ridiculous order, Captain Queeg.
2. That particular statement — I know that all of you will agree with me — is clearly a falsehood.
3. These huskies — that is, most of them — have been trained to the sled.
4. Gentlemen of the jury, the defendant — and this must be obvious to all of you — could not possibly have committed the crime of which he is accused.

Key to Exercise 32

1. He was a muscular and handsome — but cowardly leader.
2. She had tried — tried so hard to make a home for him — but she had failed.

3. I told you to come tomorrow — not today.
4. Fourteen survivors — only fourteen out of ninety-seven passengers and crew members — were brought ashore by the Coast Guard.
5. "Gentlemen may cry, Peace, Peace — but there is no peace."

Key to Exercise 33

The following phrases have been properly punctuated and s's added where necessary.

a man's world	everyone's duty	a year's salary
a nickel's worth	the monkey's paw	the Negroes' way
Joe Smith's car	girls' handkerchiefs	ladies' dresses
angels' voices	nobody's business	two months' salary
three cents' worth	monkeys' tails	Jim Harris's house
the Smiths' car	the Harrises' house	foxes' habits
a fox's lair	*Love's Labour's Lost*	Brooks' essays
that book of yours	men's furnishings	Rogers and Hart's play
the lass's tears	the poetess's sonnet	its limbs
a girl's handkerchief	Brooks and Warren's book	

Key to Exercise 34

1. Notice that Mississippi's spelled with four *s's,* four *i's,* and two *p's.*
2. He really doesn't know where to put the apostrophe in *don't*
3. You've used five *so's* and four *a lot of's* in that one sentence.
4. When that's done, he'll loaf until 5 o'clock.
5. The class of '43 will celebrate its twenty-fifth reunion in '68.

Key to Exercise 35

1. In nineteen forty-eight John L. Lewis, the cigar-smoking ex-leader of the mineworkers, called a high government official "a whiskey-drinking, poker-playing evil old man."
2. When Eisenhower, the great soldier-statesman, thought that the buildup for the Normandy breakout was almost complete, he re-formed his Anglo-American troops into three armies: one led by bald-headed General Montgomery, one by an ex-classmate at West Point, and the third by the pistol-carrying Patton.

3. If we are to de - emphasize athletics without a flare - up in the coaching ranks, we must convince the coaches that a "point - getter" in the classroom is no more to be despised than one on the football field.

4. Because of his anti - administration attitude, the hot - tempered old pro - Stalinite was leading a hand - to - mouth existence with his thirty - eight fellow conspirators, who had formed what they called a government - in - exile.

5. A well - known Irish - American labour leader has been indicted for hit - and - run driving by the once weak - kneed grand jury.

Key to Exercise 36

The following words have been correctly hyphenated into syllables.

lem - on - ade	right - eous	in - sta - bil - i - ty
col - lege	col - lar	re - fer
in - fin - i - tes - i - mal	stroll - er	ref - er - ence
ne - ces - si - ty	build - er	e - nig - ma
mis - chie - vous	bold - er	en - ig - mat - ic
call - er	eas - i - er	lend - er
cal - lous	plat - ter	ten - der - est
der - rin - ger	bon - y	leop - ard
err - ing	bon - ny	plant - er
lus - cious	din - ghy	plan - ta - tion

Key to Exercise 37

1. It is important to remember that *de gustibus non disputandum est* (there can be no argument about tastes).

2. When the piston reaches top-dead-centre ("T.D.C."), over half the gases in the cylinder have already burned.

3. The most important rule (forgive me for mentioning it again) is that good citizenship is dependent upon a respect for the rights of others.

4. A great many workers in the plant (87 by actual count) have been injured since the installation of the new machinery.

5. On April 23 (?), 1564, the greatest English poet (there is no argument about the term applied to him) was born in the little village of Stratford-on-Avon.

Key to Exercise 38

1. "It is rather for us to be here dedicated **. . .** that government of the people, by the people, and for the people shall not perish from the earth" has real meaning for us today.

2. " Duncan is in his grave;
   . . . nothing
   Can touch him further."

3. "This other Eden, this demi-paradise,
   . . . this England."

Key to Exercise 39

1. Then Jesus turned to the man and said, "Go thou and do likewise."

2. Hamlet speaks of man as "this quintessence of dust."

3. Was it not C. C. Pinckney who said, "Millions for defense, but not one cent for tribute"?

4. "Render unto Caesar the things that are Caesar's," Jesus told the Pharisees; and to the Herodians he said, "and unto God the things that are God's."

5. "Eternal viligance," he quoted the old saying, "is the price of liberty."

6. It was Adam Smith who first called the English "a nation of shopkeepers."

7. "The King is dead!" cried the palace guard. "Long live the King!"

8. The saying, "You can fool some of the people all of the time, and all of the people some of the time," has been ascribed to Lincoln.

9. Disraeli spoke of Gladstone as "a sophisticated rhetorican inebriated with the exuberance of his own verbosity."

10. "People will not look forward to posterity who never looked backward to their ancestors," murmured the old Charlestonian.

Key to Exercise 40

1. "That 'Vinegar Bend' Mizell is almost as colourful as Jerome 'Dizzy Dean' Dean," chuckled the radio announcer.

2. "When you sing 'The Road to Manadalay'," the producer told him, "try to imitate the style of Lawrence Tibbett."

3. "The defendant told me when I arrested him, 'I just borrowed the car for a little while,'" the detective testified at the trial.

4. The principal told John's father, "The boys say, 'We call John "The Wedge" because he is the simplest tool known to man.'"

5. "Which nation has in the past ten years revived the old adage, 'Might makes right'?" the U.S. delegate asked the Security Council of the United Nations.

Key to Exercise 41

1. "I have never ― " she began; then in her usual fashion, she shifted to another subject.

2. "What should I do with these notebooks ? " the janitor asked.

3. "Eureka ! screamed the scientist. " I have found the 'Philosopher's Stone'!"

4. "This room is certainly a mess , " the inspector said . "Report to me as soon as you have cleaned it up."

5. "Handle it carefully , " admonished the foreman , "for it contains TNT."

Key to Exercise 42

1. As the old priest murmured the final words, "forever and forever. Amen , " he collapsed and died.

2. He shouted "What in the ― ? " ; then the rest of his exclamation froze in his mouth.

3. Did you say, "I need four volunteers" ?

4. He chortled, "Willy is a real square" ― a rather ironical term for him to apply to anyone else.

5. Just as he was falling, did you head him begin, "God save the ― " ?

6. He was often referred to as "Nutsy . "

7. When they had finished singing "The Old Rugged Cross" , they knelt for a moment of silent prayer.

8. They sang the old hymn, "Nearer, My God, to Thee" ; then they knelt for a moment of silent prayer.

9. Was it you who shouted, "Down with the tyrant ! " ?

10. Can you believe , " they asked their scoutmaster, "that such a thing could happen at a boys ' camp ? "

Key to Exercise 43

1. "Be-bop" music has succumbed to the rhythms of "rock'n roll. "

2. When asked the whereabouts of his accomplice, the young "hood" derisively replied that the "jerk" had "kicked the bucket" from a "dose of plumbism."

3. The youthful "toughie" vowed to "exenterate" his teacher's eyeballs if the "square" didn't "get off his high horse."

Key to Exercise 44

1. Emily Dickinson's little poem, "I never Saw a Moor," is a masterpiece of condensation.

2. There is some similarity between the two short stories: Steinbeck's "Flight" and Conrad's "The Lagoon."

3. E. B. White's essay, "Once More to the Lake," is quite as nostalgic as Charles Lamb's "Dream Children," but not so full of pathos.

4. Recently a very fine article, "Why We Need More Teachers," appeared in the *Saturday Evening Post*.

5. Two of Franz Hals' paintings — "The Smoker" and "The Merry Company" — show his zest for life.

6. Ben Jonson's "Drink to Me Only with Thine Eyes" is one of the best known songs from the days of Elizabethan England.

7. The second chapter of Cronin's *The Keys of the Kingdom* is entitled "Strange Vocation."

8. The "Book of Genesis" in the *Bible* is often criticized as being scientifically inaccurate.

9. When one studies some of Milton's shorter works, such as "L'Allegro," "Il Penseroso," and "Lycidas," he wonders how the same man could have written *Paradise Lost*.

10. Everything about the room reeked of pseudo-culture: on one wall hung a copy of Matisse's "Goldfish and Sculpture"; flanking it were framed copies of Lincoln's "Gettysburg Address" and Kipling's "Gunga Din"; scattered about were miscellaneous pieces of period furniture; a phonograph in a Chippendale cabinet was playing Joyce Kilmer's "Trees." What a conglomeration of bad taste!

Key to Exercise 45

A. 1. In his mind there had never been any question about his own bravery; yet now he wavered between staying and running, as the massed tanks zigzagged across the field towards him.

2. He had suffered terribly during those two months; not once, however, had he lost faith in the doctor's ability to save him.

3. "Man is not the creature of circumstance; circumstances are the creatures of man."

4. He was distinguished for his ignorance; **or**: he never had but one original idea, and that one was wrong.

5. It is said that absence makes the heart grow fonder; that is true — if we add, "for someone else."

6. "Prose is words in their best order; poetry is the best words in the best order."

7. The law forbids a man's taking whatever he wants. Do you defy that law?

8. The battle for Khartoum was lost; Gladstone had moved too late.

9. Be sure before you act; think before you speak.

10. "Is there no balm in Gilead? Is there no physician there?"

B. 1. "The harvest truly is plenteous; the labourers, however, are few."

2. "The souls of kings and clerks are cast in one mold; **or**: the same reason that makes us quarrel with our neighbours causes a war between princes."

3. You can lead a horse to water; nevertheless, you cannot make him drink.

4. "Man is the only one that knows nothing, that can learn nothing without being taught; he can neither speak nor walk nor eat; in short, at the prompting of nature alone, he can do nothing but weep."

5. "Can the Ethiopian change the colour of his skin? Can the leopard change his spots?"

6. Never in our history has there been such peril to the nation. We must awake to the dangers before it is too late.

7. He leaned on his hoe and stared at the ground; the work that day had taken all the spirit out of him.

8. I wonder sometimes at your present lassitude. You used to be quite energetic.

9. "A poor man without a budget is like a duck without oil on his feathers; **or**: neither can hold his head above water for long."

10. "Good night, sweet Prince. Flights of angels sing thee to thy rest."

Key to Exercise 46

Punctuation marks in bold type are those which should be eliminated.

1. At midnight**,** the "policeman" walked to the "call-box"**,** and reported to the desk sergeant.
2. We were served **:** orange juice, oatmeal, bacon**,** and eggs, toast, and coffee**,** for breakfast this morning.
3. The dark-skinned**,** Italian boy tore the clothing away from the hole**,** which the bullet had made in my side.
4. Few people**,** who have never experienced poverty**,** can understand the plight of these destitute**,** Viet-Nam refugees.
5. The *"Lusitania"* finally up-ended**,** and sank to the bottom**,** of the ocean.
6. He asked me**,** "why I had never given any thought to the teaching of history as a profession **?** "**.**
7. They kept shouting the same**,** dreary question: "Why did you do it?" **!**
8. She exclaimed**,** "that she did not intend to marry me **!** "**.**
9. The "do-it-yourself" builder will have to procure **:** a hammer, a screwdriver, and some nails**,** and screws**,** before he can assemble the cabinet.
10. There is no doubt**,** that a superfluous comma**,** can hinder comprehension for a good reader.

Key to Exercise 47

1. The true story of the sinking of the submarine *Squalus* was first published in the *Saturday Evening Post.*
2. The drama critic of the *Gazette* was quite scornful of the Old Vic Company's production of Shakespeare's *Macbeth.*
3. Thornton Wilder's three act play, *Our Town,* has many of the qualities of the Greek drama, according to our literature text, *Adventres in American Literature.*
4. The London Symphony Orchestra gave a concert which included Tschaikovsky's *Fourth Symphony* and the "Overture" to *Romeo and Juliet.*
5. *A Tale of Two Cities, Ivanhoe,* and *Silas Marner* seem to be the favourite novels of high school textbook publishers.

204

Key to Exercise 48

1. My teacher considers a good dictionary a *sine qua non* for all his students.
2. "Noblesse oblige," murmured Duncan as Malcolm related the circumstances of the Thane of Cawdor's death.
3. His possession of the watch was considered *ipso facto* proof of his complicity in the crime.
4. Few people have the *savoir faire* of Parisians, and even fewer have their *joie de vivre*.
5. A vicious attack of *mal de mer* almost ruined his trip from New York to Bermuda.

Key to Exercise 49

1. The noun *Smith* is the indirect object of the verb *built*.
2. The sound of *too* can be spelled correctly in three different ways: *to, too,* and *two.*
3. Your *8's* look like *3's* to me.
4. Never use *don't* with *he* as its subject.
5. *Joe* is the subject, *hit* is the verb, and *home run* is the direct object.

CAPITALIZATION

Key to Exercise 50

Correct changes in capitalization are as shown in bold type.

1. A **W**ild **W**est show has come to **W**ashington, bringing with it over twenty cowboys, three **B**rahma bulls, a number of pinto ponies, and two **I**ndian **p**rincesses, who came along to see "the **G**reat **W**hite **F**ather."
2. Because he intends to go to college in the **S**outh, his family sent him to a **N**orthern **p**reparatory **s**chool so that he might meet people from as many sections of the **c**ountry as possible.
3. When a new **P**resident enters the **W**hite **H**ouse, his wife always has the rooms refurnished to suit her taste.
4. Although **F**rench, **L**atin, mathematics, and science had all given him trouble in **h**igh **s**chool, he made straight "A's" in **M**athematics, **P**hysics and **C**omparative **L**anguages when he went to **c**ollege.

5. His father and mother had died when he was a baby, but he always called his foster parents **M**other and **D**ad.

6. As **he** looked eastward out of the window of the big **D**ouglas transport plane, he could see the vast plains and deserts of the great **S**outhwest.

7. Last spring the **c**ity planted **o**ak and **m**aple trees along the major avenues and in **M**eriwether **P**ark.

Key to Exercise 51

1. Jack always said that he wanted "to die with his boots on."

2. "The wind has slackened," he reported over the radio; "the sea, however, is still as rough as I've ever seen it."

3. "Those are the scoundrels!" he shouted. They are the ones who stole my cattle!"

4. Hamlet speaks of man as "the paragon of animals."

5. She turned away from him and said slowly, "You go your way, and I'll go mine."

Key to Exercise 52

1. He went to the **C**entral **L**ibrary, where he read *Look Back to Glory and Gone With the Wind.*

2. *The Wind in the Willow* and *Alice Through the Looking Glass* were two of his favourite books for light reading.

3. The **P**rime **M**inister **of** **C**anada delivered a speech with the title, "What **A**re **Y**ou Afraid **Of**?"

4. Walter White was once **E**xecutive Secretary of the National Association for the Advancement of the Colored People.

Key to Exercise 53

1. In the *Old Testament* God was call Jehovah by His people.

2. O Father in heaven, who art omnipotent, save Thy people in their distress.

3. Hail Him, the heir of David's line,
   Whom David Lord did call;
   The God incarnate, man divine,
   And crown Him Lord of all!"

Key to Exercise 54

1. High school seniors all over the country look forward with great eagerness to commencement exercises.

2. The president of the company is always elected at a meeting of the board of directors; he then selects his assistants, who in turn are placed in charge of the several departments.

3. My mother told me that her brother, my Uncle Jim, was sending me through college.

4. When you reach the northwest corner of the county, the road will make a sharp turn south.

5. English and mathetmatics are more important than languages, history, and sciences at most schools.

6. At 6th Avenue, the street angles toward the east for about two city blocks; it then again parallels the main highway going to the north.

7. The House of Commons will move into its rebuilt office build- on New Year's Day.

8. *The Star of the West* was a ship fired on by the Southern soldiers stationed on Fort Sumter in South Carolina.

9. "One Confederate can whip ten Yankees" was the boast of the soldier of the South during the War Between the States.

10. The bank on the southeast corner of Board and Trade Streets has a cashier who is known all over the business district for his honesty and wisdom.

GRAMMAR AND CLEAR WRITING

Key to Exercise 55

1. After the librarian had given him the book that he had asked for, he met two of his friends in the hallway and went to the gymnasium with them.

2. Suddenly there were many enemy soldiers all around us. We became confused as to what to do. Lt. Smith, however, rallied us around his tank, and we managed to drive them back to the street corner. One of them slipped around behind us, leaped on Lt. Smith's back, and bit him on the arm, making a nasty wound. After that disaster, we had a terrible time until the reinforcements from Able Company arrived.

3. Our vacation at the beach had been a most active one all summer; but as Labour Day brought it to an end, we packed our bags and went home.

4. Four children named Kathy, Alicia, Willy, and Ruthie used to play every day in the sandbox under a tree just in front

of our house. Once I did not see them there for a whole week, and then I learned that they had gone away for the summer.

5. The trouble with our government is that the Liberals and Conservatives are constantly squabbling over minor points. . . . We should really have a government that would pass constructive legislation.

Key to Exercise 56

1. There are several reasons for her academic success: she has always studied a little more than was required; in elementary school she was given a good foundation in the fundamental subjects; and furthermore, she has considerable intelligence.

2. He had followed carefully the careers of the two boys. One had gone to Africa and had become a successful mining engineer; the other was living in Paris and had never settled down to any occupation.

3. We have very little time before class begins; therefore we should stop chatting and do a little reviewing for the test.

4. As he sat under the old oak, he heard the call of a partridge in the woods across the river, the noisy splashing of a fish near the far bank, the screeching of a marsh hen as she was disturbed on her nest, and the loud laughter of the dockmen as they unloaded the shrimp boats at the wharf down below him. He felt completely enthralled by the medley of sounds.

5. He would have liked to join the fun, but he was considered *persona non grata* by everyone in the group.

Key to Exercise 57

1. No matter how tired you may be, be ready to attack on the signal.

2. Every few minutes he glanced at his watch to check the time.

3. Jack, as well as his friend, was aware of the danger involved.

4. If a boy does not realize his mistakes and if his parents do not point them out to him, life will be difficult for him.

5. He let himself be guided by Christian principles, though he did not wholeheartedly believe in them.

Key to Exercise 58

1. Over his arm he had an overcoat that had a red lining.

2. The coach was disturbed that not all the boys got to practice on time every day.
3. Under a taxicab they found the dog without a license or a collar.
4. Worry has caused almost all of his hair to turn white.
5. They had only seven minutes to get a sandwich before the train departed.
6. All but him were terrified, and even he turned slightly pale.
7. The wrestlers felt hardly tired after the first day of the tournament.
8. That is an excellent plan which you have proposed for meeting the deadline next Tuesday.

Key to Exercise 59

1. By the use of the "infinitron," it is now possible to split an infinitive quite easily and effectively.
2. In order to be really effective, the tennis service should cause the ball to veer sharply after the bounce.
3. He was able to rouse his sleeping comrades quickly by throwing icy water from the horse trough on them.

Key to Exercise 60

1. Although he did not recognize the fact, he had ruined his chances of advancing in the company.
2. While living at Horton a life of comparative ease, Milton wrote some of his finest lyrics.
3. When we know just what you want, we can get the job done.
4. While the members of the Assembly were debating the issue, they recognized the wisdom of the governor in calling the special session.
5. Though most college professors are underpaid and actually need higher salaries, they do not complain simply because of their love of learning.

Key to Exercise 61

(NOTE: Complete the comparison; then add the elliptical clause.)

1. There is one of the most beautiful mountains in the world, if not the most beautiful.
2. Joe is as intelligent as any other boy in his class, if not more so.

3. London is just as large as Paris, even though not so glamorous.

4. Randolph's contributions to charity have been greater than Carter's, though not so well publicized.

Key to Exercise 62

1. They spent all of their money, not only on necessities, but on utterly useless things as well.

2. Dr. Faustus, it is too late neither to mend your ways nor to ask God's forgiveness.

3. Slowly, gradually, and unemotionally, the mill of the gods ground Oedipus to fine dust.

4. The besieged troops had been offered a choice; either to surrender honourably or to suffer death upon being captured.

5. She saw him run out of the store with a mask on his face and a gun in his hand.

6. He developed a liking for broccoli through necessity rather than through finding any pleasure in eating it.

7. Ackroyd is of middle age, stands as straight as an arrow, and has a commanding presence.

8. Either you must park your car in one of the designated places, or the police will give you a ticket.

Key to Exercise 63

1. Born in 1606, Milton became one of England's greatest writers.

2. He likes football and baseball, and strange to say, is also fond of algebra.

3. That newspaper, which features local political and social events, has a circulation of over five thousand.

4. Mr. Rutledge, a former teacher of English and dramatics, enjoyed watching professional football.

Key to Exercise 64

1. Change *vary* to *varies*.

2. Change *are* to *is*.

3. Change *are* to *is*.

4. Change *were* to *was*.

5. Change *have* to *has*.

6. Change *are* to *is; is* to *are; them* to *him*.

210

7. Change *are* to *is*.
8. Change *makes* to *make*.
9. Change *is* to *are*.
10. Change *have* to *has*.

Key to Exercise 65

1. We were told at school today that Washington did not really cut down a cherry tree, as we had been led to believe in grammar school.
2. He removed the suit from the box in which it had been shipped, and then deposited the box in the trashcan.
3. The personnel manager told the office boy, "I (You) have done enough in my (your) years with the company to deserve a promotion.
4. When you have finished putting the jelly in the jars and labelling them, put them in that box on the table.
5. Removing his own mask, the umpire reproached the catcher for complaining.
6. Willy told his father, "I am certain to get a letter from mother this very day."
7. This book belongs to Mr. Callaway, who has been looking for it everywhere.
8. During the French Revolution if a person disagreed with the regulations of the government, he was sent to the guillotine.
9. His worst fault was his tendency to stammer, but he spoke smoothly when he was talking with close friends.
10. He is an excellent lifeguard and helps to support himself during the summer months by serving as one.

Key to Exercise 66

1. Change *their* to *his*.
2. Change *their* to *his; cards* to *card*.
3. Change *their* to *its*.
4. Change *their* to *his*.
5. Change *their* to *its*.
6. Change *their* to *his; her* to *it*.
7. Change *their* to *his*.
8. Change *you* to *he; have* to *has; them* to *one*.

9. Omit *they*.
10. Change *their beds* to *her bed*.

Key to Exercise 67

1. You promised to be on time, and as you were not there at two o'clock, we did not wait for you.
2. As excessive smoking can cause cancer of the lung and as you smoke incessantly, you may get lung cancer some day.
3. (No logical conclusion can be drawn from the facts given.)
4. When Milton became blind, he at last found time to write *Paradise Lost*.
5. (No logical conclusion can be drawn from the facts given.)

Key to Exercise 68

1. The fact that you felt devilish is no valid reason for your dropping a block of ice down the stairwell.
2. When one is intoxicated, his brain is to a certain extent poisoned.
3. He was so fatigued because he had just run three miles.
4. We boiled the nitro-glycerine until it became jelly-like.
5. I read in the newspaper that we can expect to have sub-normal rainfall for the next two months.

Key to Exercise 69

1. Jack is the tallest boy that I know.
2. His manner of walking was as quiet as an Indian's.
3. Tokyo is larger than any other city in the world.
4. He liked apple pie better than anything else.
5. Willy is smaller than Donny, but just as strong.
6. This is one of the longest bridges in Canada, if not the longest.
7. Ruth's hair is much blonder than Julie's.
8. Charleston is nearer Bermuda than New York is.
9. He loved his dog much more than his father did.
10. It is much easier for Dan to make money than to make a friend.
11. The view from the top of Lookout Mountain is the most beautiful in the world.

Key to Exercise 70

1. Insert *that* after *said;* insert *whom* after *girl.*
2. Insert *who* after *man.*
3. Delete the first comma and insert *and* after *morning.*
4. Insert *my* after *and.*
5. Insert *the* after *and.*
6. Insert *your* after *and.*
7. Insert *that* between *us* and *he* and between *and* and *they.*
8. Insert *whom* after *boy.*

Key to Exercise 71

1. Having listened to the minister preach for an hour and a half, the congregation left the church rather rapidly after the benediction.
2. At Malmedy the SS Troopers, laughing at their victims' screams, massacred hundreds of defenseless American prisoners.
3. When the bob-sled turned crosswise and flew over the bank, the driver was killed, and the other members of the crew were injured.
4. Because of the recent two-day blizzard, the road has been blocked for almost a week.
5. After I was promoted to sales manager, it became part of my job, etc.
6. Before removing the spark plug, blow out the recess surrounding it, using an air hose.
7. One does not need an elaborate classroom to teach people to read and write.
8. Latecomers used to be locked out of college lecture halls as punishment for being late.
9. When one travels through Europe on an extended tour, nylon underwear, etc.
10. Some theatres are equipped with special hearing aids for people who are unable to hear the program otherwise.

Key to Exercise 72

1. Do the easier problems first, and then if you have time, work the harder ones.
2. The cab-driver assumed the duties of a policeman and very quickly unsnarled the traffic jam.

3. I soon finished my Latin translation, and in about another hour had worked all my algebra problems.
4. The more exercise we take, the stronger we become.
5. As we were walking along, minding our own business, a fellow in front of us suddenly went berserk, drew a knife, and began to slash at people near him.
6. He made an investigation and soon solved the case.
7. We had been waiting for over an hour to see the doctor. A man dressed like an important banker came in, strode over to the receptionist, and in a loud voice demanded to see the doctor at once, as his time was very important to him. When she gave him priority over us, we were really furious.
8. Omit the sentence, "Behind . . . himself," as it would be impossible to see John, the janitor, from the "point of view" which you have chosen.

Key to Exercise 73

1. There does not seem to be any explanation for what has happened.
2. A good many hunters "got their limit" on the first day of the deer season.
3. The shipment which you inquired about in your letter was sent by freight last week and should be delivered to you in a few days.
4. Omit the second *that*.
5. That painting on the wall, if cleaned up, will probably bring a good price at the next art auction.

Key to Exercise 74

1. Insert *therefore* or *consequently* after the semicolon.
2. Insert *nevertheless* or *however* after the semicolon.
3. Insert *however* after the semicolon.
4. Insert *otherwise* after the semicolon.
5. Insert *furthermore* or *moreover* after the semicolon.
6. Insert *furthermore* after the first semicolon; insert *therefore* or *consequently* after the second semicolon.
7. Insert *however* after *crucial situation*.

Key to Exercise 75

1. He repeated the question twice before he realized that the student was asleep.
2. As it was 5 P.M., they closed the office and went home.
3. They were members of the local country club, which was just across the road from their house.
4. As the fog was quite heavy, we were unable to see the lights of the approaching truck.
5. At a boys' preparatory school football game, she met a young teacher named Taylor.

Key to Exercise 76

1. When the house was almost quiet, a scream of anguish suddenly rang out from the guest bedroom.
2. While he was sitting by his television set, a bolt of lightning struck the antenna and burned out the picture-tube circuit.
3. Just as he was about to lean back in his chair and listen to another dull lecture, it occurred to him that a review test had been assigned for that day.
4. Moving casually toward the enemy position, he sprayed them with his sub-machine gun and forced them to vacate their positions.
5. As the old man was sitting in his boat, a huge shark seized the bait on his line and began to run with it.

Key to Exercise 77

1. A whirling tornado roared in from the south, struck the sleepy town, demolished many of its buildings, and killed eight of its inhabitants.
2. As he walked out the door, a huge fist caught him in the chest and drove him back against the door frame.
3. He picked up the unusual pebble and put it into his pocket for later examination.
4. The arrow sped on its way, struck the deer in the shoulder, and killed it instantly.

Key to Exercise 78

1. There was not, it seemed, any other way to solve the problem.
2. The fish never seemed, however, to be able to get off his hook.

3. They have, to some extent at least, controlled the spread of the disease.
4. The boy about whom I was talking is not, to say the least, the criminal type.
5. They will, moreover, never again be able to put their trust in their present City Council.

Key to Exercise 79

1. He (1) had been scolded, (2) had received no letter, (3) had failed . . .
2. We (1) have asked, (2) have implored, (3) have practically gotten down . . .
3. (1) a good defensive man, (2) an excellent blocker, (3) a superlative . . .
4. (1) the community centre, (2) its only two doctors, (3) a hurricane . . .
5. (1) the setting, (2) the plot, (3) the characterization . . .

Key to Exercise 80

1. The ship lay at anchor in the harbour. Her lines were quite sleek, and she had just been repainted. On her decks the sailors were polishing her brass and scrubbing her decks. Some of them had their shirts off, and their bronzed backs glistened in the sun. It was a beautiful sight.
2. It was a long trip down the mountain. The fog was blinding. The road, which was not protected by guard rails, was icy, very slippery, and quite steep in places. There were sharp curves every few hundred feet, with no signs to warn motorists of them. There were also two narrow bridges across deep chasms. When we finally reached the bottom, I breathed a sigh of relief.

Key to Exercise 81

The bear had just emerged from his cave when we first saw him. As we approached him, he hesitated in his slow walk. On our getting even closer, he turned back toward the cave. Seeing that he intended to "hole-up," we raced for the cave as fast as we could to cut him off, but he got there first. Since we were afraid to follow him into the cave, we turned sadly away and continued our tramp along the mountain path.

Key to Exercise 82

1. The City Council has been investigating the most efficient method of disposing of unburnable garbage. (15 words)
2. We are currently swamped with requests for information about government loans for soil conservation projects, but we will send you the requested information as soon as we can. (28 words)
3. Although he had worked long and efficiently to prevent his firm's bankruptcy, he now decided that because of its unpayable debts, it should be declared insolvent immediately. (27 words)
4. England expects every man to do his duty. (8 words)

Key to Exercise 83

1. Most people are upset by the unfamiliar, but our pastor, who is wiser than most, is not in the least.
2. It was such a tiny bit of organism that it was hardly visible; but by looking closely, one could see that it was rectangular and red.
3. It was a surprise when the old lady deliberately pulled off the road so that we might pass her.

Key to Exercise 84

1. It was a warm, sunny, cloudless day; and we enjoyed every minute of the swimming, the sunbathing, and the picnic lunch.
2. Joe usually makes B's in all his courses and is an above-average student in his class; furthermore, he is an honest, reliable, sensible, and popular boy who has been elected the student council representative from his class.
3. The business failed because orders were not filled on time, there was much employee-absenteeism, employees would take "coffee breaks" whenever they felt so disposed, suppliers were not held to their contracts, mistakes of judgment were constantly made, and there was other general inefficiency.
4. It was an animal with two heads, each horned; its black eyes bulged; its mouth constantly gaped; its yellow furry body was seven inches long and about one inch in diameter; its legs, which were polka-dotted white on a lavender background, barely kept its drooping stomach from dragging the ground. It was very strange-looking.

5. He proposed that we correct our balance-of-payment deficit by prohibiting importers' purchasing goods from a country to which the United States was indebted.

Key to Exercise 85

1. Change *was* to *were.*
2. Change *was* to *were.*
3. Change *is* to *were.*
4. Change *was* to *were.*
5. Change *was* to *were.*
6. Correct.
7. Change *was* to *were* or *had been.*
8. Change *were* to *had been.*
9. Change *was* to *were.*
10. Change *was* to *were.*

Key to Exercise 86

1. Change *will* to *shall.* (Futurity)
2. Change *will* to *shall.* (Futurity)
3. Change *will* to *shall.* (Futurity)
4. Change *shall* to *will.* (Determination)
5. Change *shall* to *will.* (Willingness)
6. Change *will* to *shall.* (Determination)
7. Change *shall* to *will.* (Form expected in the answer)
8. Change *will* to *shall* (Futurity); *shall* to *will.* (Determination)

Key to Exercise 87

1. Change to second *was* to *is.*
2. Change *was* to *is.*
3. Change *was* to *is.*
4. Change *did* to *do.*
5. Change *was* to *is.*

Key to Exercise 88

1. Delete *had.*
2. Change *may* to *might.*

3. Delete *had*.
4. Change *has been* to *was*.
5. Change *talks* to *talked* or *had* to *has*.

Key to Exercise 89

1. Change *were* to *have been*.
2. Change *had* to *has*.
3. Change *found* to *has found*.
4. Change *were* to *have been*.
5. Change *did not hear* to *have not heard*.

Key to Exercise 90

1. Change *know* to *had known*.
2. Change *made* to *had made*.
3. Change *discovered* to *had discovered*.
4. Change *have* to *had*.
5. Change *was dead* to *had been dead*.

Key to Exercise 91

1. Change *pass* to *have passed*.
2. Change *become* to *have become*, or *will become* to *becomes*.
3. Change *finish* to *have finished*.
4. Change *use* to *have used*.
5. Change *finish* to *have finished*.

Key to Exercise 92

1. Change *is* to *was*.
2. Change *were* to *are*.
3. Change *studied* to *had studied*.
4. Change *should like to have been* to *wished that I had been; prepared* to *had prepared*.
5. Change *blew* to *had blown*.
6. Change *thought* to *had thought; have shocked* to *shock*.
7. Change *might* to *may*, or *listens* to *listened*.
8. Change *will* to *would*.
9. Change *was* to *had been*.
10. Change *was* to *is*.

Key to Exercise 93

1. Change *have seen* to *see.*
2. Change *being* to *having been.*
3. Change *Crossing* to *Having crossed.*
4. Change *be* to *have been.*
5. Change *have eaten* to *eat.*
6. Change *be* to *have been.*
7. Change *live* to *have lived.*
8. Change *Being* to *Having been.*
9. Change *have been* to *be.*
10. Change *Having been* to *Being.*

Key to Exercise 94

1. Change *most* to *almost; regular* to *regularly.*
2. Change *badly* to *bad; fresh* to *freshly.*
3. Change *real* to *really; bad* to *badly.*
4. Change *some* to *somewhat; frank* to *frankly.*
5. Correct.
6. Correct.
7. Change *terribly* to *terrible.*
8. Change *quietly* to *quiet; real careful-like* to *very carefully.*
9. Change *careless* to *carelessly; slow* to *slowly; sure* to *surely.*
10. Change *quick* to *quickly; angry* to *angrily.*

Key to Exercise 95

1. Change *this* to *these.*
2. Change *those kind of books* to *that kind of book.*
3. Change *this* to *these.*
4. Change *sort* to *types.*
5. Change *this* to *these,* or *alumni* to *alumnus.*

Key to Exercise 96

1. Change *last* to *latter; best* to *better.*
2. Delete the first *more.*
3. Change *better* to *best; whiter* to *whitest.*
4. Change *most lovely* to *loveliest; better* to *best.*
5. Change *more happy* to *happiest.*

Key to Exercise 97

A. 1. Change *I* to *me; him* to *his.*
2. Change *whom* to *who.*
3. Correct.
4. Change *her* to *she.*
5. Change *it* to *its; him* to *he.*
6. Change *who* to *whom.*
7. Change *she and I* to *her and me.*
8. Correct.
9. Change *Who* to *Whom.*
10. Correct.

B. 1. Change *Whom* to *Who.*
2. Change *I* to *me.*
3. Change *whom* to *who.*
4. Change *enemy* to *enemy's.*
5. Change *I* to *me.*
6. Change *someone's* to *someone.*
7. Change *whomever* to *whoever.*
8. Change *he* to *him.*
9. Change *I* to *me.*
10. Correct.

Key to Exercise 98

1. Change *whose windows* to *the windows of which.*
2. Change *which* to *who.*
3. Change *whose carburetor* to *the carburetor of which; whose tires* to *the tires of which.*
4. Change *that* to *who.*

Key to Exercise 99

1. Change *theirselves* to *themselves.*
2. Change *myself* to *me.*
3. Change *hisself* to *himself.*
4. Change *yourself* to *you.*
5. Change *myself* to *me.*

Key to Exercise 100

1. Change *dove* to *dived; swum* to *swam; bursted* to *burst.*
2. Change *raised up* to *rose; taken* to *took; swore* to *sworn; sunk* to *sank; give* to *gave.*
3. Change *shined* to *shone; drunk* to *drank; lead* to *led; hung* to *hanged.*
4. Change *knowed* to *known; laid* to *lay; stole* to *stolen; froze* to *frozen.*

Key to Exercise 101

1. Change *of* to *have; loaned* to *lent; suspicioned* to *suspected; without* to *unless; ever* to *every.*
2. Change *real* to *quite* or *very; invite* to *invitation; like* to *as if* or *as though* and *was* to *were.*
3. Change *On account of* to *Because; size* to *sized; barefooted* to *barefoot; an awful* to *a very; like* to *as.*
4. Change *loathe* to *loath; awhile* to *a while; all ready* to *already; then* to *than; of* to *have.*

Key to Exercise 102

1. Delete *of, of,* and *of.*
2. Delete *up, up,* and *down.*
3. Delete *up with, together with,* and the final *of.*
4. Change *rose up* to *rose; out on to* to *on.*

Key to Exercise 103

1. I do not suppose that we have ever been such a great distance from home before.
2. It is a rather long way for you to have to carry that heavy sack.
3. When I sneaked behind her and kissed her on the cheek, she hit me with the wet mop that she was holding.
4. As Sam hastened down the path in his newly-bought clothes, a white-complexioned person who looked like a ghost suddenly loomed in front of him.

Key to Exercise 104

1. Many people go to bed early so that they may be refreshed for the next day's work.

2. Any person with the least common sense would not be deceived by a group of children.

3. The chemistry professor told me in the laboratory today that on Monday I would have to take the examination which I had missed.

4. After I had come back to the dormitory from the gymnasium, I found my very intelligent roommate quite enthusiastic about a book which he had been reading, and explaining its merits to a group of boys.

Key to Exercise 105

1. We humans undoubtedly will some day be able to go anywhere that rockets can fly.

2. The former criminal committed suicide after the police became relentless in suspecting him of having burgled the jewelry store.

3. I used to be able to get an invitation to the country club party almost every Saturday night; but since I had that clash with the manager, I am no longer welcome there, regardless of whom I am with.

4. I do not remember exactly when I lent you the money, but we were somewhere downtown at the time.

5. When he was attacked that time by the octopus and dragged to the bottom of the inlet, he almost drowned.

Key to Exercise 106

1. Change *crummy trick; lousy; dust-off; nice guy.*

2. Change *cool date; sharp; slob; hop-hall;* and quote *rock'n roll.*

3. Change *blob; plastered to the gills; cop; picked him up.*

4. Change *chiseler; stuck his neck out; pull a phony deal; corny; nut in the booby hatch; caught on.*

Key to Exercise 107

1. Change *irony of fate; strong as Hercules; half scared to death; harmless as a kitten.*

2. Change *goes without saying; sense of relief; near tragedy; came through; none the worse for the wear.*

3. Change *pearly teeth; rosy lips; member of the weaker sex; pretty as a picture.*

4. Change *unguarded moment; soul of honour; straight and narrow; years on end; demon rum; all too soon; horrible victim; Grim Reaper.*

5. Change *fond parents; green with envy; one and only; blushing bride; loving couple; the old folks.*

Key to Exercise 108

1. Hundreds of women dressed in mourning clothes passed the open coffin of the dead movie idol just before the funeral ceremony.

2. Please tell me what the doctor charged for setting your broken leg.

3. When you read the newspaper at home this morning, did you notice the article about the fight between the supporters of the two opposing football teams in yesterday's game?

4. In these perilous times, it seems to me of the utmost importance that we have plans for putting out the great fires that may be set by an enemy rocket attack.

Key to Exercise 109

1. That reference book—a mine of information—I used constantly in writing my last composition.

2. The thoughtful student, naturally, soon discovers that he cannot learn all the material in a course unless he studies on his own.

3. When he sat down to write his weekly composition, he started to use a subject on which he had written previously; but his mother changed his mind by pointing out that the topic was becoming trite.

4. Soon a teacher with a sad face came by and gave us a lengthy lecture on the tragedy of living too long.

5. Well, I think it a good idea to sink the well some distance from the house.

Key to Exercise 110

1. He (stated, declared, averred, asserted, protested) that one is most fortunate to have (understanding, kind, benevolent, gracious) parents.

2. We (raced, hurried, moved, scampered, dashed) to the (huge, immense, enormous, spacious) window and (gazed, stared,

peered) at the (huge, large, immense, enormous, vast, **gigantic**) crowd gathering in the street.

3. We had a (delightful, pleasurable, exquisite, thrilling, ecstatic) time at the (party, dance, picnic, reception, concert).

4. The speaker had a (harsh, grating, strident, raucous, piercing, nonresonant) voice.

5. History is a subject that I (detest, abhor, loathe, abominate).

6. The panther made a (throaty, guttural, purring, hissing) noise as it (loped, crept, slunk, stalked, sprang, leapt) toward us.

7. She is a (lovely, attractive, enchanting, charming, engaging) girl.

8. We had a (toilsome, troublous, irksome, exasperating) time working those (difficult, hard, practically unsolvable, frustrating) problems.

Key to Exercise 111

A. 1. have; regard; hour; with; whether; to.
   2. had; of; against.
   3. to; with; to.
   4. of; aloud; Hayes for it.
   5. to; with; rearing.
   6. behind; to; of shirking.

B. 1. plan to climb; wait for; as far as.
   2. all-round; whether; into.
   3. only about six years old; of her own accord; angry with; comply with.
   4. cannot help believing; due to; independent of.
   5. very much interested; try to; novel about.

Key to Exercise 112

A. 1. Besides; reputation; quite; stingy; cynical; custom.
   2. practical; annoy; already; remainder.
   3. compare; likely; common.
   4. pessimistic; censure; invented; impeding; imminent; effect.
   5. spectators; imperious; disinterested; personal.

B. 1. Incredible; conscience; contemptible; desert; immigrant; further.
2. quite; ingenuous; accept; presents; obligated.
3. implied; altogether; too; aggression; but; suspect; fewer; pacific.
4. capital; proposing; defer; later; compare.
5. healthful; envious.

C. 1. principal; stationery; coarse.
2. knowledge; noted; wisdom.
3. unusual; envious; strange.
4. almost; elapsed; morale.
5. sat; luxury; whereas; remainder (rest).
6. suspect; principal; effect; continually; archaic.

NOTES

NOTES

NOTES

NOTES

NOTES

NOTES

NOTES

NOTES

NOTES

NOTES

NOTES